Dovegate

A Therapeutic Community in a Private Prison
and Developments in Therapeutic Work
with Personality Disordered Offenders

Dr Eric Cullen

Dr Judith Mackenzie

D1614740

WITHDRÁWN

Dovegate
A Therapeutic Community in a Private Prison and Developments in Therapeutic Work with Personality Disordered Offenders
Dr Eric Cullen and Dr Judith Mackenzie

Published 2011 by
Waterside Press Ltd   **Telephone** +44(0)1256 882250
Sherfield Gables   **Low cost UK landline calls** 0845 2300 733
Sherfield on Loddon   **E-mail** enquiries@watersidepress.co.uk
Hook, Hampshire   **Online catalogue** WatersidePress.co.uk
United Kingdom RG27 0JG

ISBN 978-1-904380-54-2 (Paperback)   **ISBN** 978-908162-88-2 (e-book)

Cataloguing-In-Publication Data A catalogue record for this book can be obtained on request from the British Library.

Cover design © 2011 Waterside Press. Design by www.gibgob.com. Cover photographs kindly supplied by Serco.

UK distributor Gardners Books, 1 Whittle Drive, Eastbourne, East Sussex, BN23 6QH. Tel: +44 (0)1323 521777; sales@gardners.com; www.gardners.com

North American distributor International Specialized Book Services (ISBS), 920 NE 58th Ave, Suite 300, Portland, Oregon, 97213, USA. Tel: 1 800 944 6190 Fax: 1 503 280 8832; orders@isbs.com; www.isbs.com

Printed by MPG-Biddles Ltd, Kings Lynn.

e-book *Dovegate* is available as an ebook and also to subscribers of Myilibrary and Dawsonera (for ISBN see above).

Dovegate

A Therapeutic Community in a Private Prison
and Developments in Therapeutic Work
with Personality Disordered Offenders

Dr Eric Cullen

Dr Judith Mackenzie

Foreword Dr Barbara Rawlings

≋ WATERSIDE PRESS

CONTENTS

4: BUILDING THE PEOPLE AND THE COMMUNITY

5: THE DIRECTOR'S TALE: A SEARCH ENGINE FOR MEANING
Roland Woodward

Dr Eric Cullen and Dr Judy Mackenzie

THE AUTHOR OF THE FOREWORD

Dr Barbara Rawlings has worked in and around therapeutic communities (TCs) since 1973, including a hierarchical TC for drug users, a democratic TC for adolescents with behavioural difficulties and in both open and custodial settings. She has also carried out research into TCs as well as conducting reviews of them for both HM Prison Service and the High Security Psychiatric Services Commissioning Board. She is an Honorary Fellow in the Department of Sociology at the University of Manchester and joint editor (with Rowdy Yates) of *Therapeutic Communities for the Treatment of Drug Users* (2001), Jessica Kingsley Publishers.

FOREWORD

I agreed to write this forward long before I read the first draft because like others in the world of therapeutic communities, I have watched the development of Dovegate Therapeutic Prison with avid interest. I was honoured to be asked to introduce the story of Dovegate to the world. How humbling then to actually read the first draft and discover how very small my contribution could be to this powerful piece of work. The story of Dovegate is extraordinary—a 200-bed therapeutic community (TC) in a brand new privately-run prison?—come off it! And the way the story is told in this narrative is so fresh and alive that I could feel the tension and the elation, the gloom and the joy as I read it. It's an honest piece, warts and all, and I was left with a conviction that this is exactly the way to write about such a dynamic and innovative organization. So *this* is what it was like!

I have worked in and around therapeutic communities since 1973, mainly doing research. Some years ago I was lucky enough to spend some weeks at the therapeutic community in Gartree Prison. Once I had got used to locked gates, uniformed officers and the officers' radios crackling into life at any time, I discovered that the therapeutic community approach I was used to was well-suited to a custodial environment despite the seemingly antithetical priorities of discipline, security and hierarchy. Prison provided a full-time residential setting and the prisoners' index offences provided a rich focus and framework for therapeutic endeavour. The strong physical boundaries made it difficult for residents to leave on impulse—decisions to leave necessarily took time to take effect, and this could help residents to change their mind and stay in treatment rather than just walk out. I was fascinated by the work that went into bringing together the security priorities of custodial settings with the treatment requirements of the therapeutic community approach—two seemingly such different concerns and yet potentially so mutually supportive. This work of weaving together the prison and the therapeutic community at all levels is richly documented in this book, along with the practical and therapeutic problems that have become part of the familiar tapestry of daily life. We hear from a wide range of people here, and find that their varying perspectives can be strongly defended and not always popular — just the way it is in the living-learning environment the book describes.

Since being asked to write this piece, I have reflected a good deal on my experiences of prison TCs. As a researcher, I have had the opportunity to spend time in different prison TCs for varying lengths of time. Amongst recollections of faces and events, of meetings and interviews, note-taking and questioning that is the lot of the researcher, I think the most startling was sitting in a community meeting, digging my nails into my hands to stay focused, as one of the group, a prisoner, read out a detailed account of another group member's crime. Through the harrowing description of tormented perpetrator and helpless victim came the insistent offence-focused questions: Why did this happen? What led up to it? And how can everyone here help this person never do it again? Prison therapeutic communities are tough places, where prisoners face their inner demons while the staff and the other prisoners offer them support, encouragement and challenge. Many prisoners have had hard, desperate, sad lives and many have committed serious crimes, some many times over. In the full-time treatment environment of the therapeutic community, they can learn to acknowledge what has gone wrong for them, discover how they can change it, and find the strength to go through with that change. This very readable and lively book provides vivid insights into how this work has been organized and carried out at Dovegate.

I know both authors well. I first met Judy in 1975, when she was a hospital registrar at a therapeutic community for disturbed adolescents in Macclesfield, Cheshire, and I was a social therapist with a special role as researcher. We became friends, only later learning that each was equally awed by the other — I am still awed by Judy, even after knowing her all this time. I visited the therapeutic community she set up and ran for years at Glen Parva Young Offender Institution Unit in Leicestershire, and this was the first time I saw at first hand that it was both possible and desirable to run a democratised unit inside a security-oriented hierarchical institution. Judy is a brilliant practitioner whether working with a single prisoner or managing an entire community. I regard her as a bit of a legend and I am not alone in this.

The other legend is Eric. I knew of him before I met him, as the author of a seminal piece of research carried out at Grendon therapeutic community prison in the 1990s, which I discovered when writing a literature review on TCs for the prison service. Now, we often work together—he and I are members of the Ministry of Justice's Correctional Services Accreditation Panel (CSAP) where we contribute to decisions about the value and likely effectiveness of psychological programmes for offenders, including therapeutic communities. He too has long practical experience of prison therapeutic communities and I am frequently impressed by his knowledge and experience of forensic psychology and by his steady enthusiasm for the therapeutic community approach to treatment. Like Judy he has played a crucial role in the development of prison therapeutic communities in this country as clinician, manager, trainer and consultant.

Therapeutic communities work with some of the most disturbed and disturbing people in custody. The whole point of running psychological treatment programmes in prisons is to lower the re-offending rate—that is to make it far less likely that someone who leaves prison will commit more crime. The research shows that this intensive long-term approach can truly turn people around, and give them for the first time the strength of character and self-belief they need to live a constructive and pro-social life. It takes time, it's very intense, and the day-to-day experience for everyone, staff and prisoners, is a raw mix that feels challenging, puzzling, uncomfortable, sad, scary and very rich by turns. This book gives a real flavour of how that whole mix of emotions and experiences surfaced at Dovegate. Sitting here, at a safe distance from the interpersonal rollercoaster described in these pages, I end up feeling admiration for all those people, staff and prisoners, who engage so courageously with the life of the group, compassion for their experience of the darts and arrows of interpersonal strife and a certain envy for the real, deep, connectedness that I know is possible in a therapeutic community. So here I am, affected, warmed and humbled, urging you to read this book. It's a real experience.

Barbara Rawlings June 2011

THE AUTHORS

Dr Eric Cullen's career as a forensic psychologist included serving as head of psychology and director of research and development at Grendon and Springhill Prisons before becoming lead consultant to the private sector contractors chosen to manage Dovegate Therapeutic Community Prison.

He has also served as: a justice of the peace; a member of the joint Home Office and Department of Health Working Party on Personality Disordered Offenders; a member of the Home Office Task Force to Determine the Need for further "Grendon-style" Therapeutic Regimes; and he is the founder and was the first chair of the Association of Therapeutic Communities — Prison.

He has been a member of Advisory Panels for Prison Therapeutic Communities (TCs) at Dovegate, Grendon and Gartree Prisons. He also advised on the creation of TCs for women prisoners at Send Prison and for young offenders at both Aylesbury and Feltham Young Offender Institutions. He is a member of the Correctional Services Accreditation Panel which advises on proposals for offender treatment programmes in prisons and the community.

Dr Cullen was an honorary senior research fellow, Department of Psychology, University of Birmingham, and is co-editor of *Therapeutic Communities for Offenders* (Wiley, 1997) (with Lawrence Jones and Roland Woodward) and *Murderers and Life Imprisonment* (Waterside Press, 1998) (with Tim Newell). He is nowadays a full-time carer for Margaret, his wife, "official walker of Gyzmo the dog" and a supporter of Liverpool FC and London Wasps.

Dr Judith Margaret Mackenzie qualified in general medicine in Manchester in 1972. She obtained the Diploma in Psychological Medicine in 1976 and undertook the psychiatric rotation both in Child and Adolescent Psychiatry and Forensic Psychiatry prior to setting up the first therapeutic community for young offenders in HM Young Offender Institution Glen Parva in 1981. She has also worked as visiting psychiatrist to HM Prison Service for over 30 years, specialising in those forms of treatment for personality disorder and the addressing of offending behaviour known as therapeutic communities (TCs). Until April 2010, she was the Therapy Manager for the TC at Gartree Prison and is now therapeutic community consultant, supervisor, trainer and psychodynamic lead for the TC at Dovegate Prison.

In addition to her psychiatric qualifications, she holds an MA in Psychosynthesis Psychology and a diploma in Psychosynthesis Psychotherapy. She is a member of the UK Council for Psychotherapy (UKCP); an associate member of the Royal College of Psychiatrists and of the Association of Therapeutic Communities; sits on the Quality Control panel of the Royal College of Psychiatrists for therapeutic communities (Community of Communities); and is a former member of the Parole Board.

Judith Mackenzie is an accredited trainer for staff working in TCs and holds a Diploma in Management for Prison Medical Officers. She is registered with the General Medical Council for the preparation of legal reports but relinquished full registration to practice medicine in 2009.

ACKNOWLEDGEMENTS

Eric Cullen would like to thank, from Grendon: Tim Newell, David Wilson, Peter Bennett, Bernie Marcus, Edgar Darling, Jinnie Jefferies and Alex Alexandrowicz; from Dovegate: Roland Woodward (my original co-author) and the amazing original team from Premier; Michael Gander, without whom I would never have had the opportunity to be involved and there would be no book; Margaret, Daniel and Emma for their brilliant support; and, finally, Judy MacKenzie who stepped into the breach to help me finish the book and who managed to complete and enhance it so wonderfully.

Judith Mackenzie writes: I would like to thank those who have helped and supported me along the way and who are, in the time-honoured phrase, too numerous to mention. They include the many residents and staff of all the TCs in which I have worked. However, those who have been especially remarkable and to whom I extend my thanks are: Mary Ellis for showing me the direction my life would take; Jinnie Jefferies for teaching me about the rocks on the path; Eric Jackson for showing me there is more than one way to skin a cat; Mark Morris for getting me hooked on burgers and helping me avoid sesame seeds; Roland Woodward for lighting the lamp of possibility; Eric Cullen for inviting me to participate in the gruelling journey of writing this book; and Tom Isaac who gives shape and meaning to it all.

INTRODUCTION

The original idea for this book was as a description of a new enterprise: the creation of a new therapeutic community (TC) for offenders contracted out via the Private Finance Initiative (PFI), to the private sector. That was in 2002. Now, nearly ten years later, events have shaped a new, wider set of objectives. This book sets out to:

Describe and explain what it is like to create a democratic therapeutic community (DTC) in a private sector, purpose-built prison: HM Prison Dovegate in Staffordshire. We chronicle the first decade of the DTC's life from the unique perspectives of the lead consultant, first and subsequent directors of therapy and the consultant psychiatrist—the people responsible for the creation, direction and therapeutic integrity of the entire enterprise.

Discuss the economic, political and ethical issues as between therapy, imprisonment and profit motives from the perspective of practitioners who have worked in both the private sector and public sector for over 25 years.

Provide a range of—at times divergent—perspectives from staff, inmates (better known as "residents") and managers.

Address the wider questions of treating offenders within Department of Health/Ministry of Justice joint strategy initiatives created by the Coalition Government to "break the cycle" of re-offending; and also the great advances (and questionable changes) made over the past decade thanks in part to the introduction of accreditation, audit and reviews, and to suggest a future model for Dovegate and TCs in prison settings generally.

These more ambitious objectives evolved over the past few years as the first author became involved in advising the Ministry of Justice on offender programmes and the second author practised in both public and private settings, with the distinction of being the only independent professional to have been at Dovegate TC ever since it opened.

The economic climate of 2010-2012, in particular annual cost-cutting directives across-the-board, may well sound the death knell for a number of treatment programmes after ten years of expansion. The reduction of re-offending, the protection of the public, and the appropriate targeting of scarce resources onto medium and high-risk offenders, are among the main aims of the National Offenders Management Service (NOMS), responsible for the work of both the HM Prison Service and the Probation Service. As NOMS embarked upon comprehensive reviews of all offender treatment programmes from 2010, against the backcloth of the imposition of the greatest economic cost-cutting exercise in a generation, we look at the arguments for defending those interventions which are proven to reduce the most serious offending, even at the cost of imposing greater cuts on other activities, i.e. based on prioritisation rather than blanket reductions. After all, other treatment programmes, accredited or not, succeed in saving property or preventing injury. When a DTC such as Dovegate, Grendon or Gartree succeeds, more often than not, it saves lives.

Primarily the book is about Dovegate TC, including every stage of the bidding and building process, the recruitment and training of the staff, and the challenges of opening a new DTC. We highlight the philosophy and traditions which are the bedrock for such establishments.

It also provides a unique insight into what it was like to create, develop and sustain a therapeutic environment in a secure prison setting. Features include personal stories of the residents and staff during the first decade of Dovegate's life including extraordinary accounts from the person most responsible for Dovegate's success to date, the first director of therapy, Roland Woodward and then consultant psychiatrist Dr Judith MacKenzie (the second author of this book, who is now consultant to the TCs at Dovegate) about their experiences from the first day of operation through to today. There are other unique first-hand contributions from past and present residents and staff which illuminate the power and limitations of Dovegate. Here, the second author offers her candid views on some of the conflicting themes and interpersonal aspirations within a therapeutic regime operating inside a prison in the private sector.

Finally, in later chapters, the book summarises the growing body of quality and performance procedures which exist, including HM Chief Inspectorate of Prison reports, national audits, and the accreditation process of the Correctional Services Accreditation Panel (CSAP). It also reviews the research carried out by Miller and Brown at Surrey University regarding Dovegate's effectiveness.[1] We question the future viability of Dovegate within the private sector Geo Group, and tackle some of the wider policy issues concerning regimes and programmes which attempt to reduce crime; and we comment on the Green Paper, *Breaking the Cycle: Effective Punishment, Rehabilitation and Sentencing of Offenders.*[2] The latest director, Ray Duckworth (now director of the whole establishment at Dovegate) has, fittingly, the final word here on Dovegate's present and immediate future.

As authors we bring very different professional perspectives to our writing, one very much an empirical behaviourist and the other a psychodynamic psychiatrist. Over the years, we have often disagreed but we have grown to understand that there are many paths to the same truths. We share both a mutual respect for, and an abiding belief in DTC traditions.

Ultimately, Dovegate is an intense experience dedicated to ensuring there are fewer victims in the future. This is both the most important and the final imperative. The best prison treatment must not only help the offender, but also safeguard the public.

Eric Cullen and **Judith Mackenzie** June 2011

---

1.   See, in particular, *Chapter 9*.
2.   (2010), Cmnd 7972. This Green Paper is mentioned further in *Chapter 10*.

Dovegate

We dedicate this book to the many thousands of offenders who have changed their lives by succeeding in therapy at democratic therapeutic communities like Dovegate, thanks in large part to the hundreds of staff who have helped them to do this, and to the many more thousands of offenders who, given the same chance, will join them in the future.

Dovegate

CHAPTER ONE

DOVEGATE: THE BID, PHILOSOPHY AND PRINCIPLES

I. The Origins of a New Therapeutic Community in the Private Prison Sector

Grendon Underwood therapeutic community (TC) in Buckinghamshire had stood alone as the only total establishment-based TC in the UK since opening in 1962. Having fought many battles for survival over the ensuing three decades, there was in the 1990s a sense that at last the time had arrived to seriously consider expanding this vital resource rather than struggling to avoid closure.

In 1993, the first proof that democratic therapeutic communities (DTCs) in prison work in terms of reducing re-offending was published. This was the report of a research project, "The Grendon Reconviction Study, Part 1".[1] It inspired the commissioning of two subsequent, larger independent research studies by Marshall (1997) and Taylor (1999) which corroborated most of the earlier findings.

The intervening years saw mounting pressure to build more TCs in prisons, including strong support from the Prison Reform Trust. In 1996, the Home Office commissioned a working party to determine the extent of un-met need for the DTC approach, of which the first author of this work was a member. Their recommendation, published in 1997, was for the creation of two new TC prisons, including a proposed establishment in the private sector, then termed 'Marchington for the Community', near an agreed site in Staffordshire. The HM Prison Service specification stated that

The therapeutic community should be provided in an autonomous prison setting providing 200-250 places in conditions of category B security. Close proximity to

---

1. Cullen, E (1993), *Prison Service Journal*, No.90, 35-37.

another Prison Service establishment, preferably of category C security, would be an advantage...

Following this, private consortia were invited to tender for the contract to build and run an 800-bed category B security prison, to include a separate 200-bed TC. The contract would be for a term of 25-years. Premier Custodial Services (hereinafter shortened to "Premier") was the lead company for the consortium which the first author joined as lead consultant. Dovegate was to become only the second "whole prison" TC in the UK since Grendon opened in 1962 — and the first to be managed by the private sector.

II. The Private Finance Initiative

The 1990s was the greatest period of growth in private sector funding for previously exclusively public sector organizations, including prisons. The Private Finance Initiative (PFI) was announced in the 1992 Autumn Statement of the Conservative party with the aim of "achieving closer partnerships between the public and private sectors". It was one of a range of policies introduced by the Conservative Government to increase the involvement of the private sector in the provision of public services. The PFI involves transferring the risks associated with public service projects to the private sector in part or in full. By the time the contract for Dovegate had been awarded in 2000, almost 450 PFI deals had been signed with a total capital value of £20 billion. PFI projects signed up to by the end of 2001 committed the Government to a stream of revenue payments to private sector contractors between 2001 and 2026 of almost £100 billion. The contract to build and run an 800-bed category B prison at a site in Marchington, Staffordshire was the beginning of the Dovegate story. Crucial to the initiative was ensuring the public sector client retained oversight of the quality control standards and that these explicit standards were contractually binding.

It is interesting to note in his speech announcing the creation of the PFI, that Norman Lamont, the then Chancellor of the Exchequer, set three broad conditions of compliance in principle (in addition to ensuring that taxpayers' interests were protected) wherein:

- he scrapped the rule that private projects could only be approved "after comparing them with a similar project in the public sector" (this was astonishingly sensible given there was no way of saying whether a public sector project was even considered or ever would be);

- the Government would treat proposed projects as joint ventures where relevant, rather than obliging them to be either wholly public or private; and finally

- there was to be greater use of leasing where it "offers good value for money. As long as it can be shown that the risk stays with the private sector, public organizations will be able to enter into operating lease agreements, with only the lease payments counting as expenditure and without their capital budgets being cut".[2]

III.   The Dovegate Bidding Process

HM Prison Service, the "official side" in these negotiations, opened the process by inviting expressions of interest from private sector consortia in the summer of 1997. By February 1998, Premier, along with five other consortia, presented their "Indicative Proposals" for the design, construction, management and financing (DCMF) of the 600-bed category B training prison and 200-bed TC at Marchington. These extremely detailed submissions were in direct response to equally detailed specifications setting out what was required. The major members of the Premier consortium were:

- Premier Prison Services (later Premier Custodial Services)
- Kvaerner Construction
- CAPITA EC Architectural Practice;
- Lazard Bros; and with
- Serco and Wackenhut Corrections as joint venture partners.

---

2.   HC Deb 12 November 1992 vol. 213 c998.

Premier Prison Services Limited (PPS)

Two major international companies created PPS: Wackenhut Corrections and Serco Limited. From its start in 1992, PPS's stated objective was

> …to create a uniquely appropriate vehicle for the establishment of focused solutions to the requirements of the Criminal Justice Services throughout the country.

The 'parent' company, Wackenhut, was at the time the "leading company developing and managing private prisons in the USA and Australia" and proudly boasted that its "current share of the global privatised corrections and prison facility management market [stood] at 25 per cent of total contracts let".

The form and content of bids were gradually shaped towards the preferred model and detail by a series of successive bidding stages and there were six bidding consortia. The next crucial stage was the short-list, when the number of bidders is reduced to, normally, three or four. This is followed shortly by something called the "Best and Final Offer" from each of the remaining bidding consortia, and is an attempt to enhance the various bids competitively to the optimum level, including so as to show what the bidders hope to be unique features, innovations and costings which might gain a crucial edge over competitors. This process results eventually in the Official Side selecting the "Preferred Bidder" which is in most cases the successful entrant. There remain, however, a few final hoops to jump through, including responding to searching questions about deliverability and detailed scrutiny of the operational and construction proposals.

IV.   The Operational Drafting

One of the most memorable aspects of the entire process was assembling and working creatively with the team of consultants assembled by Premier to draft the operational programmes for the TC at Dovegate. This process began with Premier's director of special projects, Michael Gander considering relevant consultants who were available outside the public sector. When the first author was invited to join as the lead consultant, the team soon began to take shape, including Dr Jeff Roberts, psychiatrist; the Group Analytic Practice, London; Elaine Genders, Dean of Students, University College, London; and Joe Chapman, formerly a senior officer at Grendon Underwood TC.

The question of who would be the director of therapy was crucial to ultimate success, possibly of the bid itself and certainly in anticipation of the opening of the TC. At that time, Roland Woodward was the therapist in charge of a small TC for life-sentenced prisoners at Gartree Prison, a unit which he had created with the support of the prison Governor there. Roland Woodward had also been a wing therapist at Grendon, giving him more direct TC management and therapy experience than anyone else in the country. His acknowledged qualities of leadership, professional integrity and knowledge made him our first choice for this crucial post and, fortunately, he accepted. It was to be his strength of character which was most tested in the years that followed.

Treatment Model of Choice

It was essential from the beginning to combine proven treatment efficacy with traditional TC practice and add a number of viable innovations. A multi-modal model of treatment was agreed. The primary treatment model was social-psychological enhanced with elements of cognitive behavioural therapy and group psychotherapy. The history of democratic-analytic TCs in general and that of Grendon Underwood in particular had taught us that therapeutic direction was clearer and simpler, and the day-to-day therapeutic life of the community much less fraught, with a single agreed theoretical model. The conclusion of Genders and Player in *Grendon: A Study of a Therapeutic Prison*[3] was that "the therapeutic community gives predominance to social learning over psychoanalytic methods". The main architects of the treatment programme design, Cullen and Woodward, were both psychologists with a combined experience of over 25-years working in TCs and with the growing

---

3. (1995) Oxford University Press.

conviction that the relevant population were offenders whose crimes were a direct *product* of personal deficits in their relationships with other people. Growing research findings showed that treatment based on cognitive therapy and interpersonal skills was more effective in reducing future offending, which we believed was the most important objective of (and justification for) prison treatment. All this meant that we were absolutely resolute in our conviction that the Dovegate bid from Premier would not perpetuate the psycho-analytic imperative. It would also be disingenuous not to record that Premier knew that psychiatrists were significantly more expensive to employ than, for example, counsellors, but this was not a consideration for the lead consultant and director of therapy.

Bid Outline

The main headings required of the bids included:

- The consortium
- Timetable
- Design, construction and operation
- Outline plans
- Daily routines
- Prisoner employment
- Healthcare
- Management charts
- Visits
- Throughcare.

The bid specific to the TC required:

- Design of the TC
- The daily routine in the TC
- Staff training
- Relationships with Grendon Prison
- Work with other agencies.

The bids had to be in sufficient detail to ensure that they were both operationally viable (i.e. they provided a blueprint for the creation of the institution) and that they complied in full to the specifications required.

Throughout the process, in meetings within the Premier team, we were reminded that the cost margins were the crucial imperative and that although important (possibly critical to the competitive aspect), innovation and programme integrity were perforce secondary. In other words, the internal presumption was that we had to be cheaper or, if more expensive than the competition, we would have to be significantly better in our proposal content to offset the additional expense.

The Lead Consultant

Being the lead consultant carried with it a small list of not inconsequential responsibilities. Keeping the team on a course sufficiently narrow to progress on schedule yet sufficiently wide to accommodate all perspectives and stimulate creative interaction was probably the key task. I had a clear theoretical model in mind and was not prepared to compromise it. The TC model for Dovegate must be social-democratic, based on individual and collective responsibility and accountability and primarily addressing relevant criminal and interpersonal behaviour as distinct from interpretations of personal histories. There was to be a psychiatric presence to ensure that prisoners were being referred ("referrals"), assessed and did not suffer from mental health legislation disorders (i.e. an assessment/diagnostic function) and to ensure that once in therapy, if staff were concerned as to the state of mind of any resident, they had a qualified psychiatrist to whom they could refer. This determination was born of over ten years' experience of the TCs at Grendon where the psychiatrists and psychologists seemed inevitably to be engaged in polite/strained/confrontational dialogue as to the appropriate language/interpretation to use. This, together with the parallel process of the psychiatrists directing therapy and the governor grades directing prison life, meant that much of the energy for creative change was too often diverted into interdepartmental tensions as well as leaving the most professionally qualified staff spending more time on managerial issues and at meetings, rather than directly involved in ensuring effective therapy was taking place. The lead consultant was only directly involved during the bidding and building stages in the life of Dovegate TC. Once the director of therapy, Roland Woodward, was in position, he assumed responsibility for the development of the TC within the context of the creation of the overall, 800-bed category B prison.

V. Success

The Home Office[4] side having considered and compared the bids on the formally agreed criteria finally announced that the short list of three consortia must submit their 'Best and Final Offer'. Final changes, modifications and additions to the by now massive submissions were then given to the Contracts and Competitions Group to scrutinise. In 1997, HM Prison Service announced that Premier Custodial Group Ltd was the Preferred Bidder, i.e. we'd won! To have both come from careers in the public service and be engaged so intensely in the bidding process for a private sector company and consortium was an exciting and in some ways liberating experience. There are a few significant experiences we should summarise:

- Private sector contract negotiations focus the mind wonderfully towards delivering the best possible blueprint for carceral regimes;

- There is a fiscal imperative in the nature of competitive bidding which limits the quality of the bid because staffing, and especially professional staffing, is the most expensive element of the equation;

- The Official Side has full knowledge of all the competing tenders, but the bidders (for obvious reasons) are working blind, i.e. with no knowledge of any of the other bidders proposals. While this is entirely understandable, it obviates any opportunities to take the best elements of the various bids and to combine them into an "all-star" bid; and

---

4. Home Office responsibility for prisons passed to the Ministry of Justice in 2007.

- Although it is tremendously exciting to win a bidding competition for a contract of such magnitude, it would be foolish indeed not to realise that the work was just beginning. We next had to build the prison—which entailed a fascinating dialogue with a local action group adamantly opposed to the entire project-and we had to recruit and train the entire staff, apart from a few senior managers already online.

The contractor was obliged to submit detailed self-audit proposals. To this end, Premier committed to annual, monthly, weekly and daily (or other interval) audits by the management staff responsible under the direction of the contract compliance officer (CCO). The CCO was also tasked to carry out some of these audits as leader of a Task Force Group (TFG). Premier also committed to audits incorporating the requirements of:

- The Dovegate director's rules for the main prison and TC sectors
- The security manual
- Home Office instructions
- Statutory Instruments
- Applicable legislation.

The successful bid provided extremely detailed arrangements for the Controller-TC to determine compliance with the contract through daily and periodic audits. Premier were required to have in place systems which monitored every aspect of the contract including available places, programme performance measures, security, visits, etc. The controller has access to all documentation—written and electronic—as well as final executive reports in all areas agreed with the authority and within the contract for the operation of Dovegate TC (as well as for Dovegate main prison).

VI. The Dovegate TC Philosophy and Objectives

The original model proposed by HM Prison Service recommended that prisoners referred to the TC should be:

33

- sentenced adult males with a minimum of two years to serve;

- those assessed as having a disorder in social functioning;

- suitability for the TC to be clinically assessed in a formal procedure conducted by professional staff;

- prisoners to be drug-free and assessed for mental or physical health conditions which might preclude them from entering the TC;

- prisoners to have the right to decline to be transferred to the TC.[5]

Although not requested in the Operational Specifications, the lead consultant for the TC and the team of consultants who had helped draft the successful proposals understood the need for these proposals to be informed and guided by wider philosophical principles:

- A conviction that **active democratic participation** in running the community is an essential component to developing the socialisation awareness element of a non-criminal life. This meant specific individual and collective responsibilities in power through choice and engagement in the process of rule-making for the community.

- **Yalom's eleven therapeutic factors** would inform our treatment and training programmes. Principal among these are universality, group cohesiveness and interpersonal learning.

- The **Generative Power of Everyday Living.** This principle was articulated for us by Dovegate's first director of therapy, Roland Woodward and came originally from a conference of the Association of Therapeutic Communities (ATC). It is about demanding from residents that they "engage with the moment and...with the process of one person 'being there' for another person".

---

5. This was a compromise falling somewhere between declared consent and direction to attend.

- **Respect for the traditions** of past and current TCs.

- Those resident on the Dovegate TC are personality disordered offenders who are being treated. So long as they didn't threaten security, the **primacy of therapy** would be our first priority.

The Premier bid was an impressive combination of proven treatment methodology, intelligent prison parameters and a wide range of innovative proposals. The core of the TC bid included an explicit *definition:*

A prison therapeutic community offers a safe environment with a clear structure of boundaries and expectations where residents have the opportunity to understand and resolve their past and learn and practice new skills within a treatment setting involving other members and staff.

Our stated mission was:

Marchington therapeutic community will seek the improvement of each prisoner's behaviour, both in the Community and after release, by the provision of an environment which provides and requires:

- trust and responsibility;
- care and challenge;
- opportunity and co-operation; and
- self-understanding and commitment to change.

We stated five unambiguous, key *Objectives:*

1. To reintegrate and strengthen the offender's: (a) personality; and (b) ability to live in a positive, adaptive, non-exploitative way.
2. To instil a sense of communal and social responsibilities.
3. To improve each man's behaviour towards others.
4. If relevant, to reduce drug and other chemical abuse and dependency; and, as a consequence of these:

5. To reduce offending as measured by the official rates of reconviction and re-sentencing.

These objectives were chosen deliberately to include all the aspects of criminality within our target population which we believed to be relevant to a TC approach. Disorders of personality have always been, and remain, the primary description for our "presenting problem". That is, there is some relatively abiding feature of the personal clusters of characteristics which might be relevantly addressed and that this aspect was ideographic, i.e. a constant factor throughout rather than particular to one individual. Improving interpersonal behaviour within the day-to-day experience of the TCs was for us an obvious second objective. It was insufficient to have a broad stroke goal of more "healthy" personality without more specific and observable criteria which might be quantified. Equally, a social-behavioural TC would hardly be justified without this objective. The instilling of a wider communal sense of responsibility is, in other words, the re-socialisation of people who are by definition outside society, i.e. convicted prisoners.

It may be a presumption to assert that they were categorically outside society by virtue of their convictions, but it was felt that this objective was consonant with the communal nature and principles of TCs and was a relevant objective. How to measure it within the research evaluation however, was another question. Reducing substance abuse and dependency is an objective which reflects the sadly endemic nature of drug-related problems within our target population and had become of such a magnitude that it justified a separate objective. Finally, we are categorical in our conviction that lowering re-offending is not just an appropriate and defensible objective for a TC regime, it is *the most important objective*.

Main Elements of the Regime

The five main elements of an offender's experience in Dovegate were to be:

- TC treatment components involving small group therapy, larger community meetings and work with individual contracts.

- Additional core treatment activities involving improvement in cognitive skills, e.g. reasoning and rehabilitation (R&R) courses.

- Collateral treatment programmes such as anger control, sex offender treatment programmes (on the Assessment Unit), addiction courses, stress and anxiety management, psychodrama, etc.

- Work and education to include external and internal sentence-planning activities.

- Physical education as part of an holistic approach to treatment.

VII. Innovations

It was explicit within the Home Office request for "Indicative Proposals" that innovation was a factor to be considered. To this end, the Premier TC bid included a number of what we felt to be critical advances on any previous therapeutic regimes as set out under the sub-heads below.

The High Intensity Programme (HIP)

TCs have suffered from chronically high attrition rates experienced both during and after the selection process. Rates of the magnitude of over one in five leaving as a result of the assessment period were not uncommon and the normal range published for Grendon and the Max Glatt Unit[6] were of the order of 15 to 20 per cent. Following that, there were several subsequent stages in treatment where "patients" were being lost. In one report from Grendon, the loss was so bad that less than ten per cent of those originally arriving for therapy were recorded as having completed their treatment to the satisfaction of the staff. Clearly there was a problem. The High Intensity Unit was designed with two purposes in mind: (a) to take difficult life-sentence

---

6. See *Chapter 3.*

prisoners who needed more detailed and sensitive assessment before being on normal location, on one of the TC units; and (b) to act as a "time out" location for men on normal location who were either at risk of losing their place due to failing to adjust or when the TC deemed it prudent to give them a brief hiatus from therapy.

Clear, Delineated Selection Criteria

One of the most abiding criticisms of prison-based TCs in the UK has been the perceived selectivity of the TCs themselves. Critics asserted that the TCs would "select out" the worst candidates, leaving a core of relatively compliant, anxious, articulate introverts who were capable of adopting the verbal skills required to succeed in the group-based treatment world of the TC. In reality, in common with the existing DTCs in the public sector, Dovegate took "prisoners convicted of a serious violent offence [who] have a significant offending history; approximately 90 per cent of the population has a diagnosable personality disorder". Selection criteria were based on treatment needs, including:

- antisocial attitudes and feelings;

- distorted thinking used to justify/minimise the seriousness of offending;

- difficulty in recognising relevant risk factors and generating appropriate strategies to cope with them;

- dependency on alcohol and drugs;

- adverse social and/or family histories and circumstances;

- deviant sexual or violent interests; especially arousal patterns and preoccupations; and

- poor social, interpersonal skills which are often offence-relevant.

Multi-Modal Treatment

The Premier bid had an approach which:

- was holistic in its treatment, i.e. of the whole person of the offender;

- was fully integrated with each prisoner's sentence management and individual treatment action plan (ITAP);

- used comprehensive small group, large group and full TC experiences;

- employed powerful and supportive targeted cognitive and educational programmes;

- provided, additionally, need-driven individual counselling and cognitive behavioural programmes aimed at a reduction of offending behaviours;

- integrated work and education into the TC programme; and

- used an integrated assessment, sex offender treatment programme (SOTP) and resettlement unit.

Referral and Entry Criteria

The current agreed entry criteria for all DTCs are:

- a minimum of 18 months to serve; category B security;

- assessed as medium, high or very high **risk** of serious harm to others and a medium or high risk of reconviction;

- has deficits in two or more of the following **criminogenic 'needs'**: self-management; coping and problem-solving; relationship skills/inter-personal relating; antisocial beliefs, values and attitudes; and emotional management and functioning;

- **responsivity**: Must be: motivated to participate in a TC programme; willing to work as part of a community, participate in groups and be subject to the democratic process; willing to commit to staying for at least 18 months; and have reached the point in their lives when they say they are ready to change and appear so;

- no offences outstanding, nor is the offender appealing against conviction; and

- not to have failed a mandatory drug test for at least two months.

VIII. The Assessment Process

Enquiries come into the referral office, which then sends out a Dovegate TC Application Pack. This includes information about Dovegate and asks for information from the applicant.

This is returned to the head of assessment (a psychologist), who checks the application against the criteria. If all the criteria are fulfilled, the individual is offered a place for assessment or placed on the waiting list whilst further information is gathered, e.g. current use of medication.

When a vacancy arises, the individual is admitted. If there is not a place on the Assessment Unit, they may be placed temporarily on the Reintegration Unit as a holding placement.

Once on the Assessment Unit, they are given an induction by staff. They then proceed to the formal assessment programme. This consists of two small group meetings a week, two community meetings and a Job Club. In the third and fourth weeks they undertake the psychometric tests, which consist of:

- Ravens Progressive Matrices — Intelligence
- Persons Relating to Others Questionnaire, Version 3 (PROQ—3)
- Psychological Inventory of Criminal Thinking Styles (PICTS)

- Offender Group Reconviction Scale (OGRS)
- Offender Assessment System (OAYSys)
- Hostility/Direction of Hostility Questionnaire (HDHQ)
- EPQ-R: Eysenck Personality Questionnaire: Revised (EPQ-R)
- Impulsivity, Venturesomeness and Empathy (IVE)
- CFSEI (2): Culture-Free Self-Esteem Inventory Version 2 (CFSEI (2))
- Personality Attributes Inventory (PAI)
- Sex Offences Attitude Questionnaire (SOAQ)
- Personality Deviance Questionnaire, Version 4 (PDQ-4); and
- Psychopathy scan (P scan); and where possible
- Twenty-item checklist to assess risk of future violence in criminal and psychiatric populations (HRC-20).

During this same period, the officers undertake behavioural observations and take a full social history. A final report is drawn up by the Assessment Unit staff and the voting slip regarding suitability is raised. A decision is taken over a period of about a week as to the suitability of any individual resident. At week 12, there is a case conference which includes community contributions, staff feedback on contributions, self-assessment and a discussion on progress and areas to develop. The Head of Assessment then writes the final report. At this point the prisoner either progresses to a TC, returns to his sending establishment (sometimes via the Reintegration Unit), or if appropriate the assessment period can be extended.

IX. Research Programme

Incredibly, Grendon had continued to be an experiment for 30 years and had only added a research department at the initiative of the head of psychology in the 1990s. The Premier bid for Dovegate put this right by including a detailed research proposal which crucially would be run by an external university-based department and, again critically, the contract for this work would also be awarded openly after consideration by an independent expert panel. The research contract was awarded to the Psychology Department led by Professor Jennifer Brown at Surrey University. That research, published in

2010 (see in particular *Chapter 9*) proved that the Dovegate TC regime was successful in significantly reducing re-convictions over a two-year period.

Summary

The process of winning the bid to build and run the TC at Dovegate on a 25-year contract was the biggest achievement of the first author's professional career. The next crucial challenge was to create the communities within Dovegate category B prison and to sustain them. This was in many ways a greater challenge and one in which the second author played, and continues to play, a vital role.

We are proud of the achievements of the TC at Dovegate. Yet, just as a business must adapt to survive in a parlous economic climate, so TCs face ever-changing challenges to their integrity and survival. How to adapt without compromise is the key. We hope this book will serve both as a chronicle of an achievement and — given the long list of TCs closed due to short-term financial expediency by local managers and the issues raised by Ray Duckworth in Part 1 of *Chapter 10* — as an aid to survival.

CHAPTER TWO

THE POLITICS OF PRIVATISATION

I have to say that I am fundamentally opposed both in principle to the privatisation of the Prison Service and indeed in practice. In principle, I am opposed because I believe that people who are sentenced by the State to imprisonment should be deprived of their liberty, kept under lock and key by those who are accountable primarily and solely to the State.

The Rt Hon Tony Blair, *Prison Service Journal* (July 1995)

And private prisons have been delivering, by and large, a far higher standard of treatment for prisoners than the public sector.

Sir (now Lord) David Ramsbotham, HM Chief Inspector of Prisons (2001)

Notwithstanding the ethical high ground taken by the Prime Minister to be, the period of greatest growth in the private sector coincided precisely with Tony Blair's tenure. We thought it might be interesting to explain something of the main elements and stages of the process of bidding and contracting between the Home Office[1] and the private sector. The wider scenario concerns the related arguments for private versus public prisons.

Dovegate is a private sector prison and TC. It requires therefore a thorough consideration of the arguments for and against private prisons specifically set within the wider arena of the Private Finance Initiative (PFI).

I.   The Private Prison Business

It might seem odd that two authors who have worked in the private sector should want to include a chapter criticising and questioning the privatisation of prisons. There is already a great deal of recorded opinion on the subject

---

1.   Since 2007, in a prison-related context, the Ministry of Justice.

in print and on the internet. However, very little of it is from people who have worked and lived on both sides of the fence, who understand both public and private protocols. The first author was employed by a private prison company, Premier Custodial Services Ltd, having previously worked in the public sector HM Prison Service for over 20 years. The second author was until recently employed in both the private and public sectors. We are both acutely aware of the differences and of the very different pressures, as lead consultant and consultant psychiatrist respectively, for a project which involves a huge contractual obligation over a 25-year period. We offer a comparison of the public and private management of TCs within prisons, based on our unique perspectives so as to let the reader decide.

The American Private Prison Industry

Perhaps inevitably, private prisons began in the USA. It is now a $50 billion plus industry[2] which was, after a boom period of over a decade, in serious difficulties between 1995 and 2004 due to a spate of court actions, many brought by the American Civil Liberties Union, and usually concerning the alleged ill-treatment of prisoners or of other types of unprofessional conduct by staff. More recently, however, the private prisons have recovered impetus and have entered another period of expansion. Not coincidentally, this pattern has been replicated in England and Wales. There are, however, more prisoners in private sector prisons in the USA than make up the total UK prison population.

It is worth putting the scale of the American prison industry into perspective. According to the US Bureau of Justice Statistics (USBJS): "In 2008, 7.3 million people were on probation, in jail or prison, or on parole at year end, 3.2% of all US adult residents". The USA has the highest documented incarceration rate in the world at 754 persons in prison or jail per 100,000 (as of 2008). It has less than 5% of the world's population and 23.4% of the world's prison population. The rates of incarceration compare with the UK's 148 (the highest in Europe), Australia's 126 and Norway's 66.

---

2. I.e. in terms of the total value of the private sector prison estate.

In recent decades, the USA has experienced a "surge in its prison population, *quadrupling* since 1980, partially as a result of mandated sentences that
came about during the 'war on drugs'". In 2002, over 10% of all black males
in the USA between the ages of 25 and 29 were sentenced and in prison,
compared to 2.4% of Hispanic males and 1.3% of whites.

The *Wall Street Journal* of 19 November 2008 noted that "private prisons
housed 7.4% of the country's 1.59 million incarcerated adults in federal and
State prisons". These 117,000 prisoners were mainly in the "care" of one of
three big companies: Corrections Corporation of America (CCA), which
had 66 facilities as of 2009, the Geo Group and the Cornell Company.

The principle function of these private prisons in America is to house
large numbers of prisoners more economically than can be done by the State
or Federal systems and, it might be argued, to perpetuate the capitalist principle of free market economy in every sphere.

In America, there is now little debate or discussion regarding the relative
merits of State or corporate imprisonment.

Private Prisons in the United Kingdom

Largescale corporate privatisation in the UK began with the Channel Tun-
nel in 1987. It was unquestionably a political initiative of the Conservative
Government of Margaret Thatcher, a conscious and deliberate attempt to
"free up" the economy, allowing market forces to dictate and reduce public sector "inefficiencies and overspending". In November 1992, the then
Chancellor of the Exchequer, Norman Lamont, created the Private Finance
Initiative (PFI) specifically to generate an infrastructure to encourage private
capital investment in what were previously public sector developments. The
major, seismic, impetus of privatisation in companies, and public services,
e.g. transportation and telecommunications, changed the landscape of service contracting for the foreseeable future. This was followed by the Private
Public Partnership (PPP), a "third way" initiative intended to give greater
credibility to privatisation and help it to appear more collaborative and less
political. In essence, it is an alternative to either a capitalistic or socialistic
approach to public service delivery.

In England and Wales, by 2010 the private prison sector already had eleven establishments of the total prison estate of 132 and was looking to expand with another five at varying stages of the PFI process, planned to provide an additional 7,500 places. Private prisons "now account for 11% of the prison population, holding around 9,071 prisoners."[3] Were these five new and very large prisons to open in the private sector, it would nearly double the numbers, meaning in excess of 16,500 (of a current total number in excess of 85,500), or nearly 20%.

The *Guardian* newspaper of 13 July 2011 commented on an announcement by Justice Secretary Kenneth Clarke as follows:

> The decision to put nine prisons up for competition...is potentially the largest single privatisation programme in the history of the prison service in England and Wales...Already 12 of the 138 jails are run by the private sector. A further four are already earmarked to be built and run by the private sector.[4]

If these plans are realised, 15 per cent of all prisons in Britain would be in the private sector, raising questions about the tipping-point for the public/private prison management equilibrium. So what are the fundamental issues concerning the debate between public and private imprisonment? Perhaps the first ethical concern is that contracting for imprisonment could arguably involve an improper delegation to private hands of power and authority over other citizens where those individuals had been apprehended, detained, tried and convicted in public sector institutions.

Linked to this concern is that private management may put profit motives ahead of the public interest, inmate welfare, or the rehabilitative potential of imprisonment. The arguments in defence of privatisation would counter this by saying that contracting enhances justice by placing accountability to the public "client" clearly and explicitly on a contractual basis with extensive, detailed standards and conditions which must be met by law and are subject to regular independent inspections to ensure compliance and, crucially, it

---

3. Prison Reform Trust, *Newsletter*, No.57.
4. "Private companies in the USA operate 264 correctional facilities, housing almost 99,000 adult offenders" (from Schmalleger F and Smykia J (2007, 2005, 2002), *Corrections in the 21st Century*, New York: McGraw-Hill).

is less expensive and funded outside the public purse. In fact, private prison companies would argue that the rigorous contractual requirements on standards of imprisonment add a new layer of scrutiny which improves both legal due process and safeguards higher standards of individual treatment.

Yet there remain abiding concerns as to the ethics of private imprisonment, many of which were unforeseen. While the risk of putting profit before standards has not really developed as forewarned, other challenges have appeared including the litigation in American private prisons already mentioned above. Female offenders successfully suing private companies for sexual assaults against them by male staff in female prisons is but one example. When stockholders can influence terms and conditions of imprisonment based on their fears of lawsuits, the entire privatisation industry is threatened with compromise. We need to learn in the UK from the serious problems in the USA.

As already noted, the American market is estimated to be approaching $50 billion in total value. The three biggest companies CCA, Geo and Cornell, with over two-thirds of the total private sector between them, have experienced major litigation reversals. One involved a federal jury in South Carolina awarding over £3 million in December 2000 to a teenage inmate who was "hog-tied and thrown against a wall" by CCA officers. Similar lawsuits occurred in this, and other, States. There have also been two successful claims against Wackenhut employees involving male staff and female inmates. One website specifically created to campaign against private prisons quoted a report from the USA Department of Justice about problems with another CCA facility:

The [facility] has experienced pivotal failures in its security and operational management as a result of seriously flawed decisions by leaders of both CCA and DOC [Department of Corrections]…It is reasonable to conclude that certain of the most serious problems which endangered the safety of the public, the staff or the inmates were preventable or subject to mitigation.[5]

---

5. See paulsjusticepage.com/crimepays; last accessed June 2011.

The irony of these reversals is that, by the mid-1990s in America, the debate over privatising prisons was seen as over and the private sector was presumed to be the victor. As of 31 December 1999, there were 145,160 beds in 190 facilities under contract or construction as private sector adult facilities in the USA, UK and Australia, with the overwhelming majority being in the USA. In a report by the USA National Centre for Policy Analysis, it was asserted that "There is no insurmountable legal obstacle to total privatisation of prison operation". Yet, in a remarkable reversal of fortune, the private sector had seen "an industry who's grand expectations have outpaced its ability to deliver" with a decline in private prison numbers, questions raised over management abilities and the profit-making approach, and the largest, CCA experiencing a "Third quarter 2000 loss of $253 million and their stock plummeting from a high of $45 in 1998 to $0.18 in February 2001. By the beginning of 2000, "just 85,000 of the 1.9 million jail and prison beds nationwide (in the U.S.) were provided by private firms". However, as noted, this is a $50 billion market, so even this relatively small proportion in the private sector represents a huge investment potential.

In the UK, the situation is a scaled-down model of the American one. The Thatcher Government allowed the private sector into prisons "following lobbying by companies and the Adam Smith Institute".[6] When Labour came to power on 2 May 1997, there were six prisons run by the private sector. The Howard League for Penal Reform was totally opposed, Frances Crook its director arguing that "At best the commercialisation of prisons has been a distraction, at worst it might have contributed to the increase in prison numbers".[7]

Alan Travis, writing in the *Guardian*,[8] argued that the lack of private interest in bidding for the running of Brixton Prison marked the failure of the first attempt to privatise a State-run jail and that it "[came] hard on the heals of a decision to hand back Blakenhurst, one of the first prisons to be run by a private company, to the State". Travis posited that while prisons may be losing their appeal to private operators, they have "wasted no time

6. "Crime Pays Handsomely for Britain's Private Jails", Mathiason N, *The Observer*, 11 March 2001.
7. 29 April 2002.
8. 12 July 2001 and see guardian.co.uk/politics/2001/jul/12/ukcrime.socialsciences

looking further afield for profitable opportunities", citing South Africa as the next private prison area for development.

In the ensuing years, the debate disappeared, such that, in April 2009, the then Justice Secretary, Jack Straw, announced that seven consortia had been invited by the National Offenders Management Service (NOMS) to compete "for inclusion on a framework that will allow firms to bid" for five new PFI 1,500 bed prisons. This began the second great PFI initiative in prisons in the UK's history and followed nearly 18 years after the first private sector prison The Wolds. "Membership" of the process was awarded in 2010, which essentially confirms the acceptable consortia. This however must be set against the economic tidal wave of cuts imposed upon all civil service departments from the fiscal year 2010-2011 onwards. It remains to be seen whether the Ministry of Justice will continue with the awarding of contracts at the same time that NOMS is having to find cuts to their budget in excess of £1 billion over the next three fiscal years.

We believe, however, that there is still an important concern about the expanding use of private imprisonment and summarise what we see as both sides of the argument below under costs, quality, accountability, security and ethical considerations

Some Arguments for Private Prisons

Cost
Contracting to private companies or consortia allows those prisons being built from scratch to be financed, sited, constructed and opened much more quickly and cheaply than government alternatives. Private sector procedures also allow management to break from the expensive staffing levels determined across time and bound up in union-official side agreements, as well as reducing public employee (non-contributory, index-linked) pensions and benefits. Newly built prisons in the private sector can be specifically designed and constructed for more efficient maintenance and operation. Contracting-out prison building through open and competitive bidding creates an impetus to be as cost efficient as possible and makes the true costs highly visible and

more accountable. Public sector building, maintenance and operating costs are more difficult to determine due to the additional expenses of central bureaucratic administration responsible for a myriad of different aspects of the overall expense. Spending on the private prisons, according to the Campaign against Prison Slavery (CAPS) was £259.4 million in 2007-8.

Quality

Private contracting makes prisons more responsible by detailed contractually binding conditions linked to financial penalties. The nature of competitive tendering encourages creativity and innovation in programmes of offender treatment and education. In fact, the official side, in this case the Ministry of Justice[9] and HM Prison Service, build in incentives within the formal bid request documentation for more qualitative features of this kind. On the other hand, the authors know from many years of personal experience that the public mentality to change and innovation is, at best, more conservative and, at worst, a disincentive to innovation.

The conditions in private sector prisons are often superior to their, admittedly usually much older, public sector counterparts. The quality of the therapy at Dovegate is addressed by the Advisory and Steering Group, which was created as part of the original contract.

Accountability

Competition between the public and private sectors, fostered by the opportunities for both to bid for new contracts on existing prisons and through the generally competitive atmosphere which tendering encourages, acts to raise the standards in terms of efficiency and performance for both sectors. Finally, the quality of the service provided also increases through the far more public debate and scrutiny which ensues, a variation on the classic market forces principle of supply and demand. Private prisons have Controllers appointed by and acting directly to HM Prison Service. These relatively senior administrators are on-site and directly involved in regular, daily scrutiny of how well the terms of the contracts are being met. Contracts are reviewed on a quarterly basis.

---

9. Formerly the Home Office.

Security

The consequences of breaches of security for staff, especially management, in the private sector are probably directly greater than in the public sector. Contracts specifically link performance criteria in terms of security to stiff financial penalties, another strong motivation to raise and maintain high security standards. Security is not a significant factor in considering the relative merits of the two systems.

Ethical Considerations

It could be argued that, if health and welfare services can be provided competitively by both the private and public sector, why not prisons? So long as the standard of containment and treatment in private prisons matches or exceeds that of public prisons, are there any other sustainable ethical concerns. Some are noted in the section concerning public sector prisons below.

Some Arguments Against Private Prisons

Cost

There is an inevitable profit margin to be added to costs in all private enterprise. Private sector imperatives are that you have to beat the competition and make your product cheaper and you have to make a profit. This twin imperative means that private prison management is more concerned with satisfying the shareholders than running a therapeutically successful prison.

	Male Cat B	Cat C	Juvenile	Local	Female Closed
Private	£26,813	£20,855	£48,669	£33,805	£44,400
Public	£25,881	£21,976	£42,143	£31,912	£34,617

The average costs per prisoner place matched for other factors such as security category are higher for most private sector prisons:[10]

Quality

The economic imperatives of competitive tendering can reduce the most expensive resource of TCs, the staff. Professional staff, particularly medical staff, can be among the most expensive and the fact that the TC at Dovegate only has one consultant psychiatrist and no probation officers could be a false economy. One unexpected problem with the public versus private setup is that the management of Serco generally and Dovegate specifically have often failed to co-operate openly with the other DTCs in the public sector in terms of sharing professional opinion and expertise on the ground that this is commercially privileged.

The staff at Dovegate TC are paid less than the staff at equivalent public sector establishments, especially the wing therapists and counsellors. In 2008, the post of director of therapy was filled by an operational Governor grade and one of the existing wing therapists was obliged to fill both this current post and the now subordinated role of head of therapy. In spite of the improving scores in the Community of Communities' DTC audits, it is impossible to argue that the Dovegate DTC professional therapy staffing profile is as strong as that of Grendon, to which it must be compared.

Accountability

There is a risk that private companies invoke forms of confidentiality in the name of "commercial interests" to prevent sufficient scrutiny from, for example, the media.

The degree and specific terms of accountability of the private provider to the public service is entirely determined by the contract. If it's in the contract, it's required. The safeguards for ensuring compliance are the financial penalties, in many instances quite swingeing. These standards and targets cover the whole contract, every aspect of the management of the establish-

---

10. Campaign Against Prison Slavery (CAPS).

ment, and are very specific, e.g. the population levels, hours for constructive activities and staffing complement.

While this is a strong safeguard against the private sector letting standards slip, it also puts pressures on the management of the prisons which can sometimes exacerbate problems of performance standards through stress and the temptation to perform "creative accountability".

Security

Security in private prisons might be undermined by relatively high staff turnover—a result of relatively lower pay and poorer conditions of employment—thus creating an inexperienced, under-trained staff more vulnerable to concerted acts of indiscipline from prisoners. There is however no evidence to date that security is not every bit as good in the private sector.

Ethical considerations

The obvious, and oft repeated, arguments against prison privatisation include the concern that delegating authority over peoples' lives in positions of subjugations can lead to an improper use of coercive power and authority, and that the profit imperative will be placed before all else. To date, there is scant evidence of this being the case or of instances where offender mistreatment can be directly attributable to the fact that an establishment is privately run. There remain however questions as to implications of a legal nature concerning the degree of accountability between the Ministry of Justice on the one hand and contracted private sector consortia. Where do the primary legal responsibilities lie if individual prisoners take legal action for alleged mistreatment? Who is ultimately responsible for the well-being of prisoners held in the private sector but detained, tried and sentenced in the public sector Criminal Justice System?

Summary

On balance, the arguments for privatisation may just tip the scales, but concerns exist that market forces and parent companies' shareholders exercise too great an influence on the decisions made by the UK private prison sector. We have seen little of the feared effects of profit imperatives influencing how the staff on the units treat the residents, but we have seen the pressures of contract conditions set with the Home Office failing to be met and of financial penalties resulting. There is absolutely no question that this focuses the mind wonderfully and has an immediate and catalysing effect on private sector managers. Improvements are driven through as priorities, unlike anything we ever saw in the public sector; although the past decade saw a transformation in the managerial mentality when (public sector)prison Governors and boards were given personal responsibility for devolved budgets for their prisons on an annual basis. When faced with percentage cuts in costs year-to-year, managers felt the acutely uncomfortable truths which face private businessmen and the self-employed on a daily basis—cutting staff, concern over re-investment in plant, etc.

For the first author, working in the public sector HM Prison Service for nearly 23 years left a frustrating sense of institutional inertia, too many layers of bureaucratic administration which stifled initiative and a pervading concern not to make mistakes rather than a culture of enquiry.

The Prison Service introduced devolved budgets (without, sadly, the commensurate devolved power). Increased accountability without increased authority means increased stress and a potentially decreased sense of commitment and ownership. In TCs in the public sector, here speaking of Grendon Underwood, the annual pressure to reduce costs was almost always an exercise in cutting either the number of staff, the replacement of more expensive therapists with cheaper ones, e.g. psychiatrists with psychologists/probation officers/psychotherapists, and the replacement of more senior/experienced staff with younger and therefore cheaper individuals. This has led, over the years, to a complete change in the professional profile of the prison, with now no psychiatrists or medical officers at all remaining and the provision of medical/psychiatric expertise left to the local Primary Healthcare Trust to determine.

The private sector prison industry has been, in the main, a more positive and stimulating place to work. The sense of enterprise is infectious and, although there were a number of relatively senior HM Prison Service ex-governors and regional directors within the management team of Premier, they seemed to behave differently: more relaxed and cooperative, still very concerned about fiscal and personnel matters, but with a greater sense of ownership, of being part of an organization they could identify with and that they felt motivated by.

Unfortunately, there are also a number of disadvantages to working within the private prisons sector. Foremost in the first author's experience was the realisation that, whatever we proposed, the shareholders of the American parent company could veto it and could do so on questionable grounds, i.e. fear of prosecution and concern for profit margins sometimes took pre-emptive precedence over innovation and concern for residents' conditions of imprisonment. In this sense, they were of course not really that different from public sector management, but the public sector had an abiding obligation to look after those in their charge: there were never any questions that it might decline to be involved. Concern for litigious prisoners is another area that seems to feature more strongly in the private context. While it is understandable, do we really want our prison service providers being led by financial and legal imperatives over those of criminal justice?

An unexpected area of concern which occurred during the writing of this book casts light on another view of the private sector for which our public sector experiences throw up nothing comparable.

Several years ago, it was alleged to the first author that most of the management of the parent company, Premier Custodial Services, had been summarily sacked. The director responsible for leading the bidding process for this successful contract (and several others) had been dismissed with no notice and via a letter to the company staff which had been prepared before the directors themselves were told. A short time after the summary dismissal of three directors, the executive director herself was forcibly removed from office by the parent American company, Wakenhut, in an equally pre-emptive manner. It is impossible not to feel a sense of antipathy for this kind of treatment, especially when we work in a therapeutic tradition which honours dialogue, trust and integrity as essential within relationships, formal and informal.

There is a relatively strong argument for the private sector continuing alongside the public in prison contracting but abiding vigilance is necessary. It might be better if the companies bidding for future contracts were less obligated, and controlled, by their larger USA-based parent companies where the fear of litigation and the profit imperative seem to be more ruth-lessly observed. Equally, there is an argument that the public sector could contract out only the building phase to the private sector, and retain the management function.

Although considerable progress has been made in addressing concerns about accountability, ethics and transparency with regard to private prisons generally, there are additional concerns relating in particular to the running of TCs in prisons.

These issues were addressed in "Legitimacy, Accountability and Private Prisons" (2002) by Elaine Genders. In that article, she refers directly to the implications of giving priority to "'outcome-based performance measures such as rates of re-offending". She argues that even with effective mecha-nisms for oversight in place, there is a risk that:

> …this can produce a culture in which private contractors find ways of purporting to achieve targets and outputs when in reality they have failed to do so.

Genders further contends that:

> The dangers of profit-driven circumvention are especially problematic in the context of a specialist institution like Dovegate, where the reliance on expert knowledge and skills serves to shroud many of the processes and operations.

It is perhaps fortunate then that the first author is on the committee which has oversight of the therapeutic regime at Dovegate. The temptations of keep-ing "unsuitable" residents in therapy longer in order to improve a "time in therapy" index of success and of picking "safer" bets rather than the more "intractable" people are not new to TCs in prison. They have been on the agenda of Grendon and other prison TCs for at least the past 15 years to the same authors' direct personal knowledge. That isn't to say there aren't risks, but the procedures for selection and completion of therapy at Dovegate are recorded in great detail and are, unlike at Grendon, subject to contractual obligations. There are a number of indices of assessment which would allow these concerns to be addressed empirically. All this was anticipated in the drafting stages before the contract was even awarded. The transparency of these operational quality control measures and the Freedom of Information Act should serve to reassure concerns about profit-driven circumventions.

II. Politics, Prisons and Therapeutic Communities

Section I: The Politics of Imprisonment

It is an obvious and unavoidable truth that the prisons of any country are passive recipients of the decisions of the courts. The courts in turn, we would argue, are subject to strong and shifting political pressures upon them to reflect what is viewed as the will of the public or the capacity of the prison estate to contain prisoners. Until 2011, we are aware of no serving senior politician who actively campaigned to reduce the number of criminals imprisoned (i.e. until the Coalition Government realised that it had no money);[11] and it is perhaps inevitable that prisoner numbers will continue to increase. Certainly the past decade has seen the biggest increase in the prison population this century, rising by over 50% to the current figure of over 85,000. Of course the most obvious explanation for this is a rise in crime and an improved efficacy in the Criminal Justice System (CJS) processing these criminals. It is impossible to determine whether increases are due to changes in procedure or guidelines without some form of controlled study pre and post any significant changes in detection, prosecution or sentencing policy. What is true is that the appetite of the great British public for a punitive response will always exceed the capacity of the CJS to imprison people. It remains to determine how best to deal with those so imprisoned and there are particular and abiding concerns for the best disposition of serious offenders with disorders of personality.

Nowadays, the general subject of crime is at the forefront of all governments' political agendas. Politicians must avoid any perception of "softness" towards criminals at all costs, as the tabloid media represents the public as

---

11. There was a public backlash when in 2011 the Justice Secretary, Kenneth Clarke sought to reduce the time spent in prison by certain offenders, leading to a Government U-turn.

abidingly hard on crime. In few fields can the views of the "experts" usually be more guaranteed to be dissonant with the majority of the public than in the CJS. Appropriate sentence lengths (see, e.g. the Jamie Bulger case), who should set tariffs (historically speaking the Home Secretary versus the Judiciary) and the shape of prison regimes all illustrate this gulf. The public, insofar as it is represented by newspapers aiming to sell the most copies, are only satisfied with longer sentences and more austere regimes. Those who work with offenders, especially the most demanding ones serving longer sentences for the most serious crimes, who have significantly more previous convictions and register on at least one of the several personality disorders tests, tend to argue differently. The best hope for safeguarding the public in future by reducing the risks these men pose is by intervening in their lives with programmes, classes and regimes which change the offenders' mind-set from criminal to non-criminal. The judiciary, whatever their personal opinions, normally absolve themselves of responsibility by referring to sentencing guidelines.

The Purposes of Imprisonment

The possible purposes of criminal justice start with the view that the system *provides a check on State power.* It does not exist to solve social problems and it places limits on State power by means of a tight definition of criminal conduct and through placing on the State a rigorous standard of criminal proof alongside other procedural protections.

Viewing criminal justice as a system and *making the system work* has been developed through the emphasis on public managerialism. This vision of making the system work raises expectations of the crime reduction potential of intervention by criminal justice agencies. The CJS Strategic Plan agreed by the Home Office, the Lord Chancellor's Department (latterly the Ministry of Justice) and the Attorney General provides for the first time a clear strategic direction for the system in England and Wales, with the overarching goals being "to reduce crime and the fear of crime" and "to dispense justice fairly and efficiently and to promote confidence in the rule of law".

We are living through a renaissance of prison-based treatment and therapy. What works? TCs for prisoners work. And it is because they work, in terms of both improving imprisoned peoples' personalities *and* reducing

re-offending, that they are growing. There is a still greater opportunity however. If we can combine the efficacy of TCs with the equally potent courses
addressing offending behaviour and the principles and procedures of restorative justice, we have an attractive recipe for steering the purposes of criminal
justice away from punitive and humane containment towards something
which would be a proud reflection of a more enlightened, pro-active imperative. That form of community justice which connotes a problem-solving
rather than punitive approach, often relies on restorative approaches, and
is another vision for the possible future of the system. The starting point
for the restorative approach is the neglected plight of the victim and a view
that the State's role as public protector has been eroded. This view embraces
notions of reparation and restoration in seeking to focus on the safety of
community life, whereas the traditional justice system has focused on blame
and pain, considering:

- What law has been broken?
- Who has broken it?
- How should the offender be punished?

Restorative justice considers:

- Who has been harmed?
- What is the nature of the harm?
- Who is responsible for that harm?
- What can be done to repair the harm?
- How can the person responsible put things right for the harmed person now
  and avoid harming others in the future?

Restorative justice involves a more comprehensive and balanced view of
crime. At its core is the concept of social inclusion, and the idea that individuals and the community as a whole have both needs and obligations. A
restorative approach requires a more sensitive and constructive response to
victims' needs, and a recognition of the many ways in which an offence can
affect their families, friends, and the wider community.

It also holds offenders to account for their actions and offers them the opportunity to make amends for the damage done by antisocial behaviour. It seeks to fully integrate offenders as law-abiding members of the community and encourages and supports both victims and offenders in the process. It means finding better ways to repair the damaged relationships caused by crime and disorder that so often lead to increased fear and social division. The way this is done most often in England and Wales is through "conferencing" in which all those directly connected to the case, including the victim, the offender and their respective "supporters" are invited to a conference run by a trained facilitator. The facilitator invites contributions from the participants that will highlight the harm caused by the offence and promote the taking of reparative responsibility by the offender.

Restorative principles have an important contribution to make to create safer communities at every stage of the criminal justice process. *From the very first contact with a victim to the resettlement of an offender in the community after a lengthy prison sentence, there are opportunities to improve on traditional policy and practice.*

Within the prison setting, many applications of restorative justice principles are possible.[12] We know that many of the processes of the TC involve working with these principles and this chapter seeks to focus on the victims of the crimes that have brought prisoners to request the TC prison experience such as that at Grendon or Dovegate.

Victims' needs could be seen as:

- Victim empowerment which requires respect for the victim's right to voluntary participation in all phases.

- Victim empathy—all prisoners can be helped to develop empathy for victims and it is a critical part of therapy that they should understand their own experience of being victims. Through this they can make connections with their own victims' feelings.

---

12. See, in particular, Kimmett E and Newell, T (2008), *Restorative Justice in Prisons: A Guide to Making It Happen*, Waterside Press.

- Victim-offender mediation — prisons can provide a place of safety and neutrality in which, with substantial safeguards for victims (privacy; the right to withdraw at any time), victim-offender mediation can be conducted. Both direct and indirect mediation can be conducted with staff help.

- The Sycamore Tree Project[13] shows promise by facilitating personal growth in prisoners through contact with victims of crime.

- Outreach to victims' groups — prison officers and serving prisoners can serve Victim Support groups by attending meetings (when invited) to share the experience of prisons, the perspective of offenders, and answering victims' questions.

Prisons could develop all these strands. TCs in prison already work with ideas of victim empathy. Many have outreach experience and it could be fairly readily developed, but it is in the area of victim-offender mediation where the greatest challenges would lie. There are other prisons that carry out such work now to good effect, with a range of contacts between offenders and victims such as third party reports about the offender, a letter of apology and explanation, staff meeting the victim to provide a report, taped or video communication and direct victim-offender mediated meetings.

In other justice systems such as those of Canada and Australia, restorative group conferences take place within prison settings. These meetings, conducted by skilled mediators/facilitators who have built up experience in these procedures, have been very helpful for victims and offenders in moving on with their lives. TCs have the skills within their staff to develop and facilitate such conferences.

Since the Second World War criminal justice in Britain expanded alongside rising recorded crime and growth in the economy. Despite all the hopes of politicians and practitioners, changes in procedure and process are unlikely to have more than a marginal effect on the level of crime. Progress in public policy to help reduce crime is developed outside criminal justice and consists of socially inclusive policies such as pre-school education, school attendance,

---

13. This is an intensive five to eight week in-prison programme that brings groups of crime victims into prison to meet with groups of (unrelated) offenders. They talk about the effects of crime, the harm it causes, and how to put things right. See pfi.org.

61

supporting parents and children in difficulty and providing opportunities for young people entering adult life.

In terms of setting goals for criminal justice, effectiveness is difficult to define in more than narrow instrumental terms. But the overarching normative goals set for criminal justice should reach to the heart of establishing public trust and confidence. Fairness as well as justice should be seen to be done. Restorative justice is best equipped to meet the needs of victims and community members in this respect as all the research evidence is that restorative approaches report vastly improved levels of satisfaction compared with conventional treatment. The goals of justice could thus be seen as to:

- **Adhere to legality**: The European Convention on Human Rights (ECHR) which was developed as a bulwark against perversion of criminal law principles constitutes a foundation for this goal. High standards begin with principles such as safeguarding the presumption of innocence and ensuring legal assistance.

- **Provide humane treatment:** Various articles of the ECHR[14] support this aim, but as important is that ultimately the expression of humane values within criminal justice and particularly within prisons resides with practitioners. Much work remains to be done in the improvement and measurement of humane treatment, but David (now Lord) Ramsbotham when Chief Inspector of Prisons made a start by challenging the Prison Service to provide conditions that staff would not mind their own children experiencing.

- **Provide public protection**: This remain a strong instrumental aim and the "what works" agenda shows that expectations in this area must be modest. Whilst there are encouraging pockets of effective practice, the need to maintain confidence in criminal justice constrains this.

- **Provide public security:** This goal seeks to reduce the fear of crime and to meet the needs of victims in relation to both their offence and their treatment by the criminal justice agencies.

---

14. See, e.g. Article 2 (the right to life), 3 (prohibition of torture, etc.), 6 (fair trial), 10 (freedom of expression) and 14 (non-discriminatory application of rights).

In 2011, the Coalition Government announced some of the most sweeping changes to the CJS this century, affecting courts, police, prisons and probation, in an effort to bring greater efficiency (swifter processing is perhaps more accurate) and stronger sentencing as messages to repeat violent offenders, sex offenders and drug-related offending in particular. There is always a threat that those programmes concerned with treating offenders to encourage their decriminalisation will be victims of a perceived shift towards the punitive. Once the HM Prison Service "supertanker" changes direction it can take years to reverse the process.

Section II: The Politics and Promise of TCs

This section looks at the multiplicity of opportunities and threats which beset TCs in prisons. There are three principle dimensions:

1. External threats from HM Prison Service itself, including fiscal, treatment-based and issues of overall policy direction.
2. Threats from the expansion of TCs, with such a limited number of qualified and experience professionals and discipline staff being stretched/poached.
3. Internal dissent, including the hardy perennial of theoretical/professional conflicts.

We follow these with the exciting opportunities to build an integrated expanded network of co-operative TCs.

External Threats

HM Prison Service does not exist to reward innovation in offender treatment. The closest it gets is to increase funding, perhaps the biggest tangible reward for TCs. Looking back, in 2002-3 the Government announced additional funding to increase by 50% the number of prisoners completing accredited offending behaviour programmes. These programmes, initiated and developed by Prison Service psychologists, are arguably the best treatment initiative ever introduced. The rigorous standards required for running and evaluating them ensure a far greater uniformity of course than has ever existed before and the additional safeguard of creating an evaluation panel including external representation to determine accreditation is also welcome.

TCs are an integral part of the accredited treatment programme suite, with some of the most rigorous audits ever to exist. They are total environments, not specific courses run for set numbers of sessions regardless of the learning speed or behavioural changes of the prisoners attending. TCs are meant to be attended until the prisoner's personality, attitudes and behaviour have changed to the collective satisfaction of the other members of his or her community. This clinical standard is obviously not particularly amenable to the objective criteria which the Correctional Services Accreditation Panel (CSAP) sets, but this is largely satisfied by the involvement of the Royal College of Psychiatrists Research Unit and the Community of Communities quality network of TCs being responsible for National Audit Reports and the Core Model for Democratic TCs (DTCs) (see *Appendix I* to this work). Without this status, we suspect that the viability of DTCs would have been at risk some years past.

Expansion Threats

In March 2010, it seemed there were no possibilities for expansion of DTCs, given that the funding body responsible, the National Offenders Management Service (NOMS), was faced with finding over £1 billion savings over the next three financial years. In spite of this, the Review of DTCs which NOMS commissioned internally in November 2008 concluded there is a strong case not only to ensure the survival of the current numbers, but for an increase in the range of DTCs throughout the ten offender management regions. The obvious threat if TCs were to grow in the public sector would include difficulties in finding, employing and retaining suitably qualified professional staff. Given also that the largest DTC in the public sector at Grendon has chronic problems in terms of getting the majority of their uniformed staff to attend and contribute to the core therapy activities, any expansion would only exacerbate this problem. In the private sector DTC at Dovegate, it is proving extremely difficult just to sustain the levels of therapy in the existing units, without considering expansion.

Internal Threats

HM Prison Service has spent most of the past 50 years not appreciating TCs. That is most true of the uniformed discipline staff, the overwhelming majority of whom regard it as a soft option at best. Whenever there are fiscal cuts and governors are required to find immediate or annual savings on their expenditures, the TCs are at or near the top of the expendable list. This is, simply put, because the service historically had no formal obligation to reduce the risk of future offending and because it is possible to close these relatively small, powerless units with very limited opposition as opposed to that which the closure of any "normal location" prison wing or unit would attract. It has often been said that TCs are marginal, too defensive or out of step with mainstream Ministry of Justice operational procedures. This is to miss the point. They should be so, because they are better. It is for the rest of the system to raise standards to match those of the TCs. TCs in prisons become defensive through experience, and not because they wish to set themselves apart from the rest.

Opportunities

Never before has there been such a growth in TCs in the Prison Service. Until 1997, there were fewer than 300 places in TCs available, with most of these in Grendon Underwood (235). With the addition of the new drug offenders' (hierarchical) TCs, another 220 places were added to the number and, with HM Dovegate opening in November 2001, the total increased to over 700. There are another 300-plus places online in drugs TCs and proposals for a Learning Disabled TC (see also our thoughts on this in *Chapter 10*). When we began writing this work, NOMS were revising a Review of DTCs which it had commissioned in 2009, in light of the recommendations of the Bradley Report concerning best treatment for personality disordered offenders.[15]

15. This subsequently led to: (a) the development of our offender personality disorder strategy (Joseph N and Benefield N, *Mental Health Review Journal*, vol. 15, No. 4. December, 2010); (b) Consultation on the Offender Personality Disorder Pathway Implementation Plan, a joint Department of Health /Ministry of Justice process; which led to (c) related matters in the Green Paper, *Breaking the Cycle: Effective Punishment, Rehabilitation and Sentencing of Offenders*, Ministry of Justice (presented to Parliament in December 2010). The Government's official policy is contained in *Breaking the Cycle: Government Response* presented to Parliament by the Justice Secretary in June 2011. There are two new policies which may directly affect DTCs. The first concerns the exciting innovation of "payment by results": "We will

As part of the nationwide Association of Therapeutic Communities (ATC), prison TCs are represented on the Advisory Committee and are active in the annual conference of the ATC. This representation however is far from proportionate and the ATC is still largely dominated by psychoanalytic psychiatry and psychotherapy, the traditional professional perspectives. For some time, however, those responsible for the new TCs in prisons have been advocating a non-medical, psychology-based model of change. This new model is based more on the what works research literature applied to traditional TC procedures and enhanced with the judicious addition of accredited offending behaviour courses and programmes.

This often painful evolution is well exemplified at Grendon, where there is no longer an active resistance to the courses, sometimes seen as inappropriate and unnecessary interloping. Critics argue that the courses set up a conflict of treatment agenda for prisoners, sometimes offering confusing and even contradictory interpretations of their behaviour as well as recipes for change. The opportunity, if this dissonance can be overcome, is great. The overwhelming conclusion of meta-analyses on what works in terms of reducing crime when treating offenders is that of a *multi-modal model of treatment.* That is, a combination of treatment elements (i.e. more than one) run in a co-operative model of change based on proven efficacy rather than traditional, cultural received wisdom exclusive to one professional group. What

---

pioneer a world first—a system where we only pay for results, delivered by a diverse range of providers from all sectors. This principle will underpin all our work on reoffending". If this is true—and on 31 March 2011 the Government awarded the contract to manage HMP Doncaster to Serco on a payment by results pilot starting in October 2011 where ten per cent of the contract value will be "placed at risk, and only be retained by Serco if they reduce reoffending by five percentage points"—the implications for TCs (which have already proven efficacy at these levels) is significant. The second relevant change concerns indeterminate sentences (IPPs) which feature in various other chapters of this book. IPPs have had unintended, negative consequences. There has been an explosion in the number of high risk prisoners receiving them, many of whom are proving litigious. Grendon has a number of IPP prisoners and there has been pressure to take more. The government's intention is to conduct a review "with a view to replacing the current IPP regime with a much tougher determinate sentencing framework which includes ..." an increase in life sentences, less open to challenge in the courts, with serious sex offenders and violent offenders (much of the DTC populations) spending at least two thirds of their sentence in prison rather than sooner, and compulsory programmes for dangerous prisoners while in prison. A downside is that compulsion flys in the face of the DTC tradition of voluntariness and consent.

is vital is that the best of the psychiatric traditions of treatment is retained and protected against any doctrinaire approach to change.

Summary

Whatever the relative arguments for or against private sector prisons in general, and TCs in particular, it seems evident that the debate is over even though the arguments remain, and that they will continue until and unless some unforeseen generic or political seismic shift occurs. The debate while it raged was ultimately inconclusive, with its pros and cons being urged by the different sides. What both public sector and private sector DTCs have in common, however, is a risk from an annual fiscal imperative which seems to disregard or consider irrelevant the huge record of achievement by whatever criterion is applied of DTCs in prisons.

DTCs have many attributes which we argue would be well complemented by a transition towards some form of restorative justice process. As they stand today, however, DTCs, whether in the private or public sector, have a remarkably robust range of attributes which act as a bulwark against the inexorable ravages of the prisons and imprisonment mentality and financial cuts. These attributes constitute a challenging standard for prison-based TCs to achieve, not unlike a qualitative accreditation process, and the new TC at Dovegate has added a number of additional features which both enhance and complicate the process. It is essential that prison TCs create and sustain an active dialogue with the whole range of other TCs, nationally, internationally and regardless of the democratic/hierarchical dichotomy. The principles and practices fundamental to TCs are not exclusive to particular kinds of TC. It has long been an erroneous presumption that TCs were a treatment modality reserved for those "suffering" from some classifiable form of mental disorder, or dysfunction of personality. In other words, offenders (or other people) had to be labelled before they qualified for help. *This is a false and unnecessary distinction which arbitrarily excludes the majority of people, and prisoners in particular, who could benefit.*

If we provide no other message in this book, let it be that TCs are the regime of choice for any prisoner who wants to change his or her criminal lifestyle. They are clearly the first choice for those with relationship problems resulting in offending, but they are not exclusive. So long as TCs are perceived as relevant only to personality disordered offenders, this artificial misconception will remain. The positive, pro-social and supportive regimes of DTCs have so much to offer any offenders with sufficient time and motivation. Even if they didn't significantly reduce re-offending, they would still be much more positive and stable regimes than non-TC units in prison.

III. Consequences of Privatisation in Practice

The theoretical concerns and advantages of the public/private sector dimension have been outlined in *Section I* above. This section looks at how Dovegate's position in the private sector has impacted on the shop floor, in Dovegate itself and the other public sector-based prison TCs.

The cost argument has already been explored as it related to the time of the contract bid, and it has been acknowledged that a "built in cost" in such a bid for a private company will always be the requirement to satisfy the shareholders by way of a healthy dividend. What perhaps was not foreseen was the knock-on effect for TCs in the future. At the time of writing there are the glimmerings of recovery from the worst recession the UK has experienced since the 1930s. However, the prison population now stands at an all time high of over 85,000 and has to be managed against a year-on-year cost-cutting requirement.

Cuts announced from 2010 onwards for the public sector of between 25% and 50% suggest that the climate will become more stringent rather than less, so with fears of as many as 15,000 jobs scheduled to be axed from the Ministry of Justice Against the background of "If Dovegate can do it so can you", Grendon and other TCs have had to struggle to justify their higher costs. These are made up not only of the wages of individual prison officers, which at the time of writing are still higher than those of prison custody officers (PCOs),[16] but also more realistic staffing levels, with a greater number of trained civilian professionals. These levels are currently the subject of a major review.

---

16. The term prison custody officer rather than prison officer is used in the private sector.

It is likely that the outcome will be a compromise. This will have implications for the public sector as it struggles to manage with fewer staff, and possibly a restricted regime, but also for Dovegate which will have to continue to meet TC service standards that are likely to include minimum staffing levels, and it will also have to keep its own costs stable. Where the arrival of Dovegate spelt threat for the public sector, the situation is now reversed.

At the time of the bid for Dovegate, the "flattened hierarchy" described in *Chapter 4*, whilst originally based on the moral and ethical philosophy of the TC, had an additional effect of reducing costs in a way not open to the public sector with its harder to change staff structures. So also did the proposed combination of therapy and operational managers. In the public sector the operational and therapeutic lines for prison TCs are separately managed, a pattern which is reflected in the higher levels of management.

In Dovegate these two roles were combined into one (with a saving on salary across all the TCs) and roles were also combined in the joint responsibilities for therapy and operational management of the director of therapy. Some of the consequences of this are referred to in *Chapters 8* and *9*.

Civilian input was also drastically reduced — rather than a psychodynamically qualified therapy manager plus psychologist plus probation officer, the Dovegate TCs were initially staffed by a therapy manager taking a dual therapeutic and operational role, and a counsellor, both of whom were also PCO trained. The flattening of the hierarchy was further reflected in the PCO role itself. Unlike in the public sector, there was no senior position between the 'shop floor' and the therapy manager. This altered the dynamics of the whole team.

Rather than a multi-disciplinary team involving multiple perspectives and lively debate, the teams became a body of PCOs led by a single professional with help from an inexperienced counsellor. The ethos became that of an expert with followers.

Staff terms and conditions combined with attrition resulted in an extravagantly high turnover of staff particularly in the early years. Thus more resources had to be expended on training new staff with less availability to support those already working; and the therapy manager and counsellor were often the only culture carriers on some of the TCs for long periods.

With hindsight the staffing levels for Dovegate TCs were unacceptably low. They worked on paper, but in practice there was barely enough cover for operational matters and therapy intervention was squeezed to a minimum. Groups frequently ran with no staff at all. The opportunity for new and barely trained staff to sit with an experienced therapist was almost non-existent.

The essential unstructured time in evenings and weekends took place with little or no staff engagement; some evenings saw as few as three officer grades covering two chevrons of 40 residents each.

Subcultures of drugs and bullying began to develop on the communities, further increasing the burden on staff and fuelling the drive to manage anxiety on the shop floor and in management through resorting to an increased operational approach using "prison" types of discipline. Young communities and inexperienced staff found it hard to generate a culture where the emphasis was on discussion and making meaning, personal accountability and restitution. Not surprisingly, staff stress and sickness went up, further increasing turnover.

For therapy managers, who were also mostly without prison operational experience, the burden of managing the operational side became acute. With no direct operational support plus the training of PCOs in all matters therapeutic, as well as the clinical responsibility for 40 prisoners, it rapidly became clear that the task was simply "not do-able". Attrition in the therapy managers also began and by the end of 2008, nine of them had left and the Assessment Unit and High Intensity Programme were running with nominal oversight by one person.

It has always been the case until recently that prison TCs, despite the apparent lack of overt control, have been some of the safest places to work in the prison system. This is due to the transparency of interaction and the trust engendered between the residents, between the staff as a team and most importantly between the residents and the staff. The traditional prison culture of mistrust and frightening dependency is consciously eroded.

TCs have lower levels of violence, prisoner on prisoner and prisoner on staff than other similar categories of prison; there are fewer escapes, fewer offences against discipline and a higher level of perceived prisoner well-being.[17]

There are anecdotes too numerous to mention from all DTCs of staff being given advance warning of resident hostility by other residents; those same residents being challenged by their peers; and planned violence being averted due to the culture of the community.

It is against this background that the murder of one prisoner by another in Grendon has come as a shock to all associated with the prison DTCs. After so many years of positive experience it is important that there is not a reaction against TCs on this account.

It is no justification, though it is the truth, that murders in prison do happen, and on a not irregular basis. Just not in TCs. How could this have happened? The results of the enquiry are not yet known. Speculation is of course rife. Nevertheless, the comments most frequently heard are the failure to pay attention to the assessment process (particularly in respect of motivation); the erosion of the social interaction time which builds the positive relationships that protect against such eventualities; and the absence of sufficient positive role models with whom to create such relationships.

One of the ways to cut costs in the DTCs has been the increase of "bang up", where residents are locked up for key periods of the day when they would otherwise have been out "socialising". Socialising in this context should not be taken to mean simply "having a good time" though it is hoped this happens as well, but rather the opportunity to build on relationships, to get to know one another, to practise trust and personal discipline, and to observe for offence paralleling.[18] It is these periods that make a TC different from an ordinary offending behaviour programme, and which embrace much of the all-important element of social therapy.

---

17. Her Majesty's Chief Inspector of Prisons Reports.
18. For some uses of the term "parallel", see *Appendix 2* to this work. Lawrence Jones defines offence paralleling behaviour as: "Any form of offence-related behavioural (or fantasised behavioural) pattern that emerges before or after an offence. It does not have to result in an offence; it simply needs to resemble, in some significant aspect, the sequences of behaviour leading up to the offence". This aspect of TC work is vital as it enables staff and residents to see the connections between current and past offensive or offending behaviour. See "Refining the Definition of Offence Paralleling Behaviour" (2007), Daffern M, Jones L, Howells K, Shine J and Tunbridge V, *Criminal Behaviour and Mental Health*, 17: 265-273, Wiley InterScience.

Some TCs base their treatment model almost entirely on social therapy, groups being a minor component;[19] Milieu Therapy[20] was the first experimental avenue which ultimately was to spawn the now heavily (in the view of the second author, too heavily) group-based approach.

Could what happened at Grendon happen at Dovegate? The TC came perilously close when an operational manager was physically assaulted during association. One of the therapy managers was suspended for over eight months whilst allegations of bullying were investigated. Whilst it was acknowledged that for the sake of the investigation this could not be discussed on the community for fear of compromising the investigation,[21] there was initially a ban on "discussion about discussion". It is only latterly that it has been possible to discuss the resonance for so many residents of abandoning/victimising/victimised parental figures. It has not been possible at all to consider publicly what may be being enacted on a collective basis.

No general examination of required staffing levels for prison TCs has been undertaken however, and this remains an outstanding requirement today. At the time of the bid the simple numerical value was looked at leading to the perception in the management of the public sector that they could also cut staffing levels without loss of safety or therapeutic integrity.

In response to this, Grendon withdrew their probation officers from the wings allowing them to cut the overall complement. The officer contingent was reduced and the post of director of therapy became a single post combined with the previous deputy governor post and was known as director of therapeutic communities. The core day was curtailed in line with the rest of the prison estate.

Debates began to be held in the central meetings about what level of reduced service would result in a TC no longer being a TC. Too few feet were on the ground and there was a real risk of the regime being reduced to a "benign environment that ran a few groups".

In Dovegate this has been to some degree adjusted lately with the move for operational managers to relieve the therapy managers of some of the

---

19. Such as Camphill Communities.
20. Linked with, but not restricted to TCs.
21. It is for exactly this reason that remand prisoners and those appealing against their sentence are not accepted onto the TC.

more practical burdens of their role. Changes in the way the administrative support team work has also assisted with the burden of the collection of the necessary statistics from each community for audit.

An intermediate position of senior PCO was also introduced giving staff a more recognisable career structure and which recognised experience as well as ability. Staff are more supported and turnover has reduced. Due to the audit requirements, groups are no longer run without staff.

The implications of being a private prison affected other areas. Earlier in this chapter the first author argues convincingly that the likelihood of keeping unsuitable residents in Dovegate to ensure targets were met was less likely than in the public sector due to contractual agreements. Unfortunately the overwhelming financial necessity to keep the therapeutic prison full outweighed almost any other contractual agreement and the tyrant figure of 194 hung like a Sword of Damocles over the heads of successive directors of therapy.

In October 2002, the riot in Lincoln Prison resulted in the disgorging of 200 additional prisoners into the already overstretched prison system. For Dovegate TC it meant the steady admission of suitable applicants had to be suspended and empty places had to be filled as quickly as possible with those who appeared suitable on paper only, bypassing the carefully crafted assessment procedure. Although this was later reinstated, the lack of proper assessment at that time meant a number of unsuitable people were accepted onto the TCs with concomitant therapy dropout. The numbers of those deselected as unsuitable for breach of the constitution rose and as the percentage of "toxics" increased, therapy delivery became more difficult. Residents became disillusioned and the number of requests for deselection also began to rise. A vicious circle was engendered which took nearly six years to reverse, the out of therapy figures rising at one point to 38% across all the communities.

The perception grew that the imposition of the 194 clause resulted in the keeping of toxic individuals and the selection of unsuitable prisoners was inflicted by virtue of the fact that failure to maintain that number of residents cost the company money—and that, as always, was the bottom line. This added to staff disillusionment and discontent.

The overcrowding in the general prison population meant that not only was it hard to move on the troublemakers, those found to be unsuitable for therapy and those who no longer wished to engage, but also those who had made a success of their stay and were judged to be therapy complete. This was particularly hard as those that were successful were penalised, often waiting for over 12 months to be moved. At one point, one community had 50% of its resident population out of therapy.

Apart from a brief respite from the figure of 194 as a "one off" during the time of David Lynes as director, it is only in the last two years that there has been a temporary softening of this position. Even then, the capacity to move high numbers of residents out of the TC meant an equally determined effort was required to get suitable prisoners in. High turnover on the communities had a destabilising effect with a dilution of the therapeutic culture.

The situation has settled considerably now. The determination to manage local population control led to the focusing of residents' hearts and minds; the new operational structure and the appointment of Maggie Evans as senior therapist reinvigorated an exhausted staff team. Recent statistics show that the numbers out of therapy have dropped to as low as 6 per cent.

The pressures on population also led to a change in the "48 hour" rule. Under this a resident who was reconsidering the appropriateness of his place on the TC could put in an application to leave and had 48 hours to reconsider this before his request was acted upon. However, the impossibility of moving people without a significant delay meant that many who had submitted their 48-hour notice remained on the wings out of therapy for many months, "clogging" the system still further.

The 48 hour boundary is a difficult one for staff and residents to maintain as it is not uncommon for a prisoner to change his mind and request to re-engage in therapy. Refusal seems brutal and ineffective in terms of cost as it would require the prisoner to return to another establishment and then reapply, sometimes putting the possibility of therapy outside his reach because of sentence length.[22] It was decided that this boundary should be relaxed. The replacement system requires an extensive period of discussion

---

22. Prisoners must have a minimum of 18 months left to serve of their sentence to qualify for the TC. This restriction is common to all prison DTCs and is due to the finding that those who complete less than 18 months in therapy fare less well than those who complete more.

before it can be agreed that somebody can voluntarily withdraw from treatment. This period can be as long as three months.

Although this had the effect of keeping a number of residents in therapy for longer (thus assisting with the statistics required for audit), it also had the effect of reducing the degree of motivation required as a resident can tender his intention to leave therapy when things get difficult and then withdraw it when a crisis has passed.

TCs are about pro-social interaction and relationships. For therapy to be effective there need to be sufficient healthy adults for newcomers to have those relationships with. These same relationships are what keep a prison community safe. Without them, and with less recourse to standard prison means of control, staff can became beleaguered. This leads to pressure to return to prison-driven thinking and operationalisation. Behaviour gets driven underground; the features of confrontation and exploration and the opportunity for the observation of offence paralleling are lost. For the "middle years" of its development this is what happened in Dovegate.

The financial imperative impacted on other areas as it has done in the public sector but to a greater degree. The standard training delivered to all staff of prison DTCs is known as "T Cat". This training is described by the first author in *Chapter 4* and is designed to provide a common language across all prison TCs and to include the opportunity for cross-fertilisation between them. Thus the training in Grendon is offered to staff from other TCs in the public sector across the prison TC estate. Training for Dovegate staff, however, is entirely in-house and even senior trainers are not interchangeable, being outwith the safeguards built into that delivered by the public sector.[23]

In addition to a Training Committee, there are central meetings to review the assessment procedures; to co-ordinate research; to plan strategy and to share ideas and offer support (TC Liaison). These meetings have been instrumental in maintaining the quality of the public sector TCs and ensuring that policies are relevant and up to date. They also embody the democratic

---

23. The delivery of training in the public sector DTCs is regulated and overseen by the Central Training Committee. Trainers are selected through presentation and interview and subjected to a rigorous procedure for the training of trainers. There is ongoing quality control. In Dovegate there is no such oversight, leading to the risk of erosion of quality.

TC culture, comprising representatives from all TCs from all levels of staff. Attendance at central meetings is limited and at one stage dropped rapidly.

Dovegate maintains a good level of attendance at the strategy meeting but attendance at the other central meetings has been seen as less important. Other TCs from the public sector are also beginning to question the value and cost-effectiveness of these meetings and this last year has seen them greatly diminished in number, brief and attendance. It is currently the case that more decisions are made centrally without wide TC representation to the point that even the TC strategy meeting has the function of a "rubber stamp" and decisions are made prior to and without reference to wider consultation.

In her paper "Legitimacy, Accountability and Private Prisons",[24] Elaine Genders argues that these areas are difficult to evaluate in the private sector suggesting that they remain "intractable, especially in the specific context of a therapeutic community prison". She further states:

> no means have been found to prevent . . . circumvention [of checks and balances, output-driven performance measures and mechanisms of accountability] from occurring. Damage limitation has been the extent of achievement. This has taken two forms: the granting of a high profile to the research function at Dovegate, the funding of which is to be ring fenced; and the setting up of a specialist oversight committee that possesses the requisite expertise and understanding of the regime.

The two examples she cites have been achieved. The advent of audit and its consequences and the longitudinal research study undertaken by Surrey University are outlined in *Chapter 9*.

The committee meets quarterly and comprises experts in TCs from different disciplines including a representation from the central team. It receives a report from the director of therapy and also meets with therapy managers and visits communities. However, once again, the all encompassing financial imperative remains and at the time of writing the provision of funding for the chairman is being withdrawn.

---

24. "Legitimacy, Accountability and Private Prisons", Genders E, *Punishment and Society,* July 2002, vol. 4, No.3, 285-303.

In the same paper as is mentioned above, Genders quotes Dave McDonnell, director of HM Prison The Wolds:

> I remember being asked by some of my public sector colleagues (who had then been very critical of the then director-general of the prison service) what the difference was between the private and public sector. I told them that if I had been publicly critical of my chief executive as they had been of theirs I would be looking for another job.

It is true that at some periods criticism in Dovegate has been difficult to voice, this being even more so outside the walls of the institution. Questioning of decisions and processes was at times looked at as indicating an absence of company loyalty. Whilst it is arguable that this is potentially dangerous for any institution, it is particularly damaging in a TC, which depends so heavily on a culture of enquiry. Enshrined in the training and the manuals is the understanding that decisions are open to question by anybody and that everybody is required to be accountable for what they say and do.

For a while there emerged a culture of fear and threat. The effect was to stultify debate and to engender a culture of secrecy and a sense of persecution. This contributed significantly to the difficulties in managing some of the practical effects of policy and in the policy-makers receiving appropriate feedback. This area remains a potential danger for a TC in a private prison. However once again much depends on the quality of leadership. With a sound understanding of the importance of the culture of enquiry this threat can be diminished.

Beyond these caveats, results in practice do not merit such a pessimistic view as outlined by Genders. Although some of the things she warns of have come to pass, they have brought with them a positive aspect as well.

In the current situation there is once again greater openness of debate and discussion through: the re-instigation of meetings to provide an open and non-judgemental forum for communication, support and cross-fertilisation of ideas; a statement of intent that feedback is necessary and welcome; a willingness by the director to attend these meetings and the communities to speak directly to residents about their concerns; and to model Rapoport's four principles (see *Chapter 3*).[25]

The dependence on the qualities of an individual is a weakness in the system. However it cannot be said to apply only to the private sector. The examples in the public sector of the danger of ideological drift, especially when leadership passes from the therapeutic to the custodial/business side, are not confined to prisons but occur in the outside community as well. A prison governor in the public sector is as able, perhaps more able, than in the private sector to take Draconian methods including sudden and absolute closure, without reference to procedure or therapeutic need. This has happened to three of the smaller TCs in recent years.[26] There are advantages however in the relative freedom from historical structure and regulation that can make the instigation of creative solutions in Dovegate compared to the public sector seem like the difference between a thoroughbred and a carthorse.

The broad nature of the contract means there is room for creativity particularly in managerial decisions. The changing of roles and functions for example can be done on the basis of need without the restrictive forces of centralised control and protocol. One example is that when additional finance unexpectedly became available in Dovegate it was a simple local decision to change its distribution to allow a better career structure to be inbuilt for the basic grade officers. When a similar situation arose in the public sector such flexibility was not possible, resulting in the loss of personnel and expertise and the abandoning of a group of prisoners therapeutically to their own devices.

In Dovegate job descriptions can be generated on the basis of need rather than directive when conditions call for change. For example, in the original design two communities had therapy in the mornings followed by education in the afternoons with the other two communities reversing this (education in the mornings and therapy in the afternoons). This was based on the original Grendon model. When Grendon changed to having therapy for all communities in the mornings with education and work for everybody

---

25. This in addition to the regular, formal Prisoners and Residents Activities Committee meetings (PIAC/RIAC) with representatives from senior management facing questions. These became stereotyped with answers being prepared beforehand, limiting the scope for debate.
26. Glen Parva, Aylesbury and the Max Glatt Unit at Wormwood Scrubs.

in the afternoons, it took over two years to accomplish. When Dovegate recognised the need to make a similar change it took less than two months.

Most TCs consider complementary therapies to be important and Dovegate is no exception. However, the original contract did not include sufficient finance to purchase psychodrama and art therapy for each community, and where this was delivered, with the exception of one qualified psychodramatist, it was undertaken by students from the local university. These students required supervision, which the therapy managers were not qualified to undertake; the students were relatively inexperienced in their chosen field and were entirely prison naïve. The current director (Ray Duckworth) has moved the emphasis on creative therapies into the education department which has allowed the appointment of a qualified art therapist as well as opening the opportunity for complementary therapies to many more residents than was previously the case (see further for Ray's involvement *Chapter 8*).

Thus in Dovegate there is now a greater sense of freedom and optimism and a recognition that there is the flexibility to respond if things are not working. This flexibility as opposed to rigidity of response is a hallmark of a TC. It is of course a double-edged sword — the relative freedom to act allows the possibility of bad practice as well as good and for a time it seemed as if Dovegate may have been heading that way, with decisions being made without consultation or redress. However, the more enlightened approach means that there has been more consultation and consideration and there is a positive response to "thinking outside the box". Opportunities have been generated for relevant staff to get together and revisit "anything and everything" with the result that the overall mood is one of freedom and optimism.

The risks however are the same for the large establishment as for the communities themselves — there is the possibility of polarisation in one direction or the other; too punitive and rigid an approach versus too unstructured and unboundaried, with power and respect given either to operational or therapy personnel. This potential for polarisation rather than creative tension applies to all DTCs in prisons. It could be contained and capitalised on by the constructive use of the central meetings (comprising a strategy meeting, a liaison meeting, a training meeting and a research and assessment meeting). Within these meetings could be reflected the tension between the old and the new allowing the wisdom and experience of the old to temper the excitement of the new, and the enrichment of the new to enhance the sometimes negative rigidity of the old. The cross-fertilisation should enliven each party and at the same time provide a safety net for each.

The importance of the central meetings is even greater at this time to ensure that the economic cuts do not regress the establishments into a mutually hostile stand-off. Healthy competition needs to be combined with cooperation. The dangers of isolation are that Grendon and the public sector may get ground under by their history and allow Dovegate to potentially fly off on a limb with fewer terms of reference or checks and balances.

In the sense that privatisation in the Prison Service has always been seen as an opportunity to drive up standards as well as to drive down costs, then from the point of view of Dovegate TC it has been a refreshing and positive experiment, but one that could not safely have happened in isolation from the support and input from the public sector TCs.

CHAPTER THREE

A BRIEF HISTORY OF THERAPEUTIC COMMUNITIES[1]

The British tradition of therapeutic communities (TCs) is something to be proud of and to nurture. Reflecting something of the best of human and cultural values, TCs are the only proven full-time, regime-based treatment for men whose criminal lifestyles reflect some of the most destructive and dysfunctional choices modern life holds. Though TCs as we know them haven't been around for long, they have a rich and informative history which we should honour and learn from. We summarise briefly here the events, philosophy and people who have most shaped our present course. One reason why we include this in a book which is very much about the present and the future is because of the debt we owe to our predecessors who we've learned from and because we value the experiences of our history.

TCs are much more than programmes or regimes. They are *ways of living without victims* and, as such, we need to approach the subject with a healthy respect for the traditions, customs and mores that have shaped our communities to develop as they have. TCs in prisons are challenged by a range of sometimes-conflicting principles and imperatives. Fostering individual initiatives, flattened hierarchies and collective decision-making and setting these interpersonal requisites within procedures which allow prisoners—in our case residents—to run meetings where staff and managers attend, might appear to run contrary to the received managerial wisdom of incarceration.

But these TC principles and procedures are founded and predicated upon a tradition of a belief in people's ability to change when given the right environment, an enlightened and positive one. The challenge for everyone involved in the Dovegate project is to see if we can create, nourish and sustain a collective of TCs from scratch.

It is generally accepted that there are two broad categories of TC in prisons, the *democratic* model as practised in the UK and the *hierarchical* model

---

1. Readers interested in a more detailed appreciation of the history of TCs are referred to David Kennard's *Introduction to Therapeutic Communities* (1999) (edn. 2) and Barbara Rawlings' *Therapeutic Communities in Prisons: An Overview*, a review for the Home Office in 1998.

as practised in the USA. Variations on the former have become largely either socio-behavioural or the more traditional analytic (depending entirely upon whether or not the organizing profession is psychiatry or psychology).

The American model is oriented almost exclusively towards drug offenders although there is no apparent logic for the exclusivity with which it has come to be used. Equally, the democratic-analytic model that developed in Britain takes predominantly those with classifications of personality disorder although, again, the logic for this relatively narrow exclusion is elusive. The authors argue that TCs are the treatment models of choice for much wider categories of offenders and that selection should be based more on offence type and motivation to change than on clinical classifications. In the 21st century, hybrid or modified TCs have been developed and some of these, e.g. Kainos,[2] are now used in British prisons and have been accredited.

I.   The History of British Therapeutic Communities

William Tuke and the Quakers

Therapeutic communities in the UK are of one clear lineage; the analytic-democratic model. British TCs have their origins in late 18th-century York. It was there that Quakers, distressed at the death of one of their own in a charity asylum, opened the York Retreat in 1792. It was founded and run by William Tuke, a retired tea merchant. It was intended as

> a place where members of the Society of Friends [Quakers] who were experiencing mental distress could come and recover in an environment that would be both familiar and sympathetic to their needs.

The remarkable thing about this innovation was the simplicity of their beliefs and the practical potency of what they began. Although it clearly didn't

---

2.   Kainos Community is a charity dedicated to reducing reoffending "by lives being changed". See wix.com/kainoscommunity.

have the language of psychological treatment (predating psychoanalysis by a century) or any of the TC principles and procedures of the modern era, The Retreat was predicated upon perhaps the most important belief of all: that there is a positive, life-affirming experience within all of us and that if people are treated decently with respect and humanity, they will respond, ultimately, in kind. The final barrier is only that we believe that criminals are deserving of this chance.

It was apparently customary in the 18th-century to "treat" mentally ill people with physical restraints, enforced idleness and passive reflection which was meant to allow those who were criminally and mentally disturbed to come to their own rehabilitation by natural processes. The Retreat was predicated upon a more humane and, it transpired, enlightened, process. *Moral treatment* was the term adopted to distinguish the new approach. It was based on "treating the character of the individual, the whole person in his social environment". More than that, it sets the stall clearly on the premise that there is a moral element to treatment and that the causality of the "sickness", at least in part, lies *both* within the individual psyche and the social setting. The success of this approach led, in 1845, to Parliament passing laws which required asylums for the lunatic population to be provided across the country, the origins of which were to become the enormous mental hospitals of Victorian times. The Retreat continues today as a TC and a living embodiment of those founding principles.

Victorian Asylums

In the early decades of the 19th-century, asylums grew in number and size and their primary functions perforce tended increasingly towards the successful feeding, clothing, medicating and containing of very large numbers of the mentally disordered. In spite of this, a number of important principles emerged which add tremendously to the TC collective. Kennard[3] highlighted some principles from the period between the late 18th and late 19th-centuries:

---

3. Kennard D and Roberts J (1983), *An Introduction to Therapeutic Communities*, London: Routledge, Kegan and Paul.

- **Reward rather than Punish:** This axiomatic paradigm of behaviour therapy of the late 20th century informed the institutions—hospitals mainly—for the mentally-ill. Patients were to be praised and rewarded for positive and compliant behaviour rather than emphasising punishment for misbehaviour and using physical (as well as medicinal) restraints. Sadly, with the growing sophistication of psychotropic drugs, the liquid cosh found its way increasingly as a means of imposing compliance through sedation. Growing patient populations—sometimes 2,000 or 3,000 in one hospital—meant that medication became a tempting means to a quiescent, compliant patient group. This, for many long-term disordered groups, was seen as the only viable outcome.

- **Personal Attributes of the Staff:** We have a heightened concern for the interpersonal skills and personal qualities of individual staff who may work on the TC. The emphasis is perforce on their "prison-craft" knowledge, i.e. the operational and security facts and skills, but there also needs to be something of a positive role model, empathising skills, a belief in people's capacity to change (and psychological mindedness) and, most important, personal integrity.

- **Curability of Insanity:** We are deeply indebted to the era of moral treatment for introducing the principle that insanity was curable. The function of the prison or asylum then shifted from custody to rehabilitation. This, coupled with the parallel growth of a range of treatments including psychotherapy and those which follow from social learning research, meant that TCs were founded in optimism about the human potential for positive change including the "curing" of mental illness.

- **The Doctor as Member:** Leadership and power in a TC is devolved as much as possible from the doctor or therapist, and staff, to the residents or patients.

These historical principles developed within an increasingly monolithic organization for containment of the mentally-ill in what were, harshly termed, warehouses. There were of course many examples of good and humane practice but they became ever more expensive anachronisms such that the official alternative, "care in the community", was introduced by a Conservative Government that provided the rhetoric but not the funding and infrastructure to support genuine treatment in the community. It has become largely discredited in a relatively short period as a cynical, even exploitative economic exercise.

Northfields and Mill Hill

The clearest possible dating of the origins of TCs with their now defining characteristics date from World War II and, specifically to the hospitals at Northfields in Birmingham and Mill Hill in south-London. In the chronology of the democratic-analytic TC, the clearest beginning is with Wilfred Bion, a psychiatrist posted to Northfield Hospital in 1943. Kennard has written extensively about this phase of our history and we record here the innovations of:

- regarding problems of discipline (it was a military organization) as *communal*; and
- patients were given a daily session to *discuss* common issues and problems.

Bion was only there for three months and was followed by S N Foulkes, a psychoanalyst, who remained for three years and introduced:

- better co-ordination between staff, with the nurses actively involved in decision-making; and
- new techniques including psychodrama and staff training in groupwork.

After six months, the leadership of the unit was assumed by the then Lt Colonel Tom Main. "The training wing became transformed into an organization for promoting activities of all sorts". Painting, hobbies, a newspaper, drama, printing, typing and chess all had their own organizational groups. During a period of poor morale, Main offered an insight that carried the TC concept to a new level. He articulated the unconscious tensions in this new type of hospital between patients and staff and within the staff group, especially between Main and his non-medical commanding officer. Main presciently realised that their conflicts represented those of their respective

85

military and medical staff, championing causes and engaging in conflicts on their behalf. He realised that

> the *whole community*...needed to be viewed as a troubled larger system which needed treatment...Clearly we would need a total *culture of enquiry* if we were regularly to examine, understand and perhaps resolve the tensions and defensive use of roles which are inevitable in any total system.

Kennard summarised six key ideas developed by Bion, Foulkes and Main:

- disruptive behaviour problems are shared, common problems rather than the leader's problem;

- patients develop a programme of events, activities, etc. which allow them to behave normally and it is this honest behaviour which is then reviewed in the regular meetings and groups;

- community tasks are group-based thus fostering opportunities for social interactions;

- the patients, or residents, should gradually be encouraged to take leadership responsibilities both for personal growth and to encourage a stronger sense of community;

- Main's "culture of enquiry" must be established and nurtured. The community serves a containing function for the staff and residents to explore and challenge their relationships and tensions as well as the hierarchical dynamics which influence their living together; and

- understand and explore the effects of change and innovation on the organization.

More recently, Kennard and Lees have produced a TC checklist—the Kennard and Lees Audit Checklist (KLAC)—which affords communities a way of performing both a service check on their health and a standards monitor to determine the extent to which they are meeting agreed general criteria for TCs from the Association of Therapeutic Communities (see below).

Mill Hill Hospital was the second of the two origins of the modern TC. Dr Maxwell Jones began work there in 1940. He developed procedures at that hospital to help treat "effort syndrome" in soldiers which closely resembled the innovations of the Northfield Hospital but it was his later work, primarily at the Henderson Hospital, which gained Maxwell Jones recognition as the father of the TC movement. Key among these innovations were *community meetings, staff review meetings* and the *living-learning situation.*

Henderson Hospital

Widely regarded as the role model for democratic-analytic TCs, the Henderson illustrates the importance of the charismatic leader. The lineage of Maxwell Jones, Stuart Whiteley and Kingsley Norton has provided a strong sense of continuity and guidance through the over 50 years it has been in existence. Collective responsibility within daily community meetings, feedback of the gist of all the group "mills" to the assembled community, staff and patients—and the exploration of the "living-learning" situation are but three of the vital ingredients attributed to the work done in this beacon establishment. A long tradition of training staff from other TCs and of organized visits have further enhanced the Henderson's standing. The applied research work of Bridget Dolan in the 1990s was also vital in this process, particularly in establishing the cost-benefit analysis arguments for the comparative efficacy of the TC approach at the Henderson for chronic personality disordered patients. After 61 years as a beacon of excellence, the Henderson Hospital TC was closed as a treatment resource in May 2008 by the Primary Care Trust responsible for funding it.

Robert Rapaport, in *Community as Doctor,*[4] refers to the results of a questionnaire asking staff about the values that best informed the therapeutic nature of the TC. His four principles of *Democratisation, Permissiveness, Communalism* and *Reality-confrontation* have assumed axiomatic status.

---

4. *Community as Doctor* (2003), Rapaport R, Routledge.

Although they require some explanation and, in our view, modification to current circumstances, they remain a potent shorthand for some of the essence of the TC ideal.

Barlinnie Special Unit (1973–1995)

David Cooke chronicles the rise and fall of this well-known special unit which, although created as an extreme response to extreme prison distur-bance, became an antidote based largely on three TC principles:

- a shift from confrontational officer/prisoner relationships towards "something approaching" co-operative nurse/patient relationships

- prisoners were given a share of the decision-making process

- prisoners were given opportunities, through regular community and group meetings, to articulate their problems rather than acting them out with violent and defiant behaviour.

In "The Barlinnnie Special Unit: The Rise and Fall of a Therapeutic Experiment",[5] David Cooke combines a eulogy, obituary and autopsy of this powerful but ultimately failed experiment with singular clarity and truth. We took from this a number of essential lessons:

- therapeutic communities can deal effectively with even the most violent and recalcitrant of offenders, even though they have little or nothing to lose;

- staff training and morale are essential to the TCs viability and good staff-management relationships are essential to good staff morale;

---

5.   See Cullen, E, Jones, L and Woodward, R (1997) (eds), *Therapeutic Communities for Offenders*, John Wiley & Sons.

- unless the core therapeutic principles and procedures are actively maintained, *sense of community* loses its meaning and potency; and

- Cooke records an illustrative example: "more concern was expressed about why the video repair was taking too long than about the hostile and non-cooperative behaviour of a new inmate". He goes on the assert, and we agree, "gradual decline within a regime is both the hardest to detect and the hardest to remedy".

The Association of Therapeutic Communities (ATC)

One of the best things that happened to TCs in the UK was the creation, in 1972, of the ATC. With a representative steering group, monthly journal, annual "retreats" known as the Windsor Conferences, a useful and informative website[6] and an informal national and international network of like-minded friends of TCs, the ATC provides a valuable reference point. In 1996, the first author organized the inaugural meeting of ATC-Prisons, with representatives from the five democratic-analytic TCs as well as staff from the newly opened drug offender hierarchical TCs. This group provides something of the same functions for prison-based TC practitioners and the wider ATC, establishing potentially vital links with a broad range of communities and practitioners.

Some Prison-based TCs

In one sense, prison TCs pre-date even the work at Northfield and Mill Hill. The story began in 1939 with a proposal from Dr W H de B Hubert and Sir W Norwood East: "the most satisfactory method of dealing with abnormal and unusual types of criminal would be the creation of a penal institution of a special kind". The cornerstone for Grendon Underwood was eventually laid in July 1960. The then Home Secretary R A B Butler championed its cause: "The regime must be flexible with the accent on treatment…".

---

6. See therapeuticcommunities.org.

William Gray, the first medical director, provided a focal point and impetus for this neonate, vulnerable institution. The first head of psychology, Bernie Marcus, gave Grendon 16 years of his wonderful insight and humour. When Grendon struggled within a Prison Service in turmoil, it was the persistent criticism that it didn't work in reducing reoffending which was its Achilles' heel. The publication of *Psychiatric Aspects of Imprisonment,* by Gunn *et al*, in 1978[7] perpetuated this vulnerability in spite of finding significant improvements in inmates' interpersonal skills and reductions in indices of personality disorder. They did not however, and crucially, find any significant reduction in the rates of subsequent offending. Indeed, Gunn argued that reconviction was an inappropriate measure for the efficacy of TCs as there were too many confounding variables to do with ex-offenders in the community to determine the relative effects of the TC. Sadly, this widely publicised, oft quoted, and occasionally misrepresented book set back the cause of the prison-based TC for another 20 years.

Cullen, in 1992, published "The Grendon Reconviction Study, Part I".[8] In it, he proved that reconvictions within two years of release from prison was significantly related to both time in therapy at Grendon TC and to the manner of leaving, i.e. whether the man had been release direct from the TC, transferred to another prison or released without probation supervision. Those who were released directly from Grendon, who had completed 18 months or more in therapy and were under direct supervision had significantly lower rates of re-conviction than any other combination.

In Grendon, and the small prison TCs, although there is a psychiatric tradition, there has also always been an internal conflict of methodology. TCs were created as antithetical to the traditional medical model of doctor-patient primacy, emphasising collective, non-expert judgement and decision-making.

The evolution of the primacy of psychiatry at Grendon paralleled that in the wider therapeutic mainstream, with research-based efficacy and professional staff costs being the double nails in their demise and replacement by psychologists and other non-psychiatrically trained therapists.

---

7. Gunn J (1978), *Psychiatric Aspects of Imprisonment,* Academic Press.
8. Cullen, E (1993), *Prison Service Journal,* No.90, 35-37.

At Grendon, the medical staff had, uniquely in HM Prison Service, the managerial responsibility through a director of therapy. In 1985, this changed in the wave of budget devolution and the recommendations of an Advisory Committee for the Therapeutic Regime at Grendon (ACTRAG). For the first time in its history, the management changed from a psychiatrist director to a civil servant Governor. Incredibly, the initial compromise was to have two heads of the establishment, a prison Governor and a director of therapy. The latter was soon subordinated to the former. In 1991, Tim Newell was appointed Governor of Grendon, ushering in a period of growth, stability and achievement perhaps unparalleled in the history of the TC. The decade of the 1990s saw a number of significant advances, including the publication of a series of three research reports that firmly established beyond doubt the proof that Grendon worked (see Cullen, 1994; Marshall, 1997 and Taylor, 2000).

In celebrating the anniversary of Grendon's opening, John Shine edited "A Compilation of Grendon Research"[9] which taken collectively placed the question beyond dispute. Grendon works. One of the most significant researchers throughout Grendon's life is unquestionably Margaret Newton. A psychologist who worked first in the late-1960s and early-1970s and then, after a family break, in the 1990s to the present, she has quietly but professionally accrued probably the most thorough and methodologically rigorous body of work concerning the efficacy of treatment in Grendon that exists. Included in the more significant findings of her body of work are:

- Grendon residents scored significantly lower levels of psychoticism.

- Neuroticism, hostility, and higher levels of extraversion, with better sense of personal responsibility on discharge compared to at reception.

- Prisoners with personality disorders are more likely to respond to substantial periods of residence in the TC if they are aged over 30 on release.

---

9. John Shine was the successor to the first author as head of psychology/director of research at Grendon Prison. See Shine J (2000), "A Compilation of Grendon Research", Leyhill: PES.

- Reconviction after release from Grendon was linked to high scores on psychoticism and extra-punitiveness scales on the hostility and direction of hostility questionnaire (HDHQ); re-imprisonment was linked to low non-verbal intelligence and reconviction for a violent offence was related to a low neuroticism score.

In 2002, with the retirement of Tim Newell, the unexpected loss of his replacement, and the departure of Mark Morris, Grendon's excellent director of therapy, the future of this flagship of prison TCs received another major shift. The team of Peter Bennett as Governor and Michael Brooks as director of TCs guided Grendon away from years of internecine tensions between professional groups and gave stability and clarity to the direction of treatment. It might be argued however that this was achieved at a cost.

It is unarguable that Grendon has moved more towards being a physically secure category B prison than ever before, with significant reductions in the enfranchisement of the resident prisoners in the day-to-day living and decision-making of their collective lives, one of the tenets of DTCs. The viability of a TC is dependent upon a number of critical factors, with leadership but one of them. Therapeutic integrity, staff competence and motivation, direct involvement in core therapy groups by uniform staff and accreditation are other crucial elements.

The Max Glatt Unit at Wormwood Scrubs (1972–2002)

The second prison-based TC was the brainchild of Dr Max Glatt, an Austrian psychotherapist who opened this unit in the hospital of HM Prison Wormwood Scrubs, one of the largest prisons in the UK. That this 23-bed unit targeting drug and sex offenders survived until early in 2002 was testament to the tremendous efforts of countless staff and residents over those three decades who were prepared to resist the predominantly negative, sometimes hostile "host" of the large prison which surrounded them. In March 2002, the Home Office, to their shame, closed the Max Glatt Unit. The *Guardian* newspaper reported that although "the closure decision appears to run counter to official backing for more therapeutic facilities for prisoners" the official reason given by a Home Office spokeswoman was that the availability of therapeutic regimes at other prisons was sufficient to meet current demand from prisoners. The same article goes on to record that the spokeswoman went on the say that

> savings made by closing the Max Glatt Unit will go towards refurbishing and reopening the prison's E Wing, which will have 146 places.

The view of the authors is that this is a perverse and retrograde decision made by civil servants with no sense of history or appreciation of what works and who were driven by short-term administrative and financial expediency. Shame on them. There are thousands of prisoners who could benefit from TC regimes. Far from being met, the shortfall of TC places, of which there are fewer than 1,000, can be counted in the thousands. TCs are the treatment option for anyone who is motivated to change, has sufficient time to complete the treatment (conventionally at least 18 months, but possibly less) and who has problems in interpersonal relationships which give rise to offending.

Gartree (1993–)

One of the more considerable achievements of the past decade in offender treatment was the opening and success of the TC for lifers at Gartree Prison in Leicestershire. Gartree had one of the worst reputations in the country for wilful resistance (and the occasional well-publicised riot by prisoners) and yet Roland Woodward, George Hodkin and their staff team managed to create a strong and innovative TC where places are at a premium and life sentences prisoners regard it in very favourable terms. The need for TC places for life sentence prisoners has been magnified by this excellent unit which has achieved high performance ratings (see *Appendix 3*).

Feltham (1989–1997)

The Albatross Unit, a TC for male young offenders at Feltham Young Offender Institution could take up to 23 residents. It struggled with a particularly challenging population, personality disordered young men with generally poor impulse control and aggressive, inadequate temperaments.

Aylesbury (1997–2006)

"G wing" originally opened in 1996 in the Hospital Wing of Aylesbury Young Offender Institution. Aylesbury TC subsequently moved to one of the larger residential units and the responsibility for staffing was transferred from the medical staff to the discipline staff. Although both groups received the same training and preparation, this was a regrettable decision both because it shifted the primacy from care to custody and because it increased the size of the TC without increasing the resources. As with Feltham, Aylesbury TC fell victim to the vicissitudes of local management, who found a loose cluster of excuses to close it in 2006 rather than support it with the resources necessary to do the job.

Glen Parva (1981–1997) (and a note on some further TCs)

The second author was the therapist and guiding light for Glen Parva, an estimable TC for male young offenders, which, sadly, was closed on short notice but, just as with Feltham and Aylesbury, for administratively expedient and short-sighted reasons in 1996.

The central problem with all three of these TCs for young offenders was that they were vulnerable to local managerial decision-making based primarily on budget comparisons rather than merit or wider value.

HM Prison Service has also opened and is running three TCs of a quite different type in Channings Wood, Portland and Holme House. These units follow an American model for treating drug and substance abuse prisoners using a hierarchical treatment model which is much more structured in using a three-phase programme and it is time-bounded, with treatment ending after one year. They are larger than the European models for small units (which recommend a maximum size of 40) and between them offer approximately 250 places.

A TC for female adult offenders at Winchester Prison, called West Hill, with a capacity of 87 places, was opened and added a long-neglected distaff TC service to the Prison Service. It was later moved to Send Prison where it has 40 places and continues to persevere in spite of difficulties in maintaining a full roll. We wish them well.

II.   The Psychiatric Tradition

In World War II, Malcolm Pines saw the development of TCs in the UK almost exclusively through psychoanalytic eyes. In his "Forgotten Pioneers",[10] he traces their birth to May 1946 and Tom Main's article in the famous collection of papers in the *Bulletin of the Menninger Clinic.*[11] Perhaps inevitably, Pines' overview sees Freud's upbringing in a "patriarchal authoritarian society" as influencing his focus on neurotic patients within a largely personal psychoanalytic world largely free from the "influence of society". Latterly, this perspective is influenced by the views of Moreno and Adler away from the office-couch introspective towards these origins of social psychotherapy. Pines argues that the subsequent decades of psychiatric development in the UK fostered four essential factors which allowed the creation of the TC movement, the birth of which he dates from 1946 and Maxwell Jones:

- psychoanalytic psychotherapy recognising the influence of social forces;

- a "rupture" of the barriers between psychotherapy and psychoanalysis;

10. Pines, M. (1999) "Forgotten Pioneers: The Unwritten History of the Therapeutic Community Movement", *Therapeutic Communities* 20, 1, 23-42.
11. Main T F (1946), "The Hospital as a Therapeutic Institution", *Bulletin of the Menninger Clinic*, 10(3), 66-70.

- the significantly different cultural influences of the London "school" of the Tavistock Clinic and the work of Rickman and Bion; and

- the social democratic influence on British psychiatric hospitals.

The treatment of antisocial, severe personality disordered or psychopathic people who have also committed serious crimes has always been a vexed issue. In prison, the immediate question is whether the disorder or the offending takes precedence; whether the individual is a prisoner or a patient first. Of course, for HM Prison Service, there is no dispute. The need to keep prisoners secure and controlled is paramount. After this, their psychological needs may or may not be addressed.

III.   It Works

Prison-based TCs work in terms of improved interpersonal skills, the reintegration of disorders of personality, reductions in institutional offending and, crucially, reduced rates of subsequent offending as measured by post-release reconvictions (both in terms of number and severity). Among the most significant research projects are:

Cullen (1993)
Not the largest or best publicised study, this work is probably the most important in Grendon Prison's history. Cullen (the first author of this work), then the head of psychology at Grendon, was determined to answer the question of TC efficacy empirically and set up a database of men who had been in therapy between 1984 and 1989. This database, referred to as "The Grendon Reconviction Study", formed the basis for this and the two subsequent studies by Marshall and Taylor noted below. For the first time, it proved that therapy at Grendon was significant in reducing the risk of future offending and as mentioned earlier in this chapter it found further links between reoffending and: (a) time in therapy; (b) the manner of leaving. In a two-year follow-up study of 150 men, Cullen found that:

- men who had completed over 18 months in therapy were reconvicted significantly less (19%) than for those who had done less than 18 months (50%);

- controlling for time in therapy at six monthly intervals, the longer men did in therapy, the lower the subsequent rate of re-convictions; and

- controlling for the manner of their release, those who were released direct from Grendon on parole supervision (N = 43) were significantly less likely to be re-convicted (26%) than those who were released without supervision (N = 63) (40%) or those who were transferred to other prisons and subsequently released (N = 44) (55%).

It is important to note that this original research did not include life sentence prisoners in the reconviction study as they were not released from Grendon and had almost all yet to be released from prison for the requisite two year follow-up. Now that Grendon has become a virtual lifer centre (including a growing number of prisoners serving indeterminate sentences for public protection (IPPs), new comparative research is long overdue.

Marshall (1997)[12]
The Prison Service, while impressed with Cullen's research, wanted independent corroboration and commissioned the Home Office Research and Statistics Directorate to extend and test out his findings. Marshall examined the rates of reconvictions over four years for a much larger Grendon treatment sample (N = 702) and included two comparison groups. A "Waiting List Control Group" (N = 142) of prisoners who had been selected for Grendon but didn't eventually attend due to circumstances beyond their control. Members of this group made an excellent comparison as they were very similar to the treatment group in "all important characteristics". They acted as a control for the treatment effect and in terms of motivation to change. Also a "General Prison Group" (N = 1,400) which was at risk, i.e. released from prison and in the community over the same period as the treatment

---

12. For full details, see *Bibliography*.

group, and was "weighted" according to their principal offences to achieve a similar spread of offences to those found in prisoners selected for Grendon. Marshall found:

- Grendon prisoners tended to be high-risk offenders compared with other prisoners of similar age, serving similar sentences for similar offences;

- lower rates of reconviction were found for prisoners who went to Grendon than for prisoners selected for Grendon but who did not go there;

- time spent at Grendon was strongly related to reconviction, with the lowest rates for those who stayed in therapy longest. Prisoners who were at Grendon for over 18 months had reductions in reconviction rates of "around one-fifth to one-quarter"; and

- mode of release from Grendon and length of stay at Grendon had an effect on reconviction rates, with length of stay more important.

Marshall's largescale, independent research completely corroborated Cullen's earlier findings and considerably strengthened the case for an expansion of the TC model. It also put the final nail in the "Grendon is an experiment" coffin.

Taylor (2000)[13]
This third study in the Grendon trilogy added three new factors, extending the reconviction rate assessment up to seven years after release, including life sentence prisoners for the first time and exploring different rates for sexual offenders and those in prison for violent offences. Taylor found:

- lower rates of reconviction for the Grendon treatment group than for those selected but who did not go.

_____

13. For full details, see the *Bibliography*.

- time at Grendon was "strongly related to reconvictions". Rates were lowest for prisoners who stayed for at least 18 months.

- lifers and violent prisoners had lower reconviction rates.

Among the other significant research we would again mention is the work of Bridget Dolan at the Henderson Hospital, especially in indicating the cost-benefit analysis comparisons of saving people who have completed therapy from future hospital in-patient and prison costs; John Shine's work with various members of the Grendon Research and Development Unit well summarised in "A Compilation of Grendon Research" (2000);[14] Genders and Player's excellent book *Grendon: A Study of a Therapeutic Prison* (1995),[15] identifying a five-stage therapeutic career, the 18 month threshold for greatest progress in treatment and significant erosion of prison culture, improvement in prisoner-staff relationships and a range of benefits from therapy including improved social skills, greater tolerance and less alienation/isolation.

TC Governance Arrangements

The strategy for the management of DTCs is located centrally in the National Offenders Management Service (NOMS). Previously within the Dangerous and Severe Personality Disordered Offenders and TC Unit (DSPS-TC) it has now moved to Therapeutic Communities/PIPES (Psychologically Informed Planned Environments) under Rehabilitation Services Group.

NOMS commissioned a review of DTCs in 2009. It has already had many revisions and delays and has been limited to internal distribution only. The first author has read the report "in confidence". Given the economic climate and the relative expense of treating offenders, the future of DTCs is by no means secure, regardless of their efficacy or support.

---

14. See earlier footnote above concerning John Shine and his research.
15. Genders, E and Player, E (1995), *Grendon: A Study of a Therapeutic Prison*, Oxford: Clarendon Press.

Funding for TCs is devolved to directors of offender management, effectively regional managers by another name. This model is being replaced by yet another in the wake of the Coalition Government's Green Paper insofar as it deals with personality disordered offenders.[16] The official DTC Model is now agreed and in print;[17] whilst the learning disabled TC proposal was given provisional accreditation by the Correctional Services Accreditation Panel in 2010 (see also *Chapter 10*).

Summary

In a history stretching back over two centuries, the British TC movement has affirmed many positive human, interpersonal and communal truths. There is great curative strength in the opportunities afforded to us by engaging with one another, and speaking honestly about our lives, in a small group over time. When people are encouraged to share responsibilities in order to live their lives together less harmfully, most of them respond. TCs in prisons can maintain therapeutic integrity without breaching institutional security or individual rights. In fact, security is usually enhanced both by the positive influence of the TC elders on others and because the entire purpose of the community is to encourage every resident to live a good and useful life. There have only been two escapes from Grendon TC in the nearly 50 years history of the prison, by far the best security record in the country. Dovegate TC is aware of the responsibilities of a new prison-based TC to defend these great traditions.

This relatively brief review of historical highlights has hopefully explained something of the guiding principles and significant people in the history to date. Of course, we can't mention others: patients, inmates, staff and visitors-who have also made great and positive contributions; but we can acknowledge the abiding debt we owe them for their courage, honesty, enduring counsel and bloody hard work.

---

16. *Breaking the Cycle: Effective Punishment, Rehabilitation and Sentencing of Offenders* (2010)
17. Prison Service Order (PSO) 2400, Democratic Therapeutic Communities Core Model, What Works in Prison Unit, January 2005.

CHAPTER FOUR

BUILDING THE PEOPLE AND THE COMMUNITY

I.   Staff Training

It was axiomatic that staff training should be an essential first priority. To this end, the first author and Roland Woodward met over an extended preparation period to consider the best possible training model for the Dovegate TC staff, a model which was inclusive, accommodating traditional best practice along with the required updating with proven offending behaviour techniques, e.g. cognitive behavioural therapy, into a multi-modal treatment regime. In four stages, we determined to:

1. Identify the essential training needs based on the staff profile.
2. Draft a tailor-made programme over a four week training period.[1]
3. Train the therapy and Assessment Unit managers and counsellors with an approach that allowed them to train their own staff teams in two-week courses.
4. Involve the managers in revising the training programme to best suit their own staff teams' training.

The principles which guided our work included:

- the language should be accessible and as jargon-free as possible;

- a model of concentric circles of relationships best characterised our Dovegate model, essential to which was exploring personal, interpersonal and group relationships as relevant to therapeutic targets; training must be relevant to the experiences of the community regardless of their position, staff, resident, manager or entrant;

---

1.   An outline of the four week course is available in "Dovegate Therapeutic Community: Bid, Birth, Growth and Survival", Cullen and Miller in *Grendon and the Emergence of Forensic Therapeutic Communities*, Shuker, R and Sullivan, E (eds.), Wiley-Blackwell, 2010.

- people confined against their will must give informed consent to join, engage in and be challenged by the community.; and

- community members should be enfranchised, i.e. have a genuine voice in the collective and individual responsibilities placed upon them and in the day-to-day running of their community.

Our primary sources of reference were:

- Yalom's *Theory and Practice of Group Psychotherapy;*[2]
- the Association of Therapeutic Communities (ATC) Network of Democratic-Analytic TCs.
- Kennard-Lees Audit Checklist (KLAC) for our TC standards.

II.   The Support Team

The contract with HM Prison Service required that a team of external consultants be employed to assist and support the Dovegate TC staff during the first year of their existence. The consultants were meant to possess qualifications in counselling and psychology and, preferably, have some TC experience. In the event, of the team of five, two had extensive relevant TC experience, one had some brief experience but not of prisons and the other two had no TC experience. All five were very experienced senior practitioners, with both public and private careers behind them. The team members were Dr Eric Cullen (lead consultant, team leader and the first author of this work), Pauline Oliver, senior clinical psychologist, Val Evans, Norma Wallace and Eddie Rowarth, with qualifications in psychology, psychotherapy and/or counselling.

The director of therapy provided a specific working brief in the form of four objectives:

---

2.   Yalom, I D (.2005) (edn.5), *Theory and Practice of Group Psychotherapy,* Basic Books.

- **Objective One:** To help the director of therapy to gain an overview of the developing TC and the factors that are either hindering or helping that development.

- **Objective Two:** To provide support through non-intrusive observation and feedback to the staff teams of the therapeutic community.

- **Objective Three:** To record and analyse the behaviour of the staff team that reinforced the building of a learning culture and the containment of the residents' anxieties.

- **Objective Four:** To provide managers of the TC units with an opportunity to discuss and develop strategies for the growth of their staff teams.

The contractual conditions were set and this meant that all the support team (ST) were tied to a calendar of attendance where they were full-time for the early stages of the TC life and then took part in gradually decreasing frequencies. This proved unfortunate in some ways as the needs of the staff, and the potential to make a positive impact on the residents, decreased in direct proportion to the ST's presence and therefore ability to respond fully.

The TCs were styled A, B, C and D.[3] Two of them, i.e. TCC and TCD, were delayed in their opening due to problems of staffing levels in the main prison, which meant that a significant minority of those who could have benefited only received the briefest of support from the support team before the relevant contracts ran out.

In the first author's opinion, these objectives, and the response to them by the ST, raise probably the critical questions as to the eventual viability of the entire project. Creating a therapeutic atmosphere, establishing a cluster of four communities, an Assessment and Resettlement Unit (ARU), a High Intensity Programme (HIP) and an Education Department (which became EduCom), etc. from scratch was an enormous challenge. The director maintained a watching brief but felt that the communities needed to develop without his direct involvement.

---

3. These were later to be re-styled Avalon, Camelot, Endeavour and Genesis: see *Chapter 10*.

The staff teams were obliged to learn by trial and error and the support team were meant to be as unintrusive as possible and keep the director informed. To this end, they were his "eyes and ears" — a double-edged brief.

The unit managers and staff were on the one hand reluctant to confide in the consultants as they knew they would be briefing the director and negative comments would reflect badly on their positions. On the other hand, they also knew they needed the advice and support which the support team afforded to them. In the end, all the managers and most of the staff confided extensively, showing both their fears and their achievements to the support team in full measure. It must be acknowledged as well that the presence of the support team created problems of communication and attachment for the director of therapy as well. Some of the key factors which the support team observed hindering development were:

- a lack of qualified personal clinical supervision to help the new staff understand what was happening to them within the therapeutic process;

- a timetable for opening the TCs which put considerable pressures on staff, especially the manager and staff of the Assessment Unit(s). The High Intensity Programme team had a rather schizophrenic development, being required to operate as an assessment unit initially then shifting quickly to their original brief. When the first two TCs opened two weeks later (TCA and TCB), their teams felt this sudden surge of work and expectation as well; and

- just behind the scenes was a growing national pressure to fill up as quickly as possible due to nationwide overcrowding which became a media-driven factor.

Many TC staff struggled with the concepts of process/content analysis which is critical to the therapeutic process. Coupled with this ambivalence were the sometimes conflicting objectives of operational procedure and therapeutic understanding. The *content* of the therapeutic dialogue within the TC refers to what is said, by and to whom. The *process* is essentially an interpretation of the significance of that dialogue, i.e. the hidden or shaded messages behind the words. Many discipline staff found detaching themselves from the traditional officer-inmate dyad difficult and somewhat stressful, increasing what was already a somewhat vulnerable sense of entering unknown territory.

The main prison, having only opened three months prior to the TC, was experiencing a number of significant security and operational difficulties which had a traumatic effect on the TC. A major concerted act of indiscipline at the end of November, which resulted in over 60 prisoners being transferred and a lockdown of the main prison, required many of the TC staff members' involvement in coping with both the incidents themselves and their aftermath. TC staff in large numbers reported that not only were there many incidents of excessively punitive responses from main prison staff, but that they, the TC staff, had been badly treated by their main prison colleagues. Problems with healthcare, reception of prisoners and other main prison areas of responsibility were also creating negative and, in some instances, actively hostile relationships between the two staff teams. TC staff reported that they were referred to contemptuously and treated as if their prison-craft skills were inferior or non-existent. Unfortunately, for reasons of funding, the contract obliged the TC to continue a close, symbiotic relationship with the main prison.

The director of therapy had consciously chosen to remain detached from direct involvement in, and physically visiting, the TC units. While this afforded the unit managers and teams ample opportunities to learn for themselves, by trial and error, the TC "ropes", it also left managers often observing that they felt rather under-supported. The director had put in place twice weekly meetings of all managers in a "Senate Meeting" and these proved a crucial forum for both the positive and negative dynamics experienced, a microcosm of the TC's development. Factors which appeared to help that development included:

- a hugely impressive commitment from the managers and most of the staff to making this endeavour a success. The director of therapy and the TC and operational managers were, taken as a group, working with an almost unsustainable intensity within weeks of the opening and receipt of the first inmates;

- the staff teams had been trained together in TCs. This had helped to grow a sense of collective purpose. This bonding was sorely tested by the new residents, who carried with them a highly toxic mix of prison culture attitudes, scepticism and fear of the new, unknown regime;

- the preparations during the period before opening, especially the work undertaken in investing in information packs and visits to the potential sending establishments soon proved to be crucial in identifying the "seed corn" referrals; and

- the numbers of inmates in the main prison also proved to be quite high and while this made the administration of transfers easier, the prejudicial and often negatively distorted messages they received from other prisoners often served to undermine their motivation to come to the TC.

The support team members recorded reviews of **Objective One** (helping the director of therapy to gain an overview) included:

This was a difficult role to fulfil since there was a risk that we would be perceived as the D of T's "spies in the camp"...Meeting with the director once a week as a team seemed appropriate, giving us the opportunity not only to convey our views to him, but also to hear his thoughts, concerns, etc...

My introduction to the TC through [the manager] was, at first, awkward...[He] expressed "indifference" at the prospect of support and explained that this was not personal but that...experience had been that such promises of support rarely deliver.

I think we did give a very good overview of how the TC developed. Some of the feedback was not always easy to deliver or to receive...

My relationship with [the TC] was to become a significant part of my life and for the next few months where I would take on numerous roles. There was clearly a huge gulf between the staffs' and my understanding of unconscious dynamics.

Support team reviews of **Objective Two** (providing non-intrusive support and feedback) included:

Experience and diplomacy were tested to the full in our efforts to alter the learning process for the staff teams as little as possible whilst affording the benefits of such skills as we brought to the experience so that staff didn't suffer unduly. The support team provided regular and relevant observations and feedback to the staff teams via their meetings following core therapy activities and through regular (daily) meetings with their therapy managers. The strong relationship of support which grew between all the managers and their ST members was a particular feature, starting as it did in most cases from a position of some distrust and distancing on the part of the managers and some naivety/uncertainty on the part of the ST.

It was sometimes very difficult to keep to a role of non-intrusive observation — feeling frustrated at not being able to get involved in the course of wing meetings etc. — but the staff soon came to accept this as my role and welcomed the feedback given to them afterwards.

My first meeting with [the TC staff] was cool, the staff team were very suspicious but friendly... for some reason I had thoughts of the Battle of Balaclava. I offered my credentials and what I thought my role was, in terms of support for them. To the last man they were horror struck by the possibility of me joining either their groups or listening in on the residents' groups. It was decided that it was not possible for a stranger to do this and that a referral to Roland [Woodward] had to be made before any action took place.[4]

The non-intrusive observation was almost impossible to fulfil if real contact through a relationship is to be fostered. The fact that I was able to build a sound relationship with the team enabled us to work together and also enabled the team to use me for their own benefit.

Perhaps, on reflection, the term "non-intrusive" was ambiguous. Meant to restrain our more interventionist tendencies [and thus, too, significantly alter the experiential learning for the staff], it probably inhibited our early support too much. Human nature, and the STs wealth of experience, guided us to appropriate levels of support

---

4. In spite of the fact that the managers had known about the ST role well in advance and the director of therapy had sent a memo to all units with a detailed explanation of the ST's role.

which [we hope] gave direction to the new staff without obviating their personal growth.

Support team reviews of **Objective Three** (recording and analysing, etc. staff behaviour) included:

From the beginning of our consultancy, the ST created and used a daily feedback form. These forms were summarised by the lead consultant and submitted to the director of therapy at weekly intervals. By the end of our ST work together at the end of April, there were more than 60 pages of record and analysis.[5]

I thought the form that we developed for the purpose of recording the behaviour of the staff team worked well, being simple and quick to use, but giving valuable information on the content and process of meetings.

The recording of the process became a discipline that sometimes got in the way. However, it also proved to be a very useful tool which enable me to focus on what was really happening. I think this process added some support to the containment of the anxiety of the whole community.

The support team attended every core therapy activity during our consultancy. The staff meetings after the core small groups and community meetings afforded regular opportunities to experience first hand the staffs' struggles to build a learning culture and to contain (and understand) residents' anxieties (as well as their hostilities, demanding and complaining, and regressive tendencies).

Among the most significant features which the ST observed in the efforts of TC staff to meet this objective included:

- Strong, occasionally inspired, leadership from the managers who understood the interpersonal dynamics both within the Senate and their respective staff teams. Building a learning culture within a TC inside a prison was a daunting challenge. The natural tendency of prison staff to respond to challenging and

---

5.   Excerpts from these records follow later in the chapter.

sometimes rule-breaking behaviour is to punish and, subsequently, to become more controlling. The TC response is to oblige *both the individual AND the community* to address, understand and deal with the behaviour. This is a far more demanding learning pattern to put in place and sustain but it is ESSENTIAL for therapeutic change to occur.

- The, again essential, requisite of the community staff to KEEP THE BOUNDARIES. By this, we mean both the procedural boundaries of meetings being staffed and held on time (and community members, staff or resident, being excluded from the meeting if they were late), and the therapeutic boundaries of creating and sustaining a SAFE *environment* in which the residents can begin to be honest about themselves, their feelings towards others and their current rule-breaking behaviour, e.g. drug-taking and bullying. The communities were quite variable in the early success of this endeavour, but the Assessment Unit was outstanding (given an impeccable lead by their TM).

- Residents' anxieties about the TC began long before actually arriving on the TC. We experienced a worrying frequency of referrals withdrawing their applications. Some of these men were in the main prison at Dovegate and we were able to visit them to enquire of their reasons. Every one of these men said they had heard negative and pejorative stories about the TC, e.g. that it was for treating sex offenders, that it was a soft option or that it was failing and about to close. It wasn't possible to determine the magnitude of this negative influence upon referral rates, but it was a worrying aspect, one too reminiscent of our experiences with other TCs in the Prison Service, especially Grendon Underwood.

- New arrivals at Dovegate TC came onto the Assessment Unit. The first impression they gained there was almost entirely positive. We regularly spoke to these men in the first few days after arrival and their accounts were dominated by a sense of relief and amazement that such a place existed. The staff were polite, helpful and seemed genuinely interested in them! Relationships were on a first name basis and were related and unhurried. The lead given by the TM, counsellor and staff concerning the rules, expectations and lifestyle on the Assessment Unit was clear, consistent and calm. The staff came out of the office, mixed with the residents, played games with them and *listened to them*. All these factors created the ideal environment to help the residents cope with the inevitable stress of being assessed for a place on a TC and with the culture shock of leaving 'the system' and all that entailed.

Support team reviews of **Objective Four** (providing managers with an opportunity to discuss matter, etc.) included:

In some ways, this was the most difficult to assess. While the ST did discuss their staff with the TMs, much of that was to do more with immediate problem-solving, staff support and stress concerns, and with an exploration of the difficulties of bringing an inexperienced staff group up to speed vis-à-vis the resident populations' obvious criminal sophistication and manipulative interpersonal skills, i.e. their survival strategies. In that sense, the objective was met, but at the time it felt more like survival than planning for growth.

This is a difficult one to evaluate. I was certainly involved in a number of discussions with the manager of the HIP [High Intensity Programme] regarding the developing staff team, but it would be useful to get her perceptions on whether she felt she had enough support/opportunities in this area.

I think this objective was met to some extent in that the first two units to become live had the majority of the support from the support team. Although I was able to give some support to EduCom, I felt that I was not fully-used for a whole month, this being the period when I was there full-time. Once the residents had actually started education, I was cut back to three days a week. I consider that this was the time when my full support would have been most useful.

It was unquestionably true that all the ST members were a direct and regular source of support for the therapy managers (TMs) and that their staff, individually and collectively, were the source of much of those discussions: issues of coping, concerns about sustaining professional, objective relationships with residents (particularly with some of the female staff members) and of staff being able to balance the prison imperatives of security and control with the TC objectives. The TMs with the least personal managerial/prison and TC experience struggled the most. The TMs of TCC and TCD, which came on line only two months after the other units, struggled even more due to the delays in opening which left a haemorrhage of staff and the fact that the support team were coming to the end of their contracts and had very little consultancy time left.

The Lead Consultant

After only one month from opening, the lead consultant had formed clear and strong impressions which he shared with the director of therapy. The managers of the Assessment and Resettlement Unit (ARU) and the High Intensity Programme (HIP) (which was being used as a second, parallel, assessment unit during the filling up period)

> were providing clear, calm and accurate models for their staff…Upstairs, however, it was a different matter. After an initial reluctance towards the ST members, they revealed their anxieties, anger and most of all sheer weight of work and expectations they felt.

There was obvious and consistent tension and criticism towards the other therapy managers, who they felt to be making too many errors due to their inexperience and judgement. The atmosphere at the regular Senate meeting between all the managers and the director of therapy, became increasingly strained and relatively unconstructive. In spite of one or two cautious attempts to articulate this from the support team, the situation deteriorated. An additional layer of antipathy was growing between the therapy managers (six) and the operations managers (four).

The operations managers were very experienced in prison-craft and had all been with the Dovegate project since well before the opening. They were more experienced than the therapy managers. They were responsible for all the operational aspects of the prison including security, personnel (including the essential daily manning profiles), adjudications (i.e. re prison discipline), and much of the routine requirements of the uniformed staff.

Of course a degree of strain in the relationships, given what was at stake and the workloads involved, was inevitable. It is nevertheless ironic that a

group of managers tasked to create a therapeutic regime based on the principles of TCs, which they were all familiar with, should struggle so obviously
to apply these same principles to their own relationships. The second author
provides an astute analysis of this entire process and its "toxicity" in *Chapter 8.*

The relationship between the lead consultant and the director of therapy
became even more strained when, after three months, the former registered
his belief that the effects of the main prison on the neonate TC were so inju-
rious that they should report this view to the prison manager and, through
him, the headquarters of Premier Prisons.

He further recommended that Premier Custodial Group(PCG) should
approach HM Prison Service with a view to renegotiating the terms of the
contract regarding separating the TC from the main prison. The director of
therapy disagreed, arguing that to do so would be seen as an admission that
PCG were struggling to honour the terms of the contract and might cause
the Official Side to consider withdrawing the contract and inviting fresh
tenders. The relationship became so strained that at one point, the director
announced in front of the support team that he did not trust the lead consultant, and was suspicious that he had spoken to the responsible director
at Premier headquarters about his concerns, effectively going behind the
director of therapy's back. Although untrue, this understandably triggered
a breach in the working relationship which was only gradually repaired.

We were reminded of the experiences of Bion and Foulkes in the Northfield Hospital's early months as recorded by Tom Main in his seminal paper
"The Hospital as a Therapeutic Institution",[6] way back in the 1940s (see
further *Chapter 3*).

What, then, were the impressions of the support team over these critical first months of Dovegate TC's existence? The first residents arrived the
week beginning November 7 and were placed directly on one of the two
Assessment Units.

The ST kept contemporaneous notes on a daily basis of their experiences using a form created by them for this purpose. The form recorded the
activity, e.g. small group or community meetings, the time of the activity,

---

6. Main T. (1946), "The Hospital as a Therapeutic Institution", *Bulletin of the Menninger Clinic*,
    10: 66–70.

and what took place both as a narrative description — the *content* — and an interpretation by the individual ST member of the dynamics of those events — the *process*. We provide a summary of those records on a chronological, or time-chart, basis.

Month One — November

Assessment and Resettlement Units/High Intensity Programme Units

The ST member — called here A — was introduced to the staff. One manager confided within this first meeting that she felt "de-skilled" by a barrage of questions from staff, but showed a "sense of humour and a relaxed style". There were already concerns being expressed by the two managers about the volume of work required of them and that they were falling behind — after only two weeks. The following week, the units were said to be

> developing nicely, w/good clear lead from…[manager]; some concern about the ethics of administering the Multiple Sex Inventory (MSI) to non-sex offenders [a questionnaire and part of the battery of tests administered to all men being assessed to signal possible relevant treatment courses].

At this juncture, the lead consultant and member A split their support, with member A taking the high intensity programme (HIP) and the first author taking the Assessment and Resettlement Unit (ARU). The former recorded:

> Extremely impressed with…[manager] lead on the ARU and the way the unit is going; therapeutic, clear, calm, residents positively engaged in live issues…

Therapeutic Communities A and B

As already described, these were the first two TCs to open, and the therapy managers on them were those with the least prison managerial experience. The ST member on one of the TCs reported a "shaky" early feeling, with

113

"almost a mood of hysteria among staff". Both the ST consultants recorded concerns being expressed already about the relationships between the TC managers and staff and the operations managers. The lead consultant was moved to record:

> Boundaries breaching was a definite problem across units during our first week, illustrated with an Ops manager coming onto TC … meeting with TC … [the other unit] staff in tow … [and stating] "meeting suspended to talk about wages"— not acceptable.

EduCom

The EduCom Department covered education as well as vocational training. The proposals for the unit, housed in the amenities building physically separate from the residential buildings, were innovative and imaginative, involving the aspiration to produce what were effectively cottage industries like pottery and cooking so that these classes could realise a return on the investment, i.e. sell what they produced. The head of EduCom was enthusiastic and energetic if rather anxious about the new experiences ahead. The ST member—called here B—reported the teachers to be "doing well; anticipating residents, staff development and what are the best external "qualifications".

In December, the lead consultant provided the director of therapy with a Month Two summary. It made sobering reading. Areas of concern included:

- The continuing heavy workloads on the therapy managers, which already resulted in signs of acute stress and early indications of chronic fatigue.

- The individual treatment plans (ITAPs) were too ambitious and detailed for the time and continuity constraints of the assessment period.

- The use of the Multiple Sex Inventory (MSI)[7] as a screening device for all receptions was inappropriate, causing considerable anger and indignation among the non-sex offender referrals.

---

7. With the PCL-R a score above an agreed cut-off point meant almost definite grounds for

- The three week assessment period was insufficient to allow for the case conferences to be held in the third week. The therapy manager asked for, and received, a fourth week exclusively for assessments.

- A lack of clarity as to the ultimate role(s) of the High Intensity Programme.

- Early challenges to the authority of the therapy managers on TCA and TCB by a small but vociferous number of residents. There was, not surprisingly, a strong prison mentality and suspiciousness within the resident population fighting with initially favourable and positive impressions gained from the assessment experience.

- The operations managers continue to "present as a mixed blessing". Their practical knowledge and advice has frequently been very valuable but there continues to be friction with the therapy managers and some staff when they are seen as heavy-handed or boundary breaching to the TCs.

- The ST counsellors felt strongly that there was a serious lack of clinical supervision built into the programme for the therapy managers and their staff.

The positive impressions included a growing respect for the quality and commitment of the two managers of the ARU and HIP, the enthusiasm of the EduCom staff and potential of EduCom to play a vital role in the TC, and the overall impression of determination and hard work from the overwhelming majority of the staff to make the enterprise succeed.

Into Month Two

By the beginning of December, a number of general issues were recorded:

---

exclusion. This was a source of considerable discussion and ambiguity as to whether there was any clinical discretion.

- The effects of the main prison on the TC are overwhelmingly negative, particularly as experienced during the lockdown.[8] This included the director of therapy [who as part of the command team was required to be in the main for most of the working day].

- Case conferences[9] are causing splits between therapy managers, there is no continuity/overview; TMs haven't been able to trust each other's judgement. There seems to be "total'" confusion over the PCL-R process and how we are to interpret and use them regarding resident exclusion. Could RW [Roland Woodward] meet with the four TMs ASAP and sort?

- The message the staff are getting from RW about time boundaries is not seen as fair, i.e. you're consistently late and it is getting passed down.

- TCA and, to a lesser extent, TCB are making daily TC errors which are having a cumulative effect on the process…TC experience might obviate some of the obvious problems; MSI should be administered selectively, a PEI[10] on main made unacceptable remarks about the TC to the staff on the PCO ITC;[11] lockdown: "big brother is crushing neonate TC…"[12]

Other selected commentary from December included:

---

8. Following a major act of indiscipline by over 50 of the prisoners in the main, the entire establishment including the TC had been subject to lockdown conditions which meant all the residents being locked in their cells for most of the 24-hour cycle. This totally destroyed the normal TC day.
9. Case conferences were held at the end of each new resident's assessment to summarise progress and indicate whether he should stay, i.e. transfer onto a TC or go, i.e. return to the sending establishment.
10. A physical education instructor.
11. The Introductory Training Course, i.e. essential for all Dovegate staff in both the main prison and TC.
12. The MSI, or Multiphasic Sex Inventory was part of the core assessment inventory and is a standardised questionnaire with very explicit questions of a sexual preference nature. Many of the non-sex offenders in assessment found completing it offensive and this was causing resentment and tension on the Assessment and Resettlement Unit (ARU). It was subsequently decided to use it only with known current or previous sex offenders.

116

Quiet on ARU, a kind of moratorium in the transition from abridged assessment to proper role; relief and positive anticipation. 'Spot-check' on TCA was rather more relaxed with staff and residents mixing and socialising; mood on TCB rather more strained, all staff in office and rather tense ...Met new residents p.m. on ARU/HIP. They gave the now familiar mix of acute tension/fear of unknown ahead, tinged with some relief at having finally made it to the TC.

TCA—Well organized business meeting; community meeting on residents esp. one not pulling his weight; last 10 on staff-resident relationships, inappropriate behaviour on all parts; process: building the culture; not allowing it to falter. Environment meeting: how the residents deal with the empowerment they now have; met with Ther. Man. Talking about dangers, esp. female staffs' conversations with residents; ...Staff sensitivity and why it's not happening.

ARU/HIP—Preparing for expected residents; visit from injured PCO; request for someone to go to help on Reception [in main prison]. Huge resistance to going—unwilling to put themselves in place where they feel used and abused ...

TCB—Met with TM; feeling stressed as a result of operational inconsistencies, feeling unsupported by colleagues; p.m.: Case conferences [with TMs, TCB and ARU, counsellor and PCO] challenging, collaborative and constructive. Case conference with [resident] very honest and realistic.

ARU/HIP—Issues included yesterday's intake and the number of dropouts from the main; Christmas decorations, staff cover for EduCom and need for visits orderly; Process: Yesterday's decision to confine meeting to Ops issues went unheeded; ...TMs looked "pissed off"; remaining staff seemed more engaged and enthusiastic ...

Senate briefing—Ops Managers rude to TM; ...HIP: An outstanding illustration by TM of how to do it: dealt with new residents and staffs' impressions and initial concerns adroitly, explored potential opportunities and dangers, praised staff for their work to date but [resident] expressed two areas of concern. Social histories and staff working relationships ...Note: strong and growing impression that reception are source of unnecessary problems in delays, inconsistencies and obstruction;

117

also concerned at large number of referrals who are dropping out at the last minute from the main — could we discuss someone from TC going over to see all main residents waiting to come *before* date of transfer? What about someone going over and speaking to those who recently declined at last minute (to determine reasons).

This was subsequently done and the majority of last minute dropouts said it was due to negative comments from other main prison inmates (who had never been to the TC).

Staff development training: would it be a good idea for the TC staff to have a combination of: (a) regular staff training seminars, e.g. in the visits for one or two hours on particular themes; and (b) OJT[13] sessions for any available staff of all grades/groups to discuss training needs and current topics? Continuity of practice on the TCs: We have observed a number of different practices on the units on subjects like staff cover of small groups (continuity; number of groups per TC and how new residents join) and therapy managers attendance as well as the lack of regular core staff support meetings which provide absolutely essential time for the staff team to air grievances, compare notes, sort differences, etc. Relationship with the main: I cannot overemphasise how vital I feel it is for the TC to achieve greater autonomy from the main AND greater control over the referral procedures for the new assessees from there. Can this be put on the agenda of the Senate Meeting?

TCB — TM is called away to "emergency" by Ops Manager insisting meeting be interrupted for "live issue'". Case conferences: both sessions immaculately conducted by TMs, HIP and TCB, mood felt collaborative and fair…

TCA — Small groups: Group I observed found it very difficult to stay with issues on themselves over Christmas; Feedbacks: common theme — avoiding the issues; how to move away from looking at their issues — struggling to focus (process: different ways of avoidance); Staff feedback: all felt their groups wanted to avoid in some way; we looked at the group, i.e. staff, and how they mirror what the residents do and vice-versa (process: parallel process: what residents do, staff might do, support team might do, Roland might do!…).

---

13. On the job training.

Into the New Year

Briefing:[14] mostly Ops stuff; but (DofT) went round and encouraged managers to raise anything they wished. V. helpful...Main areas of concern for (DofT) meeting this p.m.: (a) ITAPs[15]— Inefficient procedures, duplication of effort and forms, and possibly over-ambitious form itself in terms of content—could headings be prioritised and could more staff on ARU/HIP be involved in completion?; (b) Staff support a big and, in my view, growing area of concern. It seems the timing, purpose and content of staff support meetings vary widely from unit to unit and there is a concern that some staff may be suffering from the "misuse" or lack of this facility; (c) State of TCA: I am increasingly concerned about staff needing support and clarity; residents needing containment, direction and safety, and...TM needing practice at/help with, reflecting before acting, tension control and decision-making; and (d) Can ST visit main next Friday please?

Business meeting, TC: Drugs—how to deal with users/dealers. Very nice discussion—evenly balanced (staff stand back and allow residents to take control—very successful); chat w/TM: Generally pleased with evolving community—some good examples this week of residents taking control...

Nearing the End for the Support Team

Well into the New Year, the first of the support team due to finish began to reflect on her time at Dovegate:

Looking at my process; ST meeting w/DofT: I went in with enthusiasm re. work I was doing and came out with a sinking feeling that maybe this isn't the right place for me. Perhaps this is bringing me down to earth (Process: Enthusiasm and energy through to "what am I doing here?")...

---

14. A meeting with the director of therapy and Senate, first thing every morning.
15. Individual treatment action plans as drafted in summary form for all residents.

…We were invited to join therapy managers for a drink after work. Discussed the need for team-building. The Senate meeting felt safe enough for members to say how they felt and put forward ideas and leave space for disagreement and anger.

…Said my goodbyes to Zena and Mathew [EduCom staff]. Offered to come in when the external verifier makes her visit (tying up loose ends. The final process Wanting to finalise what I started).

Her final entry was:

Meeting with team; positive feedback. Certificate not arrived to fax to Hospitality Awarding Body (frustration); phone calls to chase them up. Worked with group on youth work (enjoyment). Gifts given to me from EduCom team (ending process). Goodbyes all PM (ending).

The rest of the support team would continue for another three weeks until the end of April. The lead consultant's contract required him to continue for another month. Some final selected entries include:

Special community meeting: Focus was on [resident] and his paranoid behaviour, secrecy, greed, etc. (excellent feedback given by other residents — they are becoming increasingly sophisticated in their contributions). Having two new residents on the HIP this week has strengthened the feeling of community. ST — feedback and sharing (only four of us left)…With [TM, HIP] reviewing the HIP development and her future goals (beginning the end. Saying goodbye. She will be away next week. A sad farewell).

Community meeting: Chairman emotionally confessing to lying to the community ref. "passive smoking" prompting interesting range of responses from disingenuous surprise to apparently genuine loss of trust — provoked double standard issues to some good purpose — staff and most residents engaged so there was a positive feel. Second major issue bravely raised by [PCO] ref. why there was so much "traffic" to and from a resident's cell over "tea and coffee". Nice to see the "cons" experiencing some reality confrontation. Staff Meeting (immediately after): TM and counsellor very cynical, PCOs very impressed.…[2 PCOs] clearly love the work, so maybe some concern that TM and counsellor obviously critical dismissal of residents' sincerity might bruise a bit, but probably necessary. ST: we clearly sense the end is nigh for the team … [TM from dif. unit] asked to see me. Hurt and becoming alienated from the majority of the "management team"; shares thanks for the support ST has afforded him. ARU case conference: Hard-hitting, direct thorough. Resident given last chance after having confessed to smoking cannabis at Max Glatt[16] before leaving there (TMs' performance at summarising residents' problems areas/issues would be difficult to improve upon).

Meetings displaced into visits area due to delayed changing of locks on unit. Community Meeting: In spite of invasive noise from the kitchen and EduCom residents staring in, the community had a powerful, positive meeting: (a) [Deleted] threats to kill his girlfriend's mother was put on him by a new resident (outstanding); (b) [Deleted] threat to break [redacted] legs during football match. We moved, at residents' request, into much smaller but quieter room and continued w/[deleted] issues — most powerful engagement by residents (almost all involved) since TC opened. Due to display of emotions, Com. agreed to take short break then have Special … Special allows feelings to diminish, then moves onto [redacted] hiding scissors — fear, weapon … No, he says, because he cuts hair!!! Fascinating. Support team meet — It's finally time. Senate for lunch and farewells. Back to office then out once again to say more goodbyes. Finally, met w/DofT for closure then to the gate.

The Operations Managers

The operations managers were in a difficult position. Deprived of direct involvement in the creation of the TCs (in spite of one or two of them having considerable experience and expertise of TCs), they had nevertheless to engage the TCs actively in the day-to-day realities of running a prison and of ensuring that the operational requirements of the contract were met. This created considerable tensions between managers.

---

16. The TC formerly housed at Wormwood Scrubs; now closed see *Chapter 3*.

…there was a power play being acted out by the Operations Managers. The few residents that had arrived meant that procedures needed to be put into place that would later become an everyday occurrence. One of the limitations that the staff, and, at times, the manager created for themselves was to continuously ask when they were unsure. The fact of asking often meant that in the early days especially, they would receive a "prison" not "therapeutic" response to their question (from the Ops Managers)…The demands being made on the staff from the residents was relentless and this was clearly uncontainable and being passed on. The situation was often compounded by mixed messages coming back from the Ops.

I have sat in groups where Ops teams have come in for unrelated reasons, seen decisions overhaul policy made on the TC, and other disruptive manoeuvres where a liaison with the therapy manager would have been more appropriate. The "misconduct" of the Ops managers was one of the most disturbing features, which I felt unsettled the TCs instead of containing them, in the early stages. I could speculate as to the unconscious processes that drove much of this interference, but at the core was the support of Roland [Woodward], who maintained control.

All teams needed an understanding of the therapeutic process especially the Ops Managers. The relationship between the teams and the Ops Mans. could have been smoother if the need for power and control had been managed differently…There was a certain sense of empire building and an unfortunate "we are better than you" attitude was established. The brutality of prison life is a fact, however if it can be lessened, surely any such action should be taken.

Summary of Support Team Observations

At the end of the support team placement, the director of projects at Premier headquarters, who had been responsible for that team being written into the original contract, asked the director of therapy for a final report from the lead consultant on the work of the ST. All the team were invited to contribute and some of their final comments included:

Throughout my work in the TCs, I understood that I would one day be gone. [DofT] had told us that we had to be aware that they would have to continue without us one day. At times that day seemed impossible, but it was something I held in mind. I found that within a short time my relationship with K [the therapy manager] was very close. Like…a trust had built up which said a great deal for us but volumes about Dovegate. The staff team were keen to please but not sure how to work, often being confused by the residents behaviour on one side and the Ops on the other. K and I became the parental figures around the TC, she retaining the authority whilst I held the therapeutic space. I was aware this was not what was being asked of me, but I was aware that K had no room left to take what I was holding. She would manage a very difficult morning with the residents and the staff, only to be attacked by Ops, [DofT], or another therapy manager…As Dovegate grew in residents and the workload fell on the more competent, a slow realisation descended over the managers. There was a sense that they could be kind to each other, perhaps even share vulnerabilities, and still survive. During this period the residents, who had taken up much of the time were starting to be understood and therefore the knee-jerk reactions that had been the norm started to be rare responses to requests that would previously have provoked anxiety. The very containment and kindness that generated slowly started to build a tighter framework, that felt touchable and allowed everyone some boundaries to work within.

…Despite all omissions, obstacles, unintentional blocks, mis-communication and tensions between teams and individuals, the therapeutic process continued to survive. I think that some of the obstacles could have been avoided with better consultation and preparation. A reasonably good infrastructure was in place, however the training for the PCOs could have been better supported and enhanced by the provision of supervision provided by experienced counsellors. The work with residents is so intense that continuous support from an objective experienced professional is imperative.

In general I think an overall contract of six months is probably about right. In the case of the HIP however, because of its changing role in the early stages, and its complexity, I think the manager and staff team would have welcomed my input for a while longer. It was also appropriate that input to the ARU and HIP was full-time for the first two months. However, TCA and TCB did not open up for the first three weeks so it might have been more useful to have had [two named ST members] build up to their full-time to coincide with the opening of their respective units. I think it was a big mistake not to re-schedule some of the support team input in order to cater for the late opening of TCC and TCD. I feel they were let down by circumstances and wonder if we could have done something more to assist them. Reducing our input to one day a week towards the end of the contract did not feel particularly useful, since it did not offer enough continuity to be fully aware of the developing process. Support team: I felt that the support team became a very cohesive group and one which I really valued—the mix of counsellors and psychologists worked well. It provided differing perspectives and encouraged thought-provoking debate which I found enjoyable. Finally, I question whether one or both of the psychologists with TC experience should have been placed on the TCs rather than the ARU and HIP—or was the intention to bring fresh eyes and ideas to the TCs rather than well-tried Grendon ones?[17]

It was fascinating to recognise how each community followed a similar pattern in its development, even though TCD's path seemed easier. I remain unsure about Roland's description of us as his spies. The phrase suggests "them and us" to me and I don't find that useful. I am happy to acknowledge the importance of our feedback but the quasi-militaristic feel unsettled me. I would suggest that there are some ways in which the idea of a support team could be usefully extended... I think [director of therapy] was asking at one point for a "cross-fertilisation" of good practice and knowledge. This is a hard task for a management team with so many interpersonal stressors. Perhaps the ST could have facilitated this, as indeed they could have been more useful in the development of the therapy managers as a community. This would have needed a clear acknowledgement of purpose and a structure to work in—the Fluffy. Senate was too spikey for me!"

It felt very much as though the primary support relationship was with the therapy manager or, more specifically, that each member of the ST forged their strongest support links with the relevant TM. There were many instances of individual staff, managers, counsellors and PCOs asking for help in dealing with the myriad prob-

---

17. Both the support team psychologists had worked at Grendon Prison, the other main, whole prison-based, TC.

lems encountered in their work. The stress of doing such a new, unfamiliar and emotionally demanding job was very considerable indeed. PCOs were people drawn from the local community and no extent of training could prepare them entirely for the raw reality of the details of some of the worst crimes imaginable.

Conclusion

Although the support team were only with Dovegate for a relatively short period, it was a crucial one. The body of commentary from their attachments to the new communities and the record of the struggles of the director of therapy and the Senate, or Fluffy, make powerful and, we hope, valuable testament to this amazing experience.

Dovegate

CHAPTER 5

THE DIRECTOR'S TALE: A SEARCH ENGINE FOR MEANING

Roland Woodward[1]

I am Roland and I was the director of therapy of the Dovegate Therapeutic Community (TC) from its intellectual inception to July 2006 when it had become an accredited intervention. What follows is in reality a snippet of the experience of taking the journey from conceptual idea to operational excellence. It is of course my personal perception, my personal truth and like all other perceptions and truths probably flawed to mirror my own pathology. But then if it was not I would not be human and this journey was about finding the humanity within people, environments, organizations and cultures.

This chapter is about the journey from the point where HM Prison Service publicly declared that it wanted to construct the first purpose-built TC prison of 200 beds as part of the new 800-bed prison to be built in Staffordshire to the days when the Correctional Services Accreditation Panel (CSAP) judged the TC to have fulfilled the criteria of an accredited intervention.

A quick word about the structure, or lack of it, to this chapter. In telling the story of the way in which Dovegate, and my role in it, developed, it is difficult to plot it out in a neat and organized way. Mainly because life is not like that and neither was the creation and development of Dovegate TC. At any given moment the process of creation and living contain many and varied processes that intertwine, sometimes melding into a breathtaking

---

1. © 2011 Roland Woodward. Roland became Director of Clinical Services at The Retreat, York in 2010 following a spell with Affinity Healthcare. He is a chartered psychologist with over 30 years' experience of working in the criminal justice arena, including at Gartree Prison where he opened the first TC for life sentence prisoners, now highly rated for its performance (see *Chapters 2* and *3*). His main interests lie in the design of planned therapeutic environments and living systems, group therapy, personality disorder, murder, assessment of risk and management of hostage negotiations. He continues to be involved with the Association of Therapeutic Communities and the Royal College of Psychiatrists' Community of Communities Quality Network. He was Director of Therapy at Dovegate from 1999 until 2006.

harmony—or as Hannibal would say in "The A Team"—"I love it when a plan comes together"—or creates tensions and disruptions, or goes "tits up".

To write a neat account of the whole process is not possible, or at least is beyond my writing skills, so some of the account may seem out of order or even random, however it is all connected but probably connected in different ways for the different people who experienced it. I can therefore only offer my version and leave others to add their versions in due course. My version just reflects how I tried to make sense of the task and the experience of living it alongside others. It joins the accounts already published by, e.g. Cullen and Miller (2010).

My first step into the process came when I was approached by an old colleague, Eric Cullen (the first author of this work) to join a consultancy group being put together by Premier Prisons to bid for the newly published tender for what became HM Prison Dovegate. In its early stages the prison was always known as Moreton Lane. Eric and I had worked together at Grendon Prison in Buckinghamshire where he had published some of the crucial TC research papers (Cullen, 1993; 1994) and with whom, along with Lawrence Jones, the therapist at the Maxwell Jones TC at HMP Wormwood Scrubs, we had co-edited *Therapeutic Communities for Offenders* (1997).

At that time I was the principal psychologist at HM Prison Gartree in Leicestershire, where I had opened, and was managing, a 21-bed TC for *life sentence prisoners* (Hodkin and Woodward 1996; Woodward and Hodkin 1997). This TC had come about mainly because the then Governor, Bob Perry, had the vision and the maturity to understand that a TC offered some of the men in his prison the best chance of adapting to a life sentence and using their future under that sentence to positive effect. Having worked at Grendon for several years, where I had opened the assessment unit, I had a model of working which transposed well to the Gartree situation (Woodward 1991). So the opportunity to start from scratch again on a large scale was one I could not resist. The opportunity to work with the team that was put together by Mike Gander the director of special projects for Premier Prisons was a pleasure. Apart from myself and Eric Cullen there was Jeff Roberts a psychiatrist who had worked with the Grendon management, Elaine Player who had researched Grendon (Genders and Player, 1995) and

Joe Chapman, an ex-prison officer at Grendon and I suspect others who slip my memory at the moment.

Crucially for me was the explicit aim of creating a prison TC at Dovegate that was not a replica of Grendon. For me Grendon had become ossified and self-indulgent in its self-perceived role as a model of what a prison TC could be. I was determined to find a model that approached the dichotomy of therapy and security from a different angle and a model that truly was democratic in its functioning. I especially did not want the "professionals" thinking that they could "drop in as consultants" and start to have conversations about "the staff". Either all of the staff team were in the process with an equal say or they would not be in the team at all. It is for this reason that eventually all staff trained as prison custody officers, all staff did the TC training, all staff wore uniform and the therapy managers were responsible for both the operational and the therapeutic organization and delivery of their communities. The aim was to produce a living system in which all lived and all engaged in the process of understanding what they contributed to the experience of everyone else. That's a culture of enquiry. Despite the fact that all of the development team had experience of HM Prison Grendon it was not the aim to replicate Grendon and that was a challenge; to avoid slipping into "Grendonese" as a way of assuaging our anxieties about doing something new. I will return to this later in the chapter.

At the point I joined the process, the architects had come up with a drawing of the proposed TC which was innovative and succeeded in creating a community feel to the TC area. This is no mean feat when it is remembered that this TC was in a category B security prison and had to securely house men who had received long sentences for very serious crimes. The population would range from life sentence prisoners to men who had committed armed robbery and serious sex offences. Public safety had to be a key aspect and there would need to be a strong balance between all the normal physical security and the dynamic security brought to the equation by the TC focus on interpersonal relationships. The fact that the whole TC complex for 200 men was focused on what became known as the "market square" with a water feature in the form of a boulder fountain and that there were no inner security fences, with only the perimeter wall and fence bounding it meant that this category B establishment looked and felt radically different

129

from any other equivalent prison that anyone had been in. There had been a real effort to create an environment that felt and looked like a community. This aspect of the project was crucial to its success and the architects and designers need to be congratulated on the excellent work that they did. In the years to come it provided a perfect setting in which to site the larger scale pieces of sculpture that were produced during "Rezart", the annual arts festival. More of "Rezart" later.

It was at this early stage that I realised that what was being created was a "living system". In later work I developed a view of human development based on the balance and interaction between genetic inheritance, physical environment and interpersonal environment, but it came from the realisation that at Dovegate it was the physical, interpersonal and pathological elements of life that had to be balanced to provide an arena in which meaningful therapy could take place. At the core of the process was the striving for meaning, which led me to refer to the Dovegate TC as "a search engine for meaning". In order for this to actually happen we had to create a culture and place which valued and enabled individuals and groups to make a new meaning of their lives. Through the intense interpersonal relationships created by the cultural model we intended people to live within this space. That included everyone, residents and staff alike.

The task for us was to create a physical environment that supported a cultural lifestyle that we would define. In order to do this we had to know how people would live in this space and what they needed the space to do for them. To have underestimated the importance of creating the right environment would be fatal to the project from the start. Those of us that had worked in TCs for a long time knew that the spaces we created for the therapy to take place in were crucial and the space in which the ordinary everyday living was to take place in needed to reflect the open and transparent nature of TC life. We worked hard to ensure that there was a room big enough on every community to hold a circle of at least 45 people and that there were enough small group rooms which were comfortable, private and yet fitted a security ethos. Even in this process we had to deal with the realities of the commercial world. One afternoon we had to shave a not inconsiderable amount of money off the build costs which we could only achieve by making the wings of each building a metre narrower. Once again this was about balance and we became adept at reaching the balance without compromising the central tenets of the design.

At the same time as the design was taking shape the culture had to be developed. In order to win the bid for this design, construct, manage and finance (DCMF) contract we had to describe in detail how the therapeutic community would run on a day-to-day basis. We also had to design the way the TC would be started up. This meant knowing how we would market the TC, how we would assess suitability and how we would bring people into the TC in order to go from zero to 200 residents in the shortest, and safest, time. Of course this ran hand-in-hand with how we would select staff and then train them to undertake such a huge task. All of this had to be done in the context of the main prison of 600 places being opened and filled at about the same time. We were a busy group as we wrote, and rewrote our specifications for the bid and answered specific questions posed by the tender documents. It was an exciting time and one which allowed new ideas to be floated and the search to be undertaken for innovation. We had all the collected wisdom and research findings about TCs available to us, which we plundered and used to ensure that where ever possible we based our design on evidence from the research literature. Where we could find no answers to our questions we spent a lot of time working through the plausible, and sometimes fantastic, options. In the whole process my eyes were firmly fixed on the practicalities of translating what we wrote into the reality day-to-day living experience for both the staff team and the residents. This bid had to be "liveable". If it was not it would fail as people tried to live out an unrealistic vision.

It was part way through this process that I was asked if I was interested in being the therapy director of the new TC. I was at once elated to be asked and very apprehensive. It was not so much the challenge of such a large project that I relished—as I was confident, perhaps arrogant and foolish enough, to believe I knew what I was doing—but it was leaving the public sector for private enterprise. There was a perceived huge personal risk of leaving the safety of the public sector and the knowledge that if it all went "tits up" I could easily be jettisoned by the new employers. History at that time suggested that those that left for the private companies did not easily, if ever, find their way back to the public services.

I was also acutely aware that being a forensic psychologist in this role would raise some eyebrows in some quarters as it was usual to have a psychiatrist in this role. There was therefore the pressure of wanting to do it right for my profession as well as for myself.

Finally, but by no means least, was the question of the morality of private companies running prisons. Some of my reasons for going to university and then joining HM Prison Service had been rooted in political beliefs about making a contribution to services which dealt with people who were very often society's disadvantaged and because of their activities the most excluded and reviled. For the State to take responsibility and to provide for them seemed to be right. Making the argument for the private sector seemed murky to say the least (Genders, 2001). Weighed against this was the ossification of the psychologist career structure in the Prison Service, where practising as a psychologist as opposed to managing was becoming more difficult. There was of course the sheer lack of creativity and flexibility that such a huge and complex organization brings with it. Some local initiatives were exceptions to this but were often fragile and dependant on motivated individuals who when they moved on saw the projects falter. There was little room for radical systemic thinking in the Prison Service and that was especially true when considering the challenges that a TC culture brings to the prison environment (Genders and Player, 1995; Hinshelwood, 2001; Woodward, 2006).

After a lot of discussion with family and friends I agreed that I would like the post. This of course was not straightforward. The company as part of the bid had to say who they proposed for the major roles in the new organization. This meant that the bid team, mostly Mike Gander, had to go into the process of clarification with the Prison Service to ask delicately whether if they put my name in the bid it would be acceptable. It was acceptable, but I never knew whether it was with a genuine thought that I would make a good job of it or whether they were relieved to see me on my way, or even if there was a darker agenda. As I said earlier, this journey cannot be separate from my own pathology.

Having worked through the hoops my name and CV went into the bid documents as the proposed director of therapy and it was agreed that at the appropriate moment, if and when Premier Prisons won the contract, that I would resign from HM Prison Service and take up my new role.

The process of winning a bid is not straightforward and the work of refining the bid and resolving problems goes on right up to the deadline for submission. The five volumes of our tender submission were still with the printers on the day before it was made and we were still not sure we had everything as we wanted it. We were confident that we had designed a good TC and a passable prison but there was no way of knowing that we would win. What I found out later was that our construction partners, who were ultimately to build the prison, had sunk in excess of £1 million into preparations in anticipation of winning the contract. A lot of people had a great deal invested in this project, from hard cash to careers.

Whilst all of this was going on preparations were being made and put in place to explain to the local outside community, primarily people in the two local villages, what the prison meant for them. It was an attempt to try and answer their fears that building a new prison on their doorstep was detrimental to them, to explain that it in fact had advantages. The large model of the prison as it was to be was taken in a display truck to the local church car park and we met the locals. On meeting some of the local residents of one village we found ourselves being asked some knowledgeable questions about population characteristics, and the problems created by visitors to prisoners. We quickly found out that many of the villagers had retired from careers in the prison system and had worked in the nearby open prison. It was not surprising that they were less than thrilled to find that a large new prison was to be built next to the place they had retired to. It must have felt as if the experience of prison was following them.

The succeeding weeks found the construction company, us and the local councillors meeting on a regular basis to work through the anxieties of the community. They had real and legitimate concerns regarding the increase in traffic flow and the perceived increased risk to pedestrians. The outcome was a green plan and a traffic agreement which restricted the latter to and from the site passing through the village. There was an agreement that the community regularly monitored and complained about matters if unauthorised vehicles turned right out of the prison rather than left. Alongside these meetings the construction company also undertook some local community improvement schemes to cement community relations. I mention this as an illustration that nothing gets done in isolation and that from the very beginning the TC had a complex set of relationships to negotiate and manage, not only on its own behalf but in the wider organizations interests as well.

We won! At the moment that I thought would be a time of joy and jubilation I realised what a complex and hard process this was going to be. Winning the contract meant that it was awarded to us, however there was then a period of contract negotiation during which I witnessed lawyers and entrepreneurs doing what they do best, namely shifting risk. Every single paragraph of the contract had to be gone over to ensure that it detailed exactly who was liable for what and that everything had a clear and precise meaning.

Two parts of the contract stick in my mind. The first was the paragraph that obliged HM Prison Service to pay for 200 beds if the occupancy of the TC was at 194.[2] No figures appeared in the paragraph and it contained only descriptions of things in the contract and references to schedules. The closest I got to seeing how it worked was to read the paragraph backwards, at which point I more or less got it. It was a work of genius, almost incomprehensible, but worth a fortune over the 25-years of the contract.

The second element was the day we spent with the lawyers trying to define in legal terms the meaning of "clinical judgement". This was crucial as it was my get-out clause for not taking every impossible person that governors and assistant governors all over the country would try and foist on me the moment the new TC came into being. It was crucial to be able to refuse people for whom the TC experience would be detrimental. All therapeutic interventions have the potential to be harmful if applied to inappropriate people and so this clause was needed to protect all concerned. The "clinical judgement" element was included in the referral exclusion criteria and was therefore crucial. I am not suggesting that governors or prison managers generally are bad people but they are human and if you have been trying to manage an extremely recalcitrant person who has not responded and not been transferable, the existence of a new TC is a golden opportunity to palm them off. It is a golden opportunity for the person concerned of course; to

---

2. This is the critical "194 clause" mentioned in later chapters, the 'Sword of Damocles', which was subsequently renegotiated so that the critical occupancy figure became 190: see *Chapter 8*.

go somewhere new and try something new to sort their life out. An opportunity too good to miss. As it turned out we found a way to include "clinical judgement" which proved very useful when the odd person arrived in our Assessment Unit spitting expletives, threatening to kill us and denying they ever volunteered to come to the TC. It was certainly true in one or two cases that they were ignorant of where they were and why they were there despite all our literature and information stating clearly that people had to volunteer to enter therapy.

Not until the Prison Service and its lawyers, the bankers and their lawyers, the insurance companies and their lawyers and Premier Prisons and its lawyers were satisfied that they had covered all the bases and shifted as much risk as possible onto everybody else, did the contract finally get signed. This occurred on Monday 27 September 1999. I have on my desk at home a small brightly painted piece of yellow security steel bar with an engraved plaque on it stating the date which was given to me as part of Premier Prison's ritual at winning another contract. So now the real work started. All of this preparation was part of the TC's history that no-one but a few of us knew about. It was important to us but as I soon learned anyone coming along later would be blissfully ignorant and only interested in their beginning in the process and the relationship with Dovegate TC. After all you can only know the water from the point you step into the river.

I joined Premier Prisons on 31st July 1999 and spent two weeks visiting the companies assets which included prisons and electronic tagging contracts. During this induction the gifts of company membership where bestowed on me and I collected a laptop, mobile phone and car. However there was no office as yet because the building site was being set up and so I was asked to be part of the support team to a new Secure Training Centre for juveniles that was being opened at Hassockfield in Consett, County Durham. This small secure establishment was brand new and took young people from 12-years-of-age upwards. The opening, management and the destructiveness of the young people there is a book in itself, suffice it to say that it was an interesting time which fully occupied me until I was able to move onto the Moreton Lane building site.

That first two weeks produced a rude awakening into the practicalities of the world of money on a big scale. I was asked to produce a presentation to the bankers on what a TC was. I was initially told that I had a couple of weeks to prepare, however in the middle of my first week I was told to be at Lazard Bros, our investment bankers, at ten o'clock the following Tuesday. So on my seventh working day I presented myself at Lazard's in London. The doorman had a suit on that must have cost a fortune and made me feel decidedly scruffy as I wandered through their marble hallways and up to their walnut-panelled board room where one wall slid aside to reveal a huge screen. My chief executive officer (CEO), finance director and our Lazard liaison person joined me and I ran through my presentation with them. At one point the Lazard's man stopped me and said, "Can you find another way of saying that?" When I enquired why, he patiently explained to me that it was important not to say anything that might raise anxieties in the people I was presenting to as "we need to keep them content and happy as we were asking them for an £8 million investment in the project". It must have gone reasonably well as we got the money, but it made me realise the nature of the world that I had joined.

The building site at Moreton Lane was in part a large temporary building made of portakabins in which I was found a small office with a desk. At this point in time the builders were setting huge flanged headed columns into the ground which would support the ground beams upon which the main buildings would be mounted. The developers had excavated huge ponds to the rear of the site and used the spoil to build up the level of the site by about a metre. This apparently was necessary, because the water table on the site was so high. Clearly the builders had already undertaken a huge amount of work by the time the contract process was concluded. The large ponds that I mentioned were to become a significant feature of the site. The then managing director of Premier Prisons, Kevin Lewis, was a tough Australian ex-soldier who liked to fish, wanted to stock the ponds and make an extra buck selling fishing licences. However, the county ecologist put a stop to that and explained that we had to plan and build an ecosystem. Apparently if we did this right the fish would arrive naturally. To this end the planting of the area was meticulously worked out to provide the best waterside environment which would promote the establishment of an insect population. After that all else would follow and it did.

During this time the implementation team came together and the first operational staff were recruited. Peter Wright was appointed the first director of the prison overall. He was a bright and moral man who had clear perceptions about what was to be achieved and how it was to happen. We were in agreement that in order to make a success of the whole prison it was crucial that it was clear that he and I were in agreement as to the relationship between the main prison and the TC. We knew from the onset that there would be tensions between the two parts of the prison as we were aware that we were presiding over the establishment of two cultures within one wall, which although separated by a clear physical dividing barrier, would interact and generate a degree of "them and us". Depressing as it may seem, the research literature still suggests that where there is a perception that two or more groups exists, we as humans cannot resist taking sides and feeling that our group is in someway "better or righter" than the other group. We knew this and were determined to try and model the cooperative relationship that we would strive to create across the whole organization. Initially, I think we succeeded but as time moved on and new managers came into the company and to the contract it became more difficult to maintain this model. Later when Peter moved to another establishment I lost a valued friend and ally. The process by which a host organization is able to co-exist with, maintain and nurture a TC is a complex and demanding one, doubly so when in the prison situation (Woodward, 2006).

On the TC side a small team of key people was recruited. Claire Moore a forensic psychologist who had worked for me at some time at Gartree joined, as did Marya Hemmings as an operations manager. Marya had been one of the team at Gartree TC (Hemmings and Rawlinson, 1995). To this team we added "Jewels" Cooper as my personal assistant, who arrived ostensibly to type, file and organize and ended up managing the administration team and budgets and ultimately joining the Senate.

As a small central team we set about the task of finding the team of people who would become the therapy managers, counsellors and operations managers. To this group was added an education manager, Zena Schubert who was someone who would play an increasingly central role in relation to the community.

The core team worked alongside a growing team of staff who were slowly but surely putting operational processes in place and recruiting the required staff. At that time we had been provided with a portakabin of our own on the newly completed section of car park close to the slowly growing wall of the prison. It was an idyllic time due to the fact that for a few short weeks everyone knew what was going on as everyone could hear what was being organized. The level of interaction was very good and cooperation across groups was exceptionally high. In future years those of us who were part of the portakabin group not infrequently wished we were back there. Although the task was huge, the excitement and sense of group cohesion was a delight.

It was about this time that Peter Wright and I sat down to think about what the "Vision Statement" was going to be for Dovegate. We had the usual plethora of models. All of them sickly sweet and too long for any-one to remember, let alone care about. Somewhere in the conversation we remembered Alan Sugar's (no title then) apocryphal vision statement of "I want their money", which set us to thinking about what was at the core of our aspirations. As I have said before, Peter was bright and moral and so it did not take us long to come up with "Lawful, Safe and Reasonable". That was it, and it worked. It became a touchstone by which we and the staff tested our actions and our decisions. In prison when dealing with difficult people in every imaginable interpersonal situation it is impossible to provide detailed guidance on what to do. People need something clear and in their heads at the time to guide them. As we said when training hostage negotia-tors and telling them they could not take notes, "if it's not in your head at the time then it's no use". Lawful, safe and reasonable lodged in our staff's heads and they would challenge us as managers with it at times. Likewise when people came to us and asked if they had done the right thing we would ask them if they thought they had acted within lawful, safe and reasonable bounds. It was one of the things about Dovegate that initially was different, it was prepared to be creative and flexible in order to try and make living and working in the prison setting understandable and bearable for everyone.

At this stage we watched the building grow and occasionally had the opportunity to change things. In one instance we were able to swap two of the pre-cast concrete wall sections over to ensure that the administration office in the TC had windows along one wall. These three ton panels that could only be moved in almost windless conditions were all pre-cast, including wiring ducts, so swapping them around was not a trivial process. It was during this process that Fixtures, Fittings and Equipment (FF&E) came up at one of the regular project meetings. These meetings gave the company managers the chance to measure progress on the project and to press the team on issues of concern. FF&E or "everything that goes in a prison once it's built" had not been delegated and by some strange process that I still do not understand I became responsible for working with the builder's buyer, Dave, to spend £2.5 million. So whilst putting together a TC of epic proportions I also shopped for everything from soft furnishings to control and restraint equipment for the entire prison.

I mention this because it was important that what went into the TC had to reflect the TC culture that we were prescribing. Apart from themed internal decoration where wall colourings were matched with bedding, some of the furniture was crucial. It is funny how sometimes you know that something is right and that in the future it will have an impact. One such item was the round table to go into the TC's meeting room in the central administration area. I insisted on a round table 12 feet across. My management team, which became known as the Senate was going to sit in a circle to conduct business so I needed a table big enough to seat at least 15 people. The issue was one of ensuring that the way the management worked was the same as the way the residents worked in therapy. All through the design and my term of management of the TC I insisted that what was good enough for the residents had to be good enough for us. If we insisted that residents sit in circles to do their therapy because that ensured full observation and participation of everyone then we as managers, therapists or whatever must do the same. It was all part of the culture that said we as managers or staff had to model what we wanted our staff and residents to do. There could be no attitude of "We can do differently because we are not residents". If we wanted people to be open, honest and transparent with us then the same rules needed to apply. In something as fundamental as a table those principles needed to be demonstrated. In the end I got my way, even though it meant making the table in three parts and fitting them together inside the room.

Once it was in place, almost every one who saw it or used it, liked it.

One other thing that the table reflected was the non-hierarchical nature of a TC. With a round table there is no top or bottom for a chairperson to sit at. It was another principle that all who came into the Senate were equal, and at his point I need to clarify something that was special to the Dovegate TC.

In every prison TC that I had worked in there was always an unhelpful tension between the "therapy staff" and the "discipline staff", which was shorthand for the differences between therapy and security. Although there was talk of dynamic or relational security there was always conflict between the two elements. I had thought hard about how to overcome this accepting that there was always going to be discussion about risks in a prison TC. My solution was to do several things but primarily to fuse the therapeutic and the security roles as much as possible within the therapy teams and in the TC. Firstly as part of the culture everyone wore uniform. In so many prisons I had heard men and women say that they would only talk to the professionals, or the civvies, as the "uniforms" were not trained, did not understand and were just "screws". Prisoners did not value the uniformed staff and were able to dismiss them. With *everyone* in uniform this became more difficult to do. Secondly, all the managers, therapists, councillors and other civilian staff were trained as prison custody officers. I wanted all my staff to have the same understanding and skills of each other as far as possible. I needed them to know that they had a shared training and that when a therapy manager, an operations manager or indeed myself took the decision to, for example, move a resident using control and restraint (C&R) that we understood what that meant for staff and that we could, and did on occasions, do it ourselves.

The crucial element in this drawing together of the two strands of security and therapy was to make the therapy managers operationally responsible for their communities. They were responsible for all their team and all aspects of both therapy and operational functioning. The therapy manager and his or her team would make the decisions about everything in their community on a day-to-day basis. Where the team decided that there were issues that they alone could not decide or wanted to refer for guidance, the therapy manger would bring those issues to the Senate. Back around the round table the Senate would work through the issue and come up with a solution. This would go back to the specific community and to the wider community for action and where necessary further discussion. In this way we supported each other and lived out the process of making sense of new issues that arose. The fact that the Senate had on it therapists, operational managers, educationalist, administrators and a psychiatrist reflected the view that every role in the TC was equally important and had equal weight. This was truly a multi-disciplinary model of therapy that worked by consultation and discussion.

For the record I want to mention who those first people of the Senate were. Apart from myself there were the operations managers Marya Hemmings, Dave Gander, June Oliver, Alex Livingston, therapy managers Emcee Checkwas, Dave Lynes, Kristina Sheffgen, Claire Moore, Alan Miller, Joanne Lackenby, psychiatrist Judith McKenzie, and EduCom (education and commerce) manager Zena Schubert. After a relatively short time "Jewels" Cooper joined us as the administration manager. This group of people achieved something truly extraordinary in opening and developing a new TC with a new model and making it work.

I can hear people raising their eyebrows and wondering where the emotions went. What happened to those all too human angers, irritations, exasperations, rivalries, jealousies and all the other variants that intense human interactions produce? Well generally, as a group we were able to speak our minds and say what we wanted to say, not perfectly but "well enough" to get the work done. We did of course have the "Fluffy". Other management teams and therapy teams have "open sessions" or "sensitivity sessions", we had the Fluffy which at times was anything but. It was an early innovation partly drawn from a sense of self-deprecation as we played with the perception of others that we were the "fluffy care bears" in the prison. It actually came from Harry Potter's Hagrid character. In the first Harry Potter book, Harry is confronted by a three-headed dog guarding an underground chamber. Those of a literary bent will recognise the allusion to Cerberus the three-headed dog that guarded the Underworld. Having been nearly killed by this vicious creature, Harry relates to the half giant, Hagrid, his experience with the dog, to which Hagrid retorts, "You mean Fluffy". It was obvious that our sensitivity meeting that was meant to deal with our unconscious material could only be called one thing. What could be more appropriate than the three-headed monster that guards the lower level of our being. Hence, Fluffy.

Within these meetings we attempted to do for ourselves what we asked the residents to do and that was examine our relationship with each other in as honest and transparent way as possible. We saw this as crucial if we were to avoid projecting our own fears, angers and anxieties into our teams and hence on to the residents. It was our response to the recognition that the processes that affected the residents in therapy equally affected us and we needed to deal with that. Again what was good enough for the residents had to be good enough for us, the team responsible for containing the anxieties of our staff and residents. Like our residents we found that these experiences could be both painful and touchingly supportive.

As we got closer to the opening of the TC some crucial elements had to be clarified and acted upon. One of them was the work and activity profile of the TC. In the initial bid we had said that the residents of the TC would provide the labour force for the entire establishment's laundry. This worried me and for a while I was not sure what it was until I realised that it was going to create a point in the organization where the resentments, angers and jealousies of the establishment would be played out against the TC residents.

I realised that while the TC residents were providing a service to the whole establishment they would be subject to the projections of the rest of the inmates and staff. They would be blamed and targeted for all sorts of issues that would have had nothing to do with the quality of laundry services. There are consistent and pervasive perceptions of TCs that run through both prisoner and staff populations. They are seen as being filled with "nonces", the prison slang for sex offenders, and as such reviled and targeted in the prison system. Staff in TCs are seen as being "care bears" and subsequently thought of as being "soft" both as people and in their treatment of prisoners. Alongside these views are the ones that see TCs as being the soft option that cherry pick the best prisoners, wrap them up in cotton wool and fail to observe normal prison security. In fact, "unmanly". None of these assertions are true, I can hear some readers saying to themselves. "Oh yes they are!" And there you have the tensions and the issues in a nutshell.

Placing a big TC in an establishment alongside a big category B training prison with the only "touching point" being the laundry was asking for trouble. I discussed these issues with Peter Wright and we agreed that the laundry work would go to the main prison. It was a decision that proved to be right both in terms of the dynamics and of providing sufficient work places for the main prison.

The second issue related to work and activity was about what kind of activity we would provide for the residents apart from the usual domestic roles that would be available. The issue came to a head quite early on in the building of the prison. Whilst walking around the partially built TC administration, visits and education building I came across a large first floor room that was about to be wired. When I asked why the sockets were different I was told a three phase supply was going in to support light industrial processes. Every project has a piece of lunacy and this was the TC's. On a first floor room with no access apart from a small lift to fulfil the disabled access regulations the suggestion was that we run some sort of light industry. This seemed wrong to me on two counts, one putting this kind of work on the first floor in the middle of the education area just seemed stupid in that the work would not be meaningful, even if we could find some and the noise and nature of the work would disrupt the education around it. It did not fit the philosophy of the TC. We wanted to create a culture of learning, not only about self but also that activated the lifelong learning process.

I knew from Melvyn Rose's experience of Peper Harrow, near Godalming, Surrey in his book *Transforming Hate Into Love* (1997) that the academic achievement of people that went through a TC which was education-based far exceeded expectation in later life. People that Rose followed up after 25 years had made academic achievements far beyond what would have been predicted for the group. The message seemed to be that if an individual could be engaged in the learning process that the engagement would provide motivation to go on learning far into the future. I believed that if I could harness this process in a TC then it would be a powerful asset to the residents and to the TC. I also realised that the research was telling me that one of the most important factors in affecting reconviction rates was the ability of ex-prisoners to find work, preferably meaningful work. This meant that education in itself was not enough, it had to be coupled to a model that related to work skills.

For many men who leave prison the only work they can do is work that they generate themselves and so they need some kind of business sense to go with it. The men coming to Dovegate TC were going to be of at least average intelligence, psychologically-minded and motivated to change. As a group therefore, they needed a model that raised or inculcated expectations of themselves and their capabilities. This was in opposition to the often unsaid but acted-out stance that prisoners should take any job going and be thankful that they have one regardless of what it is. Alongside the perhaps more damning view that prisoners generally were not ever going to do much more than manual or menial tasks, there was a general "dumbing down" of prisoners. It was clear to me that it was time to "bright up" our residents and make new things available to them. Again I discussed this view with colleagues and looked at what options were available to us. The result of this was "EduCom".

EduCom was a mixture of education and commerce. The model provided for the learning of skills within a commercial framework. It meant that wherever possible the educational content would take place within projects that were run as commercial enterprises. In these commercial enterprises the residents would take roles as managers, directors, sales people and production and design teams. Also, wherever possible, the tutors would be their peers, so that as residents gained skills they passed them on to other residents. As a result of conceiving this model, the light industries area never got built and was converted into a commercial centre to run a desktop publishing business, with an IT skill learning centre as part of it. The training kitchen that provided excellent food to the staff and for all our family days and other celebrations was likewise imbued with a commercial element. Our ceramics concern was run in a similar way once residents had learned how to research their pieces of work and projects. EduCom thrived, firstly under the management of Zena Schubert then under Mat Dimbleby, who took his place on the Senate when he succeeded Zena. Great credit must be given to both of these people for the way they developed the model and the degree to which they expanded the peer tutor model. As we had predicted, peer tutors were far more successful than staff at tempting and then hooking previously education-phobic residents into engagement with learning. Of all the things that we achieved at Dovegate, EduCom is one of the things of which I am most proud of as well as the EduCom team.

I need to backtrack a bit to deal with staff training. The chance to open a new TC is a rare opportunity to take a complete staff team and train them.

I had opened a new TC at Gartree Prison and written about this aspect of the work (Woodward, 1997). Much of the work that had gone into the opening of Gartree's TC went into the training for Dovegate. The crucial thing about the training is that it is the articulation of the philosophy and treatment model of the TC. The training is the translation from theory to the practical and operational day-to-day living in the TC. It is the medium by which new staff make new meaning of their contribution to a new work situation that has an intended therapeutic aim. As no intervention is neutral, it is imperative that everyone delivering it understand the reasons why things are done in the way they are and even more importantly are able to contribute meaningfully to the development and evolution of the TC. In short, the training provides the rationale and the means of delivery for the therapeutic nature of the TC. The training has to be accessible to all the staff team and to make sense to them. This requires a balance of materials that contain the required information and methods of turning this information into understandable and usable daily interpersonal interactions.

The new staff team were going to be drawn from newly recruited prison custody officers (PCOs) and a mixture of professionals from psychiatry, psychology and counselling. In order to ensure that the training started from where all the staff team were, it was important to select materials that explained the model in clear and accessible English in the least technical way possible. TCs of the past had often been instigated by charismatic professionals who had been trained in psychoanalytic schools of thought and were fortunate enough due to their professional standards to get away with doing "something new". The experience of my time at HM Prison Grendon and opening the TC at HM Prison Gartree had taught me that the psychoanalytic models of people like Foulkes (1964), Lacan (2001) and Bion (1961) were not very accessible to people coming to the work for the first time. Experience has shown that using the work of Yalom (1995) and his research and explanation of group experience and psychotherapy it was much easier for people to make sense of things. It was also much easier to devise training materials from this perspective.

The practicality of this approach had to be thought through and a training programme devised that could be delivered to the new team. To this end Eric Cullen (the first author of this work) and I locked ourselves away for a couple of days to agree the content of a two week training course. Thus was born SNOG and KISS. It stands for Simple Not 'Orrible Groups and Keep It Simple Stupid. These titles were to be criticised at a later stage for their lack of "professional image" which of course missed the whole point, but what can you expect from overly sensitive professionals who get miffed when they find "non-therapy professionals" like prison staff demonstrating that they can deliver therapy without the years of study and navel-gazing that they have been through? Not that study and training is not without merit. Where would all our careers be without it? But if one of the central tenets of a TC is that people change their lives through the interpersonal relationships they have within the TC, then new meaning needs to be within the context of normal language and experience, not in a rarefied atmosphere or universe of psychological abstraction. It needs to be in the here and now which is live and direct and liveable.

Eric and I devised our two week course and then delivered it to the trainers who were going to deliver it to the new TC teams. The idea of this was that the tutors to be could pull the material apart and give feedback on its accessibility and add ideas about delivery and presentation. Eric and I earned our money in those two weeks, but the response from the training team was immense. They came up with really creative embellishments and ideas. New materials were produced and the whole course finally written up into a manual (Woodward *et al*, 2000).

Part of the training was a regular experiential group that focused on the life stories of the participants. The team of trainers took the supreme risk of sharing their life stories with the teams they trained as a model for the work that would come. They also contained the teams as they chose to participate in this part of the training, or not. In essence the teams needed to know and to have some experience of what it is like to have someone else "talk your life" and so that issues that they thought they had locked safely away could suddenly be released by the work they were going to undertake with the residents of the TC.

Anecdotally the ability to engage with this part of the training often predicted those staff who would blossom in the work and those who would struggle. In hindsight, I wish we had included a piece of research to test this.

As I did concerning the original Senate, I would like to acknowledge the original training team who were; Marya Hemmings, Claire Moore, Emcee Checkwas, Annily Jameson and Gustavo Angeli. The work of this team laid the foundations for all that followed in a very real and practical sense. It did a huge amount to inculcate the TC culture and to provide the foundation upon which much of the operational processes of the TC focused.

Once the team had been through the training themselves and made the modifications the task of training the staff began in earnest. As the training pairs delivered the training the team came together at the end of each day with Eric and myself to review the day, debrief the teams and to analyse the dynamics of the process. From the very beginning there was a clear focus on the team trying to understand the dynamics that were in play and what was going on. It was a core theme of all our work and delivering the crucial training at this stage was an opportunity to model the way of working that we wanted all our staff to adopt. One of the key ingredients of the training was the message that "It is not rocket science" (or "It is not psychology" as a rocket scientist would say). The staff needed to know and believe that they had the skills, understanding and attributes to be able to take on the role of TC staff and succeed. I think to a great extent we achieved this, certainly when the researchers from Surrey University got going. I think they found evidence of a clear TC culture and communities that were recognisably therapeutic.

Which leads me to "The Research Project". Whilst all the practical preparation had been going on one of my tasks was to tender and award the research contract. In the original prison contract we had negotiated a ring-fenced sum of money for a seven year research contract to be undertaken by an independent body. The original research specification was similar to the work undertaken by Genders and Player (1995) at Grendon Prison and published in their book. The work was done from a mainly sociological perspective by participant observation with the addition of some analysis of the routine psychometrics that had been collected over the years by the Psychology Department. The research specification for Dovegate TC was focused mainly on social processes and a description of the TC process. I thought that this was an inadequate specification and rewrote it to include a reconviction study, a personal change study and a study of the therapeutic process as it related to individuals reaching a point of psychological change readiness.

The project was put out to tender and as it was worth a total of £750,000 it attracted several good calibre bids. After what felt like a long process in which I was pleased to receive support from several people, but particularly Ron Blackburn, Emeritus Professor of Clinical Psychology at Liverpool University, whose expertise and good sense were indispensable to the process, we awarded the contract. Ultimately Professor Jennifer Brown and her team from Surrey University won and the process of integrating them into the life of the TC began. It was a golden opportunity to give a research team unparalleled access to a prison programme and to fully integrate the process into the community.

We established a research office in the community and afforded the team open access to all the areas that they needed. In adapting our assessment process we took into consideration the information that the research team required and ensured that all new residents coming to the TC understood that research was part of the community function. The results can be found in a number of papers and a final report by Jennifer Brown and her team (2006 and 2010). It was one of the things that we got right at Dovegate and I think that as a model of building research into a project the experience was a good one.

I realise that thus far I have said nothing about the actual opening and consequent running of Dovegate TC, which I think is indicative of the massiveness of the task that was undertaken and the complexity of the process of opening something that had never been done before on this scale and never in combination with concurrently opening a new category B training prison. However these processes are the foundations from which the current Dovegate TC came about and are the historical roots of the place. It is this history, which was crafted with a lot of thought and effort by very many good and bright people. That is the heritage of the TC from which lessons for the establishment of future TCs can be drawn.

I am going to divert to a process that was crucial to the development of the TC, in fact it allowed the TC to come into being and it was something that no one had thought of, no one was aware of at the time, in fact an unconscious process that we had to wait some two to three years to discover for ourselves. Once discovered it explained some of the things that were happening in the TC at the time and enabled us as a team to progress and crucially for me to eventually let go of the TC and my role in it. It was the psychological contract that the Senate members made with me in my role as director of therapy. It was never discussed and never agreed but it became apparent after a couple of years when the Senate began to struggle with itself, i.e. we began to struggle with each other. It was at this point that we realised that members of the Senate had given part of themselves up in order to make the TC work from the start. As one person said, "It is like I put part of myself on the table and left it there. I trusted that you knew what you were doing and was willing to follow your lead".

It became apparent that others had done the same because they had not had TC experience before and in order for the process to work they gave that part of themselves up. We became aware of this at the point that the Senate felt they had learnt what a TC was about and they wanted to reclaim the part they had put on the table. It meant a renegotiation of the relationship between the Senate and the director of therapy. I had always espoused the view that a TC should never be led or started by a charismatic leader as the TC tended to wither if such a person left. I always took the view that a TC required a strong set of internal structures and processes that were not dependant on any one person. I had worked hard to build an organizational structure that was not dependant on me and had taken a very strong stance on how I would not interfere with individual communities. To have the feeling that I had been seen in part as a charismatic leader in style came as a bit of a shock.

Clearly this was a healthy development but begged the question about what the relationship should now be as the team felt that they were presently able to develop their communities in their own ways with confidence. The issue for me was how to maintain the Senate process and—for the group to go on modelling for the community as a whole—how we wanted them to relate and operate. There was a lot of discussion and a lot of tension for a time but I think we reached a situation where there was a new understanding of how we needed to operate.

The new phase we moved into was not without its tensions and conflicts. There were still times when my role demanded that I was proscriptive about some issues, which created conflict, but in general the Senate continued to achieve its aims and fulfil its purpose. Part of this process was that the original director of the prison, Peter Wright, had been obliged to move to another of the company's prison contracts and that the director of Doncaster Prison, Kevin Rogers, was due to take over at Dovegate. It may have been the anxiety that this caused that brought to the surface issues of leadership, survival and autonomy for the Senate. Whatever the cause, the period when this was worked through was one of both maturity and personal anxiety on my part that I had failed to be aware of such a primary process and been able to facilitate it in a more informed way. However it was a lesson we all learned and one that I think all of the Senate have taken with them on their various journeys. Certainly when I left to start up new services in another environment the nature of the psychological contract that I was asking mental health nurses to take up in the establishment of new forensic services was one of my first concerns.

The main prison opened on the July 3 having trained approximately 300 staff including me as a prison custody officer as part of the TC inclusion policy. We finally opened the TC itself on 12 November 2001. The plan was to take 32 new residents a week and put them through an assessment and then allocate them and move them into their communities, which is more or less what happened. By Christmas we had two of the four communities operational, as was the Assessment Unit and the High Intensity Programme Unit, a smaller unit which was intended to provide a slower entry to the TC for people struggling with joining a larger group. EduCom had opened and was functioning and all the usual prison life had begun.

For me this was a tricky period in the TC. Not because of the pressures of opening and the worry of whether people would want to come to the TC having seen the promotional video featuring Paul Ross and the information packages. No, my concern was the support team. It had been decided that a support team of independent therapists and counsellors would be employed on a short-term contract to support the therapy managers and the Senate in the opening process. This had seemed like a good idea at the planning stage. It had been decided that Eric Cullen would lead a team consisting of Pauline Oliver, Eddie Rowarth, Val Evans and Norma Wallace to support the team, which included sitting in the Fluffy. I know for a fact that some of the Senate found the support of this team very useful and helpful, in fact I believe that one or two of them maintained contact after the support team had left the TC. For me they posed a real dilemma in that they became an unforeseen dynamic in the overall process of the TC. It felt that it was difficult to get the Senate to operate on its own and that somehow a dependency had been built in that had to be worked through. The Fluffy was not about the Senate dealing with itself but the Senate being observed by the support team, which was not helpful. "Ah," I can hear the reader saying, "this is about power." And it might be, but from my point of view they were a mixed blessing and it led me to wonder for a while who I could trust and what processes that had been put in place were functioning properly. It was a personal relief when the Senate finally sat together as the Senate and began to work for themselves without their "temporary adults" around. I am sure their experience of the support team was different to mine and if it truly helped them to get through that initial period then I have to be pleased, however my experience was different, that's all.

Being the director of therapy of a TC is a strange position to be in. The leader of a TC, especially one that consists of four 40-bed communities, an Assessment Unit and a High Intensity Programme Unit is particularly strange. All sorts of projections and expectations come your way. The Prison Service has a particularly keen sense of what a leader is and when that is not met, then things can be awkward. When your own team have difficulty with you then it can be really tricky. I decided very early on in the process that I was not going to be a charismatic leader and that the way to ensure the TC evolved was to build an organizational structure that delivered assessable quality through quality network standards. The later part was relatively easy as we took the Dovegate TC into the Royal College of Psychiatrists' Quality Network for Therapeutic Communities, the Community of Communities (C of C).

By joining this quality network right from the start it ensured that there was a credible external agency who would support us in achieving accredited standards of practice and ultimately accreditation as a recognised intervention. I also ensured that supervision took place right through the organization and that there were structures that ran the TC on a businesslike footing. The truly difficult part was not to interfere. It was not long before my managers started to ask me why I was not visiting the communities, saying that the staff would like me to, despite the fact that each month I held a briefing for all staff and presented our current situation, issues and award for the employee of the month. My argument over and over again was that the responsibility and authority for running the TCs lay with the therapy managers. It was their job to contain the anxieties of their teams and to lead the work of processing the dynamic of their communities and their staff teams. I said over and over again that I trusted the team members to be reasonable, rational adults, to act within our vision statement of "Lawful, Safe and Reasonable" and to continue to make use of all the TC mechanisms that had been built into the process. I was determined not to play some sort of parental role which became symbolised by the parent going round patting people on the head and saying how well they were all doing.

I wanted teams that were mature enough to know that they were doing the right things and to draw their confidence from the relationships within the staff teams and with the community members that resulted in the changes they saw in their community members. I wanted them to realise that they were trusted and were colleagues, not staff, engaged in therapeutic work in which we were all equal. Eventually they got it and at least one of the therapy managers was telling me that I had got it right and that it had been possible to point out to the team how lucky they had been to be allowed to be adults. I think I got this right but from the outside I got criticism from the rest of the organization about visibility and "managing by walking about" and other such stereotyped views of what leadership means to most people. Within this is encapsulated the stresses that exist when a TC is embedded in a host organization where the culture and needs are different (Woodward, 2006).

So whilst I was busy not patronising and infantilising my teams I had time to think about the wider activities of the whole TC. TCs can be deadly serious places and too much therapy makes a "theraputon", a term coined at Grendon. I have learned from other prison managers that it is always useful to have something going on outside the normal routine of the prison and I applied myself to wondering what it should be for Dovegate TC. It was not long after we had opened all of the TCs and were reaching our capacity when I suggested in a "this is what we are going to do" kind of way that we were going to have a two week arts festival during which therapy would be suspended and all residents would take part. Rezart, a contraction of resident's art, was born and would become a regular annual event. Committees were formed, Arts Council project money won through a dance theatre partnership called Motionhouse (Brown et al, 2004) and everyone geared up for the festival.

A bewildering range of arts projects were put together, from sculpture to poetry, from film-making to electronic gaming and a drama group, plus much more. The idea was to create an art for art's sake festival. I wanted to create an environment where residents could "trip over" arts activities and do them just because they were fun to do and crucially with no therapy attached to them. The hope was that if people in the TC found new activities that they enjoyed that they would incorporate them into their lives and therefore have an additional way to occupy their time—and of course a way to express themselves.

The festival consisted of two weeks of creative activity at the end of which would be a performance day. The groups that formed worked on their projects. Each group had staff attached to it and they helped to create with the group. The first year was dazzling. At one point, I became aware that some chairs had had an angle grinder and a welding set applied to them. I did not ask how that had been possible in a prison, I had a feeling I might not like the answer, or at least other people would not feel as creatively excited as me. The result was a life-size therapy group sculpture that was set in the grounds. Some of the men gave a dance performance incorporating certain moves of a professional calibre and the poetry was splendid. The drama group toured their production around the communities to packed audiences. The final triumph of the fortnight was the performance by Motionhouse of the piece that they were currently touring the country with. We brought in three tons worth of stage and rig and set it up in the "Market Square" where they performed to 200 men who were spellbound and fed homemade sweets by the creative catering group. It was the first time that the whole community of 200 men and staff had seen themselves as a complete group. It was a defining moment in which the TC established an identity, a vision of itself and saw what as a community it was capable of. As one resident put it, "For a few hours I was in a world outside of prison and understood what could be". That's art for you.

Over the years from the opening of Dovegate there were the usual set-backs and developments that organizations go through but generally the TC achieved both therapeutic excellence as measured by the Quality Network and HM Inspectorate of Prisons. It acquired a new family centre building and developed its gardens, its aviary and added to its sculpture collection. Staff came and went. There were the usual crises in the staff team when grievances or disciplinary issues arose. Some were dealt with smoothly, others created more of a crisis in the life of the TC. The TC was also successful commercially; by and large we held our capacity at a high level and made a substantial contribution to the bottom line of the budget.

The company changed the director of the prison for a second time in the summer of 2006 and in that July I decide that after 30 years of working in prisons it was time to move on and out of them. The landscape of the Criminal Justice System was changing the company I had originally joined; Premier Prisons had become part of Serco and therefore a small part of a large conglomerate. There were new challenges in the world of forensic mental health provision that were available to me and I needed to get out into the world before I became institutionalised and brutalised. An older and much wiser colleague of mine who I worked with at Grendon had said to me when I was discussing leaving Grendon and the feelings I had for the place, "Roland, you have done your share". I think I got to the stage where I felt that I had and that if my "share" was good enough then enough of the Dovegate TC would remain to continue to help people change their lives.

There is much, much more that could have been written but knowing when to stop and what to save is part of being a director of therapy in a TC. All I can finally say is that being the director of Dovegate TC was a period of my life where I made life-long friends, saw people achieve amazing things and regularly had my belief in the ability of people to change their lives demonstrated beyond doubt. What more could a person want?

CHAPTER 6

STAFF AND RESIDENTS' TALES

No book about the emergence of a new prison TC would be complete without the first-hand opinions of residents and staff. This chapter contains unedited responses from both to questions such as: How do you experience Dovegate? Are there things you would like to change? How does it compare to an ordinary prison and (where appropriate) to Grendon Prison? Staff were also asked to comment on any historical reflections.

My[1] long time friend and colleague, and personal holder of a Butler Trust Award, Jinnie Jefferies, still refers to herself as a "dirty shirt worker" when talking of her work in prison TCs. She thereby acknowledges that the purpose of all the research, planning and discussion is to provide the best for the people who it is all for: the residents; and she recognises that none of it could happen without those workers at the coal face, who manage the day-to-day highs and lows.

I.   Residents

Resident A

The first resident quoted is serving two years and ten months. This is his second time in Dovegate TC and he is still going through the assessment process. He feels differently about therapy this time round, seeing things that he didn't before, finding it both easier and harder.

> When in therapy it is all about your feelings and thoughts, but it's hard to ask because it's all there all the time, it feels weird saying it, I've heard it numerous times, I can say it in a different way but still say how I feel.

---

1.   I.e. second author Judith Mackenzie

Question What went wrong last time?

Answer Everyone had recommended parole which was unheard of. Eventually I got a D Cat and then I went back with my ex-girlfriend. I basically called her all the names under the sun and got a recall. It didn't work but I kind of needed the relationship, but I'd changed and she hadn't. Previously I would have dealt with her violently. At the end last time people would say I've changed and I said I haven't. But I had a choice and I made a bad one.

I was aggressive — I had a lot of abuse in care; I was anti-authority. David Lynes was director of therapy and he looked straight through me and saw behind all that. The things I was taught as a child were all the wrong things and now I'm being taught the right things — I would shout and bawl at people to get respect and maybe not get what I wanted.

Three months assessment is a lot better than three weeks. It is harder to behave yourself for three months than for three weeks, and more people on the communities are in therapy. If half were out of therapy it was very hard — you were pulled two ways especially if you'd only just started therapy.

The difference between the TC and the prison is that on the main the staff interaction with convicts is (like) very little — neither want to talk unless they have to. It makes it very difficult doing five years IPP.[2] If you have a problem you can't talk to the staff compared to the approach on TC. Here you learn to drop all your masks and get to express yourself. Going back to the main you have to put the mask back up — the TC staff say you don't have to but you do or else you'll be bullied and taken advantage of because they take advantage of people who are vulnerable. Perhaps you don't put on every mask.

Before my recall I went to a job agency — I told them I was a con and was honest and I got the job. When I came out after my recall I was honest again but didn't get the job. How d'you explain that?"

---

2.   An indeterminate sentence for public protection.

Question Would you recommend the TC?

Answer I have done. But you only get out what you put in. I could have been more honest last time and I caused a lot of heartache. Before I came to therapy I didn't care for anyone except the family, if I hurt someone else it didn't hurt me at all. Now I cry at what right did I have to do the things I've done. I need to talk about things I didn't talk about before. I didn't exactly lie I just didn't ...

Question Why not?

Answer Shame, guilt, to tell my group I've been a different person to what they thought was hard—but I should have done. I can't live my life taking out other people—it will be hard and people are not going to like me, but I want to do it.

Resident B

These comments are from a mandatory lifer who has served 28 years on a tariff of 14 years.

Twelve years ago I was in Grendon. The first time I did two and a half years on the wing, the second time I did six months there. I left due to having a positive MDT[3] for cannabis. I was using on and off throughout, trying to fit in. I was a bit disillusioned with Grendon at the time—people were using (drugs) on the wing. In groups they would say what staff wanted them to but out on the wing it was completely different. There were two of my small group, and I was thinking, "You bleeding hypocrite—what's coming out is crap," but I felt I couldn't challenge them because I was doing the same thing. If I wasn't doing the same thing I'd like to think that possibly I could have been more challenging but more than likely I wouldn't have been, no. It made me not want to talk because it seemed, maybe I was being paranoid, but I tried talking about the index offence[4] and growing up and that and

---

3. Mandatory drug test.
4. In effect the main offence (or sometimes offences) for which someone has been sent to prison; also one which is the primary focus of work with the offender in the TC. See the example in relation to Resident C.

I was heavily challenged, and it came across as being dug out. They wouldn't believe what I was saying and it made me angry.

I was disappointed because when it was just too late I started with psychodrama and this does have an effect and good things happened and painful things, it's what therapy was supposed to be about.

The staff could have been more challenging and open — they knew there were drugs in the wing but did nothing about it; they should have brought it out saying "I believe it's you" etc. and been more proactive in drug-testing although we did lose a family day for it.

The other time, I was deselected because I threw a television at an officer — I was on report and it was adjudicated on the wing and I got seven days loss of privileges and a fine. I was followed to my cell by two officers to get the TV and I threw it and went to kick the TV as the officer bent over. I was given the information I was being shipped out by a prisoner who heard it when he was cleaning outside the office, and I went to Parkhurst.

Question How do you find Dovegate?

Answer To be perfectly honest I didn't want to come — it's a recommendation of the Parole Board that I'm here. I've lost my C Cat twice. I've been four weeks here; there are some similarities to Grendon but mainly it's very different.

Staff are more adhering to the rules here. If in Grendon you break the Constitution nine times out of ten they say "stay and work through it" but here if you break the Constitution there are no grey areas and it's on your bike. This is far better for me so I know I'm going to be challenged and held accountable. There are going to be guys not here for the right reasons but the majority seem to want to be and that's good for me too. So if I get through this assessment I want to get Avalon[5] because they are the most serious about therapy and that's what I need.

---

5. One of the four Dovegate TCs after they were given names rather than being referred to as TCA, TCB, etc. See *Chapter 10*.

Being here has changed what I expected, I thought it would be like Grendon but it's not, it's smaller and we're pushed into a corner more. The first day I walked onto the wing and as soon as I walked through the door I felt the changing atmosphere—it was good and friendly, the majority of guys said hello. We are a community here and it's a better vibe.

I was surprised that after two days when I got my milk stolen, the thief told me that it was him. I didn't know what to do but in the end I told the chairman and it was brought to the community meeting and the guy owned up. I thought if that had been happening in Grendon it would have been turned on to me, it was a prison thing, and I expected the same here but actually guys were just saying well done. And I found after a bit that there was support for both the thief as well as me—the amount of support is phenomenal, not like Grendon at all. I dreaded doing the index offence in Grendon—it was question after question and felt like the Inquisition but it's not like that here, it's more comfortable and so I'm able to be honest and come up with things that I couldn't do before.

Resident C

I came from Swinfen[6] to do more work more than two years ago. The first thing that struck me when I landed here was that different environment compared to what I was used to. The first week was friendly—it was a bit too friendly and I was a bit wary—if a person in my last prison was like that they could be up to something—it took weeks to get used to it. Less so with the staff but I am used to things being more regimented and staff are abrupt in prison. But here we are on first name terms and in the great scheme of things it's almost like becoming an equal. We're not looked down on or bossed about, we're civilised with ourselves and others.

The next step for me is to work on the agendas and business meetings. The first time everyone was in a circle I was impressed with the way people spoke and it gave me a chance to let my barriers down and show that's where I'd got to too.

---

6.   Swinfen Hall Prison, now a Young Offender Institution, near Lichfield, Staffordshire.

The agendas were a bit of a shock because residents had to deal with things going on and be straight with one another. I had a few situations myself. Someone wanted to bring me into a gang thing but I wasn't having it. The main point was that after two weeks I needed to do it for myself, and I didn't want that sort of person around me any more, I'm no longer into the street thing.

Two weeks later, it was my case conference and I was nervous all day. I got through it because I really wanted to do this, my family was behind me. Anyway it was a good day getting through, a huge pressure off my shoulders. The pressure was not about having to do courses but what to do if I didn't get through. It gave me a chance to start focusing on the therapy. I learned to keep a diary before I came here and I've applied it to my therapy diary. It takes a while for issues to come through and in the first group I only gave a brief summary.

It's funny how things change, now I'm the oldest one on the community but back then I was still finding my feet. Situations in here brought emotions out of me. Growing up if I had something robbed off me, I'd go about it a certain way—you back yourself up and get angry. I got my T-shirt stolen here and all those feelings came back from years ago. I thought "I'll take a special"[7]—I was fuming. My old pals would have been, "What're you gonna do about it", but this lot were, "It is only a T-shirt", and "What's behind it, i.e. the T-shirt, for you?" Actually my Nan bought it for me and spent her pounds for it and it all came out about my family and how protective I am of them and that links into something else from years ago when my mum fell out with someone and was set about with knives and so on—I remember the helplessness of being a kid—I tried to phone the police but it got smashed out of my hand and I thought that was it for my mom. I was only seven or eight.

Then another thing was linked to the first instance—I remember as a child [describes a serious incident][8] and that resulted in me having feelings about sex offenders right into my teenage years. And other risk factors developed—drugs, alcohol and peers and this links into that—I needed the protection of the gang—it lifted problems from me on the street.

---

7.   A special meeting.
8.   Square brackets are used throughout this chapter where something has been added or altered.

My index offence was aggravated burglary/murder—it was convenient to do—I needed to step up to the next step to prove myself to my peers and I feared rejection which overrode the fear of doing the offence—I was thinking the police won't kill me but they [other gang members] might.

It's all linked.

I feel I've come a very long way—I wish I could go back with the knowledge I've gained and be different. I'd be less angry at the world and have a positive approach. I've dissociated myself from gangsters; I could have done it before but I lacked support. It's given me an interest in working with offenders.

The problem at the moment is this is where everything I've done in therapy has been great but now I'm waiting to go, I've been signed off[9] for six months waiting on a transfer. I want to move on—I feel like a fifth wheel in the group and it gets me down.

I'd advise anyone coming here to think carefully because of the movement thing but otherwise great.

Resident D

This resident is serving four years imprisonment for public protection (IPP) and had done six weeks of assessment and three weeks pre-assessment on the Resettlement Unit.

If I'd known the Resettlement Unit existed and I had to spend time there before coming on assessment I wouldn't have come. You're mixing with people who are screaming they are poor copers but they're not, not all want the therapy after finding out on pre-assessment—you have a foot in therapy and 40 per cent normal prison.

---

9. Completed therapy (aka "out of therapy") and awaiting a move to (usually) a normal prison location, but unable to move on: a source of tension, but this was also intertwined with the TC's need to stay virtually full due to the "194 clause". See, in particular, *Chapters 2* and *8*.

It is different though, there was a change in attitude—there is challenging and consideration, for example music and ball games and it's a respect issue. If you were in another prison the challenge would be physical—Turn it down or else!

Parts of it are hard—I had known another prisoner who is here for six years and had to put him on the agenda—I didn't like it but I did it.

I was in Grendon for six weeks of hell in 2007—I went to [X] wing and I didn't enjoy it in the slightest—the first interview I had with a CARAT[10] worker, he judged me wrong. There you decide what you are going to do before the meeting—he was on every group I was in—our guys had groups at different times. [At that time Grendon was undertaking assessments on the TCs].

It is massively different here—the first person I met I thought, "Oh my God someone actually being nice". It was a culture shock. In Grendon it was always I couldn't have that; here it's been positive. I don't recognise myself from the resettlement report from Grendon, it meant I had to fight to get here.

Resident E

Resident E was in Grendon for three years, leaving in 2000. He had been in Dovegate for a year and had a 12-week assessment period. He was released on life licence in 2003 but recalled to prison for associating with known criminals and had served six years on recall. He says:

Grendon was a lot more in your face with lots more reality confrontation and it was all the time—out of groups, all the time, people say "take it to your group". But here what little is done, is done on groups and then people go back into their egos and "wannabe gangsters" and they're just not confronted.

How people see themselves is not being addressed here—their place in society is not talked about and it is not dealt with in the here and now either.

---

10. CARATS is the Prison Service scheme in relation to drug-testing and alcohol-testing.

The relationship between staff and prisoners was more active and more engaging in Grendon, they would spend time with you and there was more interaction with staff away from groups.

I didn't want to come here—I was sent here for one-to-one work and never intended to come back to TC but I was stuck here by then so I agreed. I wish I hadn't because of how things work here. It's a numbers game isn't it—there are eleven people signed off here and they're stuck here—the financial interests of the company comes before anything and that can undermine the therapeutic process. Those people who completed two years ago are still here—we've got five empty places and people are being signed off. Some people's risk is gone up. They're in a worse position than when they started—everyone in therapy is dreading completion. I've been here a year and only seen one person move progressively, it's starting to take over every meeting.

There are staff who are good and try their best but they're more into it at Grendon, there they are career officers. When groups are over it turns into a normal prison wing here—the officers are never out of the office.

Groups are being cancelled all the time because of lack of staff. People feel bullied a lot by the threat of reports by the therapy manager. The therapy manager's never on here, he just turns up on community meetings to bully and then disappear.

Question Why did you not go back to Grendon?

Answer I was up for it but I thought it would be similar here—but they don't recognise people as individuals. I have a grievance against HMP and the private sector. Overall there is a lot of free time here, nothing for people to do, no interaction between wings or with staff, so you spend all your day gossiping and it's terrible for it.

Resident F

To be honest I thought at one time I was ready to leave therapy as I had a better insight into myself but I didn't and it was only through the staff I realised they were right. It's not been easy, it's some of the hardest time I done in prison. I came into therapy knowing I needed something; I had a lot of baggage. I came out of therapy for 18 months and was behind the door on here [i.e. lodging on the community but not in groups] and then I had the opportunity of coming back in. I was blaming everyone for me not moving. I had expected a progressive move on my 3E [lifer] board and I refused to put my 48 [voluntary withdrawal from therapy] and refused to attend groups. I got depressed. My wife died. It took all that for me to realise I hadn't really grasped it. It was a good thing and a wake-up call for me. I had done two years and had my end of therapy board and was recommended Cat C, a progressive move and I was thinking get me out as soon as possible. But if it hadn't been for that 18 months back in therapy I still wouldn't be where I am now. I know now I won't re-offend even though it's a big statement to make.

I used to think everything was everybody else's fault and I kept things inside me for over 40 years so I know I'm different now.

I got insight into losing someone when my wife died and that helped me develop victim empathy. It took 18 months.

I believe therapy works but not inside the main prison. If this was separate from the main prison it would work better — here people focus on things that are controlled by the main, like the visits. When you're doing therapy it can be a false sort of thing, with people sitting in on it; are they looking at you behind the door — they become a friend and you rely on them — it can be detrimental.

In a normal prison you know where you stand, or in Grendon when officers have to lock you up, and facilitators do the groups — whereas here officers do everything. You think they're not an officer and expect leniency and then its, "Hang on what's going on here?" The first thing that they are is a prison officer.

The good side of it is it is more relaxed — it isn't us and them and I'd always fight their case for them. You never have enough staff because the main takes priority. People who come straight here they think this is prison — when they move on they're a little bit shocked. I recommend therapy for anybody but only if they want it—I needed a whole lot. It's the best thing I've ever done; I have insight I know I have, if I had moved on before there's no saying whether or not I'd've come back.

Resident G

Resident G was in Grendon for two and a half years and had been in Dovegate for four years. He said:

There is a big—not a massive difference. They don't have Cabinets[11] here so minor squabbles go on the agenda and it gets backed up [i.e. too many items on the agenda to process]. In Grendon the business meeting was Monday and Friday, Wednesday was a break and there are two small groups and two community meetings. We knew the structure and you knew where you stood with the timetable. Here if you're not at work you're banged up. When I left Grendon the group had wanted me to talk about abuse and I wasn't ready to explore it. So I was called a liar. So then I said, "Okay it didn't happen" and I was still kicked out. It was proven positive once my sister gave evidence.

I have touched on it here and spoken about it but I was told I shouldn't be taking it back into the group as they wouldn't support me so I will do it on one-to-one.

If I look back on my previous life I can see the majority of mistakes I've made. The victims of course and you just regret it. Therapy allows you to explore with the support of your group.

I'd change Dovegate by introducing the Cabinet to ease the pressure off the agendas and I'd make less bang up. The out of therapies or the withdrawn should be moved away as soon as possible—they don't mix and it's not helpful. Communication between staff and residents—they do talk together here but management to staff and management to residents, there is no communication. Sometimes you get different answers from different groups.

---

11. In Grendon, senior residents form a "Cabinet" to undertake key posts on the community and influence decisions, including the keeping of boundaries and the monitoring of distress.

I'd change Grendon by putting in more jobs, but Grendon would invite people in from outside, for example bikers[12] and zoos[13] and so on.

Prison and Dovegate are totally different. In prison you're just a number or a pay packet to staff not a person. I have admiration for staff here; it's hard to listen to us. Neither [type of prison] is easy but the system is easier than therapy; that's the hardest thing I've had to do.

Resident H

Resident H is serving life imprisonment with a tariff of 15 years. He has spent eight months in Grendon and 24 months in Dovegate and is signed off. He thinks things didn't work well in Grendon because he wasn't ready as it was too early in his sentence (2005).

It's different here—it got voted into read out Boards [assessments] in groups which was done in Grendon all the time—I have encouraged people to do the no-confidence rule [no secrets]. Here you can go all the way through therapy without touching the main issues—they don't feel they have to talk about every-thing—they want to be signed off and if they don't get it they threaten them with solicitors. And they tell officers things but won't say who's done it and the staff won't either—they say it's because they have a duty of care. Fine but there's no violence here! But people are manipulative—if they can say things and not be challenged they'll do it.

In Grendon on small groups a guy said "one offence" and the therapist told him he wasn't saying it all and it took him out of his comfort zone. There are people minimising[14] here. They should compare the account of themselves in court and the officers should challenge with reports of contrary information. Some individual officers will do it but some are too wary of solicitors and they don't know where they

---

12. Motorcyclists whose hobby has become a passion, often associated with a particular lifestyle and groups of like-minded others.
13. People from outside the prison who come to "gawp" at prisoners.
14. For example playing down the type or seriousness of their offences, possibly blaming others.

stand on it. People are selective about what they share. Although they are voted to share at three monthly [assessment] they don't all do it.

Residents can't challenge because they don't have the information. I could have been challenged a lot more here, and I've been a bit disappointed. Staff think maybe others are scared because I know how to speak. I tried to overshow I'm approachable. It's always the same people that speak.

I hope I get a progressive move, but my rewards are from other means even if I don't get to C Cat.

If I could change things here I would say they should have two main facilitators who are consistent on the group and it should always be them whereas here we can end up with different staff every day. You can't build up trust and you can't take things forward if you don't feel comfortable.

Also there's not a lot of resettlement—you can be signed off just to sit behind a door and you get into aggro because there is nothing to do. New people who are just starting look at it and think "These people are supposed to be finished and look at them".

I try not to be gloomy—it's here or the main—and you do need a winding down period from small groups. At this stage we should stay in the community meetings and get more light-hearted and have perhaps reminiscence sessions.

Dovegate hasn't got a lot wrong with it, there's lots I wouldn't change and it has lots of positive things, but just some small things—for example all the speculation on drug use—you need to get the VDT[15] people in or the dog[16] or something.

I'd change things in Grendon because finance is hard for them—I'd not change the therapy but some aspects like there was a lot more challenge. In both cases though most therapy is done by the inmates.

---

15. Voluntary drug-testing.
16. I.e. a dog trained to sniff out drugs.

If it had just been on the main the courses wouldn't have gone into any depth — for example I don't think I'd've learned to control my emotions where I can now. But here I can trust the group and facilitators. I have a strong group, I know the words are coming from the right place with a lot of care. It is a place to do therapy — you can do ETS[17] and CALM[18] but they're just tick boxes, but you come here to learn.

It would really benefit if the whole gaol was TC. Sometimes when you're in the main the main officers mock the process — it didn't deflate me because I've done therapy before but if you weren't strong-willed it could be difficult. You know that "us and them" that you get with prisoners and staff? Well you get it with staff and staff between the main and here. Prisoners get caught between them like having two parents at war. They say things like, "Your staff, they're all lazy, just sit all day in the offices".

I've had a couple of traumatic things happen here — two deaths and a court case and the support I got from staff and the community was really good. Before I wouldn't have been able to deal with my emotions especially about my son and it has been a massive thing for me.

II.   Staff

It was extraordinarily difficult to obtain comments from staff despite their being approached directly and by e-mail. Even with all possible caveats relating to anonymity, many refused. Even some with whom I have worked since the start of Dovegate, and with whom I had considered I had a good relationship, found themselves unable to reply with a simple "yes" or "no", preferring to act as if the request had never been made. The reason for this can only be speculated upon. It could simply be that they were much too busy and such a request fell a long way down on their "to do" lists.

---

17. Enhanced Thinking Skills.
18. Controlling Anger and Learning to Manage it: a standard NOMs accredited offending behaviour programme.

Perhaps they did not have the trust either in myself or the security of the system to be certain that they could not be identified. The fullest response is from a relatively new member of staff. It is also possible that a residue of the time when there was a culture of threat remains. At one point this was so severe that individuals warned each other that their emails would be read and to be careful what they wrote to ensure that nothing could appear as criticism or lack of loyalty to the establishment for fear of instant dismissal. People were careful of what they said and to whom and rumours of plans of a concerted effort to "cull staff" and close the TC abounded. This had an obvious impact on the culture of enquiry and open debate, and transparency and honesty was limited for a while.

It is hoped that the ethos to include openness, disagreement, discussion and group decision-making will continue to improve, as has been the case in recent years.

Quotes are reproduced in full below (as written), and thanks are due for the delightful and moving comments from those who did feel able to contribute.

Staff Member A

Coming to work at HMP Dovegate Therapeutic Prison was a choice. I didn't know much about therapeutic communities at that time, and I hadn't decided to look for a TC, but it was still a choice. I had enjoyed working with female clients through my career so far and it took a lot for me to branch away. Having heard about the job opportunity, I then started to look more into this treatment model and the small flavour I got really appealed.

The choice was made, but the reality was different. I have found my experience of working in the therapeutic prison here stretches me in lots of different ways. The style of intervention has really helped me to draw on my experience both of working in a prison setting and also working in a secure mental health hospital. There were aspects of both that I missed when working in each environment, and I have found a marriage of these in a therapeutic prison. However, it is a marriage that creates a tension between the risk management and the opportunity for therapy and intervention. This, as may be expected, does not always make for the easiest place to

169

work. It is challenging for the residents but also challenging for the staff emotionally, personally and how to allow the residents space for therapy to happen, by not managing the risk ourselves.

My first introduction truly onto a TC was a strange experience; being with 40 prisoners (and not many staff) and the prisoners voting on whether they wanted me to stay in their meeting. They were uncomfortably frank and had an open discussion about this. They examined the purpose and value in my staying for myself, as well as them. Being in the spotlight and having this scrutiny on such an innocuous subject, really puts into perspective the experience for the residents, having their mistakes and behaviour scrutinised by the 39 other therapists on their community, and the staff facilitators.

The Assessment Unit itself brings with it the challenge of introducing what this therapy is about; demonstrating the boundaries and expectations, increasing [the prisoners'] motivation to change and assessing their suitability for a TC. It is really hard sometimes to tell someone at the end of 12 weeks, that this is not the right place for them; as for some they see a TC as their "last chance" to change. Personally, I don't believe this is the case, there will be other treatment interventions out there; but that doesn't take away the validity of their own belief. A TC is a hard journey for anyone to go through, and an average of 18 months a long time if this isn't going to be effective. This is why the assessment process is long, intense and in-depth; we need to get this as "right" as we can. It is also great to congratulate the residents who, at the end of 12 weeks, having put so much into their assessment, can go forward onto a TC. Those who really want to change, are relieved and over the moon to be going forward, whilst in no doubt that this is the beginning of a hard, long and intense process.

I love my job. It is hard work, but the residents work harder. I make decisions, but not many without residents' input. The residents have a lot of support from the community to participate and cope with the stress that a TC can bring. I too have a lot of support from the community, the staff team and supervision. We work together to make it work.

Natalie Parrett, Psychologist, Head of Assessment

Staff Member B

Hope this is the kind of thing you wanted.

I have worked at HMP Dovegate for seven years, six of those in the TP [therapeutic prison] in an admin role. It is a challenging environment, but then you see the change residents make over the time they are here (the way they question, discuss and ask for things) is pleasing to see.

It is great how all the staff pull together on the TP and work together. It took a while to get use[d] to challeng[ing] each other, but helps to have a better working relationship.

Hannah Gildart

Staff Member C

I arrived to HMP Dovegate TC on the 30th of March 2001, after being living in England for less than three months. Part of my job interview that day included a guided tour of the communities and I'd been asked to wear high-vis vest and a builder's helmet for that purpose, as the site was still under construction.

During the presentations stage, I listened to the presentation [the] DTC director prepared first. Mr. Roland Woodward convinced me then of shared attributes in between Dovegate and my previous experiences working in TCs in South America. After months of trying to get used to snow and morning fog, something eventually felt like home.

Sometimes—even when it feels a safety helmet is still required—it is like being at home.

Kind regards,

Gus

Staff Member D

I started nine years ago as an officer and recall really wondering what the TC was about, and initially seemed quite scary as residents were so much told what to do as i experienced on the main, they were asked and answers were discussed. The line of yes and no i had learned had become a very grey area. After starting to get use[d] to this and actually understand what a culture of enquiry was this seemed much more natural and comfortable. As the years progressed and i understood more about the link of past issues to current issues etc the work seemed to make much more sense and wet my appetite for further therapy training, which i did.

I experienced Roland [Woodward] as very driven, but somewhat of a dictator, however i only really experieced this as an officer and was not in attendance then of any managment meetings etc. I think the difficulty at that time and also with David Lynes was having a director of therapy that was wearing the two hats of therapist and opperational side (bloody dual relationships)

I think, at present and for the past year or so i am experiencing the TC or now TP . . . as working more effectivley and there are clear leads of operational management and clinical management, which i think has been much needed. There has been some improvement in communication, however i think that as a management group we perhaps have more of a storming stage ahead in terms of speaking our minds and having the minerals to do this and speak about what is not being said. A bit like the name that we cannot say in Harry Potter (Volermore, or something like that).

On a final note, i love my job and what i do and perhaps even more once it will hopefully be secure. I am very grateful to Dovegate in terms of the support i have received in terms of qualifications and funding for these to help me get to where i am today.

Hope this is something like what you are after, forgive spelling mistakes as it just flowed and i dont want to change the flow through corrections

Ian

CHAPTER 7

THE DOCTOR'S TALE[1]

I.   First Do No Harm: TCs Can Be Dangerous

Therapeutic communities engender great passion in those who become attached to them. Proponents espouse them as powerful, healing positive places in which to learn and work. What is often overlooked is that any system that has such power can also do harm. This chapter looks at some of the ways in which TCs can be harmful to those who work in them; to the environments in which they exist and to those for whom they purport to care, with particular reference to Dovegate and Grendon. It leans heavily on the ideas and terminology of psychodynamic theory, which is not universally accepted, or even acknowledged, particularly in Dovegate and for this reason a brief glossary is included in the appendices.

It seems to me that we are dangerous.[2]

In the therapists' support meeting a group worker was describing how full of rage one of the prisoners had been on her group that day. Whatever she had said to him was turned back on her but she persisted in patiently reflecting back to him what she saw until he rounded on her in a fury, nearly screaming with rage. *She was patronising and uncaring, [he] was never listened to properly and it was pointless even trying to work in the group.*

The therapist was clearly upset, still a little shaky from a threatening experience. Another member of the support group suggested it must have been quite frightening for her. She turned on him in a fury of her own: *Had he not heard what she was saying? Didn't he care? How dare he look down his nose at her! It was pointless even trying to come to this group for support.*

---

1.   As related by second author Judith Mackenzie.
2.   Arthur Miller, from his stage play "After the Fall" (1964) (4th edn. 1967), Viking Press.

This scenario will be familiar to anyone who works in a TC and there is now a widespread understanding that one of the roles of the feedback session or post-group is to "detoxify". The parallel process/projective identification here is obvious. Without the support group the therapist may have taken the unprocessed rage and hurt into her next working environment or possibly taken it home (the casualty rate of marriages in TCs is high).

In fact the example given above occurred not in feedback but in the therapists' support meeting in Grendon on a day when the wing feedback had been cancelled for operational reasons. It was fortunate that it fell on a day when the therapists meeting was taking place. How often though do these processes continue unconsciously through an organization at every level?

It is axiomatic in psychodynamic thinking that the client comes to therapy in order to "repeat the early maternal care system in the hope that this time it will be different". The model describes the psychological equivalent of the physical process of nurturing the infant. Thus complex nourishment is taken in by the mother in the form of everyday food as we know it, converted by her into milk and given to the child with its unsophisticated digestive system in a form which can be absorbed and used.

Similarly the mother (or primary carer) takes into himself or herself the unprocessed emotion experienced by the infant, and also the "slings and arrows" of the external world and processes them so that they can be returned to the child in a manner in which they can be integrated and used.

Where this does not happen successfully the infant becomes prey to overwhelming feelings of rage or terror, which at a later date may be recapitulated as psychopathology or acted out in avoidant or offensive/offending behaviour.

Such deficits are of course ameliorated to a degree by social interaction and later learning. What all theorists agree however is that for this to happen successfully there needs to be at least one benign and boundaried figure available.

It is the provision of just such a figure in the form of the community and the individuals who comprise it that makes the TC such a powerful force for change.

As much as the importance of reparation and the "corrective emotional experience" applies in individual therapy, it also applies to groups and TCs and the structures that support them.

II.   The Staff Team/Senior Staff Group

As relationships happen *between* people it is unrealistic to expect that those delivering therapy, whether inmates or staff can do so without themselves being affected.

The concept of parallel process is regularly used in supervision as a means of both understanding the dynamics of the therapy itself, and also providing an arena in which those same powerful feelings are "detoxified".

Whatever name is given to it—projective identification, re-enactment or parallel process, some attempt needs to be made to understand how our clients (and in the case of prison TCs, extremely dangerous clients) or bits of these clients can get inside us and move us apparently outside our conscious control. This is alluded to in *Chapter 8*, "Three Wise Men".

Penny Campling[3] has emphasised the necessity of staff gaining insight and understanding, although never suggesting that analytic principles should relate to the patient group. Mark Morris in his paper, "The Big Therapeutic Community Senior Staff Group"[4] puts the case very strongly when describing the situation in the Senior Management Group in Grendon:

> The question arises how the senior staff dynamics are affected by the dynamics present on the wings. It seems that the assumption is that the senior staff group are unaffected. The community staff groups act as a buffer between the dynamics of the residents and the senior staff group. The alternative is that the opposite happens; that the community staff groups act as a lens which concentrates and focuses some of the dynamics onto the senior group which burns like the paper in the children's experiment with the sun.

TCs can be as toxic as any other organization, but perhaps never more clearly is this the case than in a prison. Here the client group is operating at a primitive psychological level using defence mechanisms of splitting, projection and denial.

---

3.   Personal communication.
4.   Morris, M (1999), "The Big Therapeutic Community Senior Staff Group". Internal publication, HM Prison Grendon.

To contain this degree of pathology, which has already been acted on in the most violent of ways with many inmates being incarcerated for murder, requires a high degree of psychological sophistication and maturity in its staff team, particularly its senior management team.

The motivations of individuals in coming into this work are diverse. However it is probably true to say that for all of us there is a degree of resonance with some aspects of the prisoner population.

It falls to the senior management team to process and detoxify not only their own material and that of the prisoners, but also that of a large staff team who are also being assailed by the activation of their own previously hidden fears and impulses. How essential then that the senior management team holds this context with kindness—and how impossible a task this can seem.

How helpful it would be if they too had access to the kind of 'good enough mothering' they want to provide for the residents.

In practice they fall into the same maladaptive patterns as their charges—feeling threatened or insulted at the thought of an outsider they insist that they do not need it (after all they are therapists!). And so when they can no longer contain the overwhelming projections they proceed to act them out. As many of these projections are murderous, despite the very best of intentions and passionate commitment to the task, symbolic murder or something very like it is often what eventually takes place.

Sadly of all areas in prison TCs this area is perhaps the one both most neglected and resisted. The result is some of the most vicious aggression being acted out in so-called civilised groups that this author has ever seen.

In his paper, "The Big Therapeutic Community Senior Staff Group", Mark Morris describes his own experience of these unprocessed forces in Grendon:

> This senior staff group civil war is not history; it continues to sap the strength and creativity of the senior staff group.
>
> *He's a psychopath.*
> *They couldn't organize a piss up in a brewery.*
> *He was a disaster, nearly got the boot.*

He was on the fiddle in a big way—is clever, it's about money—did a lot of damage—a
waste of space—cracking up.
They want this place to be a C-Cat trainer.
Watch your back!
They're either never there, unintelligible or mad.
He is a snake.
He's power mad.

And so on. These quotes are not from residents, they are from members of the senior staff group about other members of the senior staff group. The dynamics are quite severe; staff permanently feeling they are on the point of being sacked; staff permanently on the point of resigning; staff genuinely thinking that other members of staff are out to forward their own interests. As currently conceded and structured, the senior staff group might be incapable of running one of the wing communities.

Mark Morris goes on to say,

The Grendon senior staff group has nowhere to metabolise its dynamics, nowhere to process the various fantasies, misconceptions and anxieties that will emerge in the course of the work. Instead this group consolidates its malignant dynamics in the various staff sub-groups: governors; therapists; probation officers; psychologists. In these cells, paranoia and distrust breed ... how do the slings and arrows of outrageous transferential therapy manifest themselves at a level once removed from actual client contact? Grendon has seen the answer several times over; the dynamics are intense and overwhelming. The senior staff team tears itself apart.

In Dovegate this malignancy came to the fore relatively quickly—I quote one therapy manager about one director of therapy who said with a face twisted with malevolence, "I hate him! I can't stop thinking of how much I hate him. I wish he would lose his job and leave with nothing—I want to hurt him". Many therapeutic communities are small TCs within a wider organization, and have discovered that they sometimes function better if they have a common enemy, and in the early stages Dovegate TC followed this tried and tested path, the common enemy being the main prison.

However the moment the beleaguered second director of therapy crossed the Rubicon and began speaking collaboratively (for survival) with the shakers and movers in the main prison, this artificial defence collapsed.

Although by the time the second director of therapy left it was recognized that there were major problems within the Senate, in the absence of an informed psychodynamic approach, the response was to bring in an organizational expert. His analysis of the organizational dynamics was useful and accurate; however without access to the Fluffy, the sensitivity meeting where the inter-relational dynamics were most concentrated, he was handicapped in terms of intervention.

It is probably true to say that by this stage the situation had become so severe that this response was the only viable one. Nevertheless it was entirely organizational and within that of course included the attribution of fault to individuals who were duly sacrificed. The concept of scapegoating was not acknowledged, indeed this lack can be seen to be part and parcel of the so-called forward thinking of a business model.

It should not be pretended that this is unique to Dovegate. The casualty list is frighteningly long. Reference has already been made to Grendon in which to this author's knowledge there were at least six serious casualties of this process all at a senior level. Even in the smaller communities there have been examples of similar consequences — these are not minor inconveniences but major life events. They include psychological damage severe enough to require admission to mental hospital, physical sequellae, for example heart attacks or accidents such as the second director falling off the roof.

Mark Morris comments on the severity of the dynamics in the big TC especially where the client population has committed such extreme offences:

> These are extreme dynamics. These are life and death dynamics; the hatred is murderous; the contempt and disregard is utter, and has concretely been so for the index offence.[5]

If it is so that in the big TC these projections are so magnified by the time they reached the senior staff group it is not surprising that there are casualties.

---

5. The main offence(s) for which someone is in prison as per their prison records.

There remains an urgent need for this process to be examined over and above the trivialising polarisation into "chaps and saps",[6] casually transported from the physical to the psychological framework. To do so is to ignore the tremendous forces at work against which it is impossible to stand alone.

So in the example given for Dovegate above it is important to recognise that this is not about a personal view, nor a statement about a degree of incompetence or malignancy on the part of an individual but an example of the process at work. Indeed similar sentiments involving the wish to hurt were expressed at various times by various people about all three of the directors.

Prison TCs are about victims and persecutors. The process of therapy requires that an individual move from an internal stance of being either a victim or a persecutor, to recognising and forgiving themselves for being both.

The criminal feels a persecutory or oppressive guilt that is extremely harsh. Faced with such horrendous judgement or attack he can only conceive of defending himself by mounting an equally violent assault on some enemy and thus project his persecutory violence into [others].[7]

Acceptance as a staff member on the TC means the individual must have sufficient ego strength to manage the recognition and integration of his or her own impulses and hidden desires.

The phrase — "The truth will do" — applies to staff as much as to prisoners. This is why so much emphasis is placed on the collectivism of post-group meetings and staff support. The same processes apply — honesty, feedback, communality and shared decision-making.

The question is repeatedly asked in staff groups, "Who or what does he represent for you?" The answer may reveal fear, yearning and sometimes envy.

One civilian became unhealthily attached to an angry alienated man who at the same time projected an air of vulnerability and damage. At the same

---

6. Colloquial prison expression for "tough guys" at the top of the pecking order and weak ones at the bottom, respectively.
7. "A Schema for the Transition from Cruel Object to Tender Object Relations among Drug Users in a Prison Therapeutic Community", Ronald Doctor, Consultant Psychiatrist in Psychotherapy and Clinical Director West London Mental Health NHS Trust, in *Dynamic Security: The Democratic Therapeutic Community in Prison* (2007), Parker M (ed), London and Philadelphia: Jessica Kingsley Publishers.

179

time she fearfully rejected another man with similar pathology who concealed his vulnerability beneath gruff aggression. Her own history revealed a brutal father who ignored her except when she exhibited characteristics similar to himself, and then abandonment by an equally brutal partner. The split transference was acted out in collusive acts with the first prisoner and rejection of the second. It was further translated within the staff team provoking counter-transference reactions of fear, protectiveness and punitive thoughts bordering on hatred. Fortunately a trusted senior officer (who of course had seen it all before) joined the team. By providing an external unifying centre he challenged and supported both the staff team and the civilian, who he was successful in persuading to engage in her own therapy.[8]

The training package given to all staff in Dovegate was originally called SNOG and KISS; acronyms for "Simple Not 'Orrible Groups" and "Keep It Simple Stupid" (see further in *Chapter 5*). Every attempt was made to deliver in a straightforward manner a common language that described as much as possible of the day-to-day working on a TC. In developing this package the team was somewhat handicapped by having to ensure that the training corresponded at least to some degree with the model of change and theory manual in the developing accreditation documentation.[9]

The constraints on time and money however mean that the training can at best deliver an outline of the structure and process. The more complex and painful issues have perforce to be dealt with in supervision and the post-groups.

One of the difficulties of working with such severe offenders is that it can lead to a sense of "they are bad people, and we are good people". This is a perpetration of the splitting that is a feature of working with personality-disordered inmates. It is also a form of acting-out on the part of the staff. If staff cannot integrate their own "internal murderers", they can never hope to bring their clients to wholeness. The clients will always continue to represent the split off part of the staff. This can be an immensely difficult task

---

8. This scenario is so common that several examples have been conflated into one.
9. Writing a manual that describes the model of change and the way in which a therapeutic community effects change on its residents was a mammoth task. Everybody had a different idea of what was essential (of course). There was an attempt to include as many ways of working as possible. The result was a model more resembling a camel than a horse.

for staff to do. Recognising the impulses to kill, maim and hurt or even sexually abuse others, integrating these parts and developing compassion for them is an essential part of a staff member's ability to empathise with his or her charges.

Damage to staff on the shop floor is sometimes less obvious. They are at risk of the same dangers as are residents by means of parallel process.

However TCs are a living and learning environment in which everybody is subject to change. This can often be traumatic for the individual and once again illustrates the need for regular supervision and staff sensitivity meetings if it is not to be channelled into acting-out with damaging effects for the team and the community as a whole.

It may also be one of the reasons that marriages of staff in TCs founder so frequently. Where one partner changes dramatically and the other does not this will always be difficult; where the first partner is embraced in an intimate supportive environment that encourages self-disclosure and exploration, the situation arises where the community becomes "mistress".

It is noted that proponents of TCs espouse their work with "an almost evangelical zeal" (*Community Care*, 2009). Perhaps job descriptions should come with a health warning, or at least that partners should be included in the interview procedure.

III. The Resident

Staff will have been drawn to this work partly because of an unconscious recognition of these aspects of themselves, and a wish to heal them. At the same time they are likely to be in denial of them and will hope to keep them safely encapsulated in the prisoners for whom they care, unconsciously perpetrating the resident's regressive state.

This is one way in which prisoners can be damaged.

The second is through the re-enactment of their original trauma. The strength of the transference engenders an equally powerful counter-transference, so that for example a resident who has been in receipt of perhaps dismissive or belittling attitudes in the primary caregiver, will elicit those feelings of superiority in the staff member. The staff may find themselves overlooking that resident and not noticing his needs, and if not explored in supervision this may manifest itself in a repeat of the original trauma.

The irony of course is that re-enactment is encouraged in the group as a process to be studied and experienced differently. Recapitulation of the family group is one of Yalom's core curative factors; a corrective emotional experience, a key feature of nearly all forms of therapy.

The early trauma that allows such a severe response as murder is difficult to process safely at an individual level. This is one reason that individual work is not encouraged on the TC, and where it does take place must always be fed back to the group and the rest of the staff team to allow containment and dissipation as opposed to collusive escalation.

This same dynamic to some extent in part explains the process in the staff and senior staff teams as described above. In addition to projected hostile impulses which then get acted out, there is also the counter-transferential response. The majority of residents have experienced early trauma of some kind; they may have witnessed abusive parental/care-giver relationships, been subject to abuse themselves or experienced abandonment or neglect. These same responses will be evoked in their care givers; and multiplied further in those who care for them (by extension by the time it gets to the senior staff group it is potentially toxic indeed).

The third way in which prisoners can be damaged is through rejection from the community, which in itself is likely to be a re-enactment.

Residents can be deselected from therapy for a number of reasons, some of which will include the discovery that therapy is more difficult than they thought, an unwillingness to translate intellectual insight into behavioural change, or the counter-transference in the community.

In the example above a prisoner may find that he is continually overlooked when it comes to applying for jobs perhaps, and that if this is brought to the community's attention they may respond with comments about his ability to undertake it.

This is where the importance of the assessment procedure lies in the exclusion of those unlikely to be suitable on the grounds of for example mental health, intellectual ability or motivation. All of these can make it difficult for individuals to make satisfactory attachments to the peer group, without which the holding aspect of the community cannot be accessed.

"Learning healthy attachment" is a key end product of therapy; yet at least some capacity to experience it, or to risk attempting it must be present as well as the capacity to tolerate frustration and disappointment.

If the small group and ultimately the community as a whole cannot accept and attach to the individual, he risks sharing his deepest fears and vulnerability only for the community/small group to reject him, thus reinforcing his worst fears and making it harder for therapeutic intervention to succeed in the future.

This is not to say that those individuals with specific deficit in for example intellect or ego strength cannot work in a TC; but the structures and procedures must be contextualised to allow them to successfully do so.

It is known that early dropout is associated with a negative outcome, with low IQ and high levels of psychopathy. Both of these factors make acceptance by and attachment to, the peer group difficult.

An area in assessment that is often neglected is the evaluation of ego strength in an individual as it is this that will allow him to go through therapy without the risk of falling into a cataclysmic depression or psychotic breakdown.

Regression is a feature of therapeutic enterprise particularly those involving emphasis on large groups, and regression will go to the "area of residual weakness". This can be to Klein's paranoid/schizoid position or early depressive position and without the compensatory "holding" power of the group and/or the capacity of the individual to manage anxiety can result in the abandonment of therapy, the construction of yet another "false self" or the "breakdown" of the healthy features of the existing personality.

A particular area of concern in Dovegate is the mixing of sex offenders with other prisoners. This was the original model in Grendon, although latterly Grendon has designated a special wing for those convicted of sex offences against children. There are arguments for and against this: it buys into the ongoing stigmatisation of paedophiles and the hierarchy of offending that allows armed robbers to believe that they are "at the top of the pile". One armed robber believed that he had not harmed anyone directly, stating in a community meeting, "But I'm always nice to my victims!"

Dovegate espouses the position that all offences are offensive. However laudable this may be in theory, in practice most staff share the views of their charges that paedophiles are the lowest of the low. There is usually a shocked response if they are asked to contact their own inner sex offender!

This is reflected in Dovegate's statistics which shows that early dropout of sex offenders, particularly when these offences have been perpetrated against children, is higher than in any other group and fewer go on to complete.[10]

Anecdotal responses from outsiders, for example solicitors, suggest that their perception is that those of their clients who have committed these offences are more likely to be scapegoated and persecuted than others.

There is a need for further research in this area to include for example whether or not these people are less likely to attain positions of kudos, for example chairman, within the community, and also the responses of staff and residents to them.

IV.   The Resident/Staff Axis

To a certain degree therapy is reciprocal. We are all to a greater or lesser extent wounded, and mention has already been made of how staff may have been drawn to this work in an unconscious attempt to heal themselves through healing others. There is nothing wrong with this and the process is part of the folklore of many professions–

The Wounded Surgeon plies the Steel.[11]

By our pupils we'll be taught.[12]

John Klauber[13] says ,"Patient and Analyst need one another … The analyst (also) needs the patient". Therapy, as has been said throughout this book, is a relationship, and for it to be authentic the therapist must bring all of

10. Internal unpublished audit (Miller, A, 2005). See also generally Miller, S, Brown, J and Sees, C (2004), "A Preliminary Study Identifying Risk Factors in Drop-outs from a Prison Therapeutic Community", *Clinical Forensic Medicine*, August: 11(4); 189-197.
11. T S Eliot. "East Coker", Quartet No2, *Four Quartets*.
12. Oscar Hammerstein. "The King and I".
13. Klauber J (1982), *The Elements of the Psychoanalytic Relationship and Their Therapeutic Implications*, New York: Aronson.

himself or herself to it. As we experience healing, we remain open to our woundedness and use it in the service of the resident, thus embodying the principle of the Instillation of Hope.

Where this can go disastrously wrong is when the process remains unconscious and produces an unhealthy maintaining of pathology, allowing the staff member to "get away with" not doing the work themselves and perpetuating the pathology in the resident. As residents move on they are replaced by others with similar pathology and a "maintaining cycle" develops in the member of staff. This stultifies the growth of the staff member and means that true healing cannot take place for the resident.

An intermediate stage is where the "pathology" or wound in the staff member begins to emerge and the staff member begins to use the therapeutic process for his or her own ends. As most residents in a prison TC have been both used and users, it is clear that this is another way in which their own wounds can be deepened and their difficulties potentiated. Most TCs are beginning to recognise this and to address it through the means of supervision and the provision of external counselling and support. We are not yet at the stage of offering therapy to all staff members (though there is an argument for all senior staff to have undertaken it) but it remains the case that "we can only help others develop as far as we have developed ourselves".

There is a tension in this process for prison TCs as staff have to be aware of conditioning. This means the understanding that prisoners being prisoners will seek to use others where they can and can compromise staff in a variety of ways including the use of emotional relationships in order to make sometimes illegal gains for themselves. These can be a threat to both security and therapy. Awareness of conditioning requires the member of staff always to view the prisoner as "other".

It takes a good deal of experience to hold both this stance and to engage in the therapeutic relationship, holding the tension between an awareness of possibility of conditioning, resisting collusion and engaging in a real relationship. Nevertheless,

> What will help the resident and the therapist to develop is emotional understanding. The therapist's job, then, is to make emotional contact with the resident…[which] together with understanding, nurtures man's soul and he can grow and develop to

full capacity. Intellectual understanding alone cannot nurture—what the resident requires is inter-subjective emotional understanding.[14]

V.   The Community(ies)

If there is potential for damage to residents, shop floor staff, therapy managers and senior managers, what of the community itself? Much has been written about the dangers for TCs of "explosion" and "implosion" relating to a failure of structure or process respectively.

TCs are also the subject of envy, especially when they are part of a host establishment and this may have straightforward consequences. Privileges may be withheld; small mistakes can excite a disproportionate response. The host establishment too may see itself as hard done by.

Without the advantages (as the hosts see it) of a 'docile' population, and plenty of interesting fun things to do with them, they may see themselves as long suffering supportive martyrs to the cause who have to "pick up the pieces" when things go wrong.

The host establishment is usually relatively poorly staffed and in reality does have to take those that the indwelling community rejects. Thus the TC can move from a position of symbiosis with its host to one of perceived parasite. Dovegate began by exciting exactly that kind of envy but was protected by a director of the main prison who not only had a belief in and understanding of the TC, but also his hands full with a new and turbulent prison and was grateful for the protection that the TC afforded in the eyes of the contractor and customer.

As the TC began to fall from grace it took the role of scapegoat for the main and vice versa. The main came to be seen as devouring and persecutory; the TC as fodder for its unbounded needs.

At the time of writing it is emerging from this dangerous period and beginning to engage in a relationship that is more symbiotic.

14. Symington, N (1986), *The Analytic Experience: Lectures from the Tavistock*, Free Association Books. The terms "resident" and "therapist" have been inserted by this chapter's author to replace "analyst" and "patient".

There is a recognition that some of the difficulties are rooted in envy and ignorance, but rather than retreat into a persecuted and persecutory huddle "behind the wall", there is now a commitment to transparency, shared services and ongoing education.

This chapter should not be read in a spirit of despondency! Its purpose is to highlight some of the dangers in TCs and particularly prison TCs so that awareness can lead to a more informed attempt to create a safe environment at all levels (custodial and therapeutic; for staff and residents).

That Dovegate and other TCs have to a greater extent achieved this already is eternally to their credit.

CHAPTER 8

THE THREE WISE MEN

In the late 1960s, Robert F Hobson (Bob Hobson) gave an open lecture to the Institute of Psychiatry entitled "The Therapeutic Community Disease".[1] Drawing on the experiences of Tyson West he explores within it three stages of difficulty in a growing TC. He entitled these stages:

- The Coming of the Messiah
- The Enlightenment; and
- The Catastrophe.

It is axiomatic that the stance enactment of the leader and its outworking informs the ethos of any TC. This is even more so within a large TC which encompasses several smaller TCs such as Grendon or Dovegate. Here the structures in senior management and the way their edicts are carried out inform and are informed by what happens on the communities.

Stuart Whiteley describes the leader as being in the role of a stable parent figure.[2] He talks of the working style of the focal leader in which

> both patients and staff, and their different levels of interaction, are looking to the leader for this parental stability with which to identify and by setting a model for interaction and intervention, the leader can also make it possible for others, both staff and patients, to move into leadership tasks, in what is then truly a multiple leadership situation as they imitate or follow on from his initial lead and thus keep the therapy in motion.

He describes this focal leadership as being

---

1. R F Hobson, "The Therapeutic Community Disease", Lecture given to the Royal College of Psychiatrists.
2. J S Whiteley (1977), "Dilemmas of Leadership in the Therapeutic Community and the Large Group". Paper given to the Scientific Meeting of the Group-Analytic Society, London.

189

based on the transference relationship and, although the overall leader may set a pattern and hold a focal position for the total group, other staff members in their respective sub-groups hold similar positions as do the patient members of the community in their particular areas of responsibility and interaction.

Since Dovegate opened there have been three directors of therapy, all of whom have brought their own individual gifts to the task of leadership; the three sections of this chapter relate to the differing effects of each.

Crucially, the director of therapy of a large combination TC such as Dovegate needs to possess three essential abilities:

- Such a key position requires a *lived and internalised* understanding of the therapeutic process in TCs. David Kennard describes the internalisation of the good authority which frees the individual, whatever his or her position, from the tyranny of the rulebook whilst maintaining the safety and structure of the TC itself,[3] and of course this internalised authority is what we hope will be reflected in the individuals who are ultimately released into society.

- The second essential is a *lived and internalised* understanding of the operational requirements of a prison.

- The third essential is a *lived and internalised* understanding of the psychodynamic processes in small and large groups as well as on an individual basis.

Each of the three directors possessed at least two of these capabilities to a greater or lesser degree. The different emphasis and understanding in each of them however has had a pronounced effect on the culture of the community as a whole.

Bob Hobson's theme puts me in mind of the "Three Wise Men" with their gifts of gold, frankincense and myrrh.

---

3. David Kennard. Personal communication.

I. Gold: "The Coming of the Messiah"

The Roland Era

The first director of therapy was Roland Woodward. A gifted man with extensive experience in TCs, he brought nearly all of the core characteristics to the huge task of opening and nurturing the emerging TC. It is perhaps due to this rare combination that this era is looked back upon by some as the golden years.

He had experience both in Grendon (a compilation of six communities as a therapeutic prison in its own right) and Gartree, a small TC within a larger non-TC prison, and he paid continual attention to the core values (now enshrined in the accreditation process).[4]

Roland designed a structure that departed in several key areas from the original model embraced by Grendon.

Unification of Therapeutic and Operational Lines.

One area that is traditionally seen as problematic in prison TCs, and which promotes endless debate and discussion, is the tension between the prison officer/group facilitator role. At Dovegate this is reflected in and reflects the tension between the main prison and the TC.

Grendon opened in 1962 with a single medical director who acted as both senior therapist and Governor. Since then, until Dovegate, in prison TCs, the operational and therapeutic lines have been separately managed and this pattern is reflected in the higher levels of management. There is usually a Governing Governor and Therapy Lead.

Roland as director (governor) of the TC was also its lead therapist and once again the two roles were embodied in one person. This model was passed down within the management structure to the communities themselves.

Therapy managers therefore were responsible for the operational line as well as providing the therapeutic lead. This allowed them to contain the competing anxieties from both parties.

---

4. See *Appendix 1* to this work.

The early days were filled with tension, hope and excitement. I arrived in the brand new TC buildings only two months after the core staff team had moved from the temporary premises of the "Wendy Hut". There, key personnel had formed a close-knit group of skilled, informed and enthusiastic culture carriers. The Wendy Hut, a prefabricated building outside the prison gates had housed the designers and architects of the new TC.

At the time of my arrival the basic systems were being put into place — staff were being appointed and trained using the writings of Yalom as a common language to carry them forward and transmit the ideal.

The first residents were greeted with a mixture of trepidation and delight. It is hard to know which was the more fazed as each group, staff and prisoners, took the measure of each other and tried to match expectation with reality. Then Brian, later to become a unit manager, stepped forward grasping the first uncertain prisoner by the hand, "How are you mate? I'm Brian. Welcome to the ARU.⁵ Let's get you settled in eh?"

"Brian!" echoed the stunned prisoner — "what happened to Boss?"

The ARU was fully staffed and headed by Claire Moore, a psychologist with previous experience of running a prison TC. She had a clear vision of how therapy should progress and how it would incorporate essential operational aspects of running a TC within a category B prison. More importantly she was able to communicate and model this for her staff team who were not only new to TCs but to prison officer work as well, having had only six weeks of prison custody officer training.

The ARU was to become the model and prototype for the other TCs opening in its wake, firstly TCA and TCB, then six months later TCC and TCD.⁶

The ride for the new fully-fledged TCs was less straightforward. Their therapy managers had varying amounts of prison and/or TC experience but none had the heady mixture of both that had proved so successful on the ARU.

Roland's vision of the growth and development of the TCs depended on the therapy managers and their teams learning through mistakes and

---

5. Assessment and Resettlement Unit.
6. Later to be given proper names: Avalon, Camelot, Endeavour and Genesis: see *Chapter 10*.

taking ownership of the process. He did not want other cultures from other places imposed upon his developing children. Whilst this allowed a degree of autonomy and required a rapid learning curve it also deprived them of the knowledge and experience that was available and which could have helped them iron out some of the initial difficulties. This has been expanded on by the first author of this work in *Chapter 4*.

The result was predictably mixed. Avoiding the cloning of Grendon meant a fresh, innovative approach. However the anxieties of the therapy managers resulted in a polarisation towards either permissiveness or over-control, which was reflected respectively in the wobbliness of the TCs and the anxiety of the operational managers. These latter were four senior staff who held the overall operational line as it related to the main prison, but only one of whom had prior TC experience. None of the others had undergone the full TC training that was delivered so religiously to their junior staff. This led to the topsy-turvy position of managers knowing less than their juniors and may have contributed first to the loss of structure when Roland left and later to the rebound condition of increasing 'prisonisation'.

Nevertheless enthusiasm, optimism and commitment prevailed and combined with the motivation and hope of the residents, carried the TCs forward over the obstacles that could well have caused others to founder.

Specialists — and All Staff in Uniform

The second area of difference (although this is more likely to have been due to the public/private issues referred to in *Chapter 2* of this work, rather than any philosophical commitment) related to the multi-disciplinary team. Whereas Grendon had a core complement of eight to ten prison officers, a probation officer, a psychologist and a psychotherapist, each of the Dovegate TCs had a therapy manager and a counsellor plus eight prison custody officers (PCOs) who were also required to cover nights. Everybody wore uniforms and everybody was trained in the prison PCO role.

Whilst on the one hand this contributed to the understanding that "nobody was better than anybody else", and "everybody could do everybody's job", and thus should have resulted in a democratic team, the reality turned out, as is so often the case, to be different in practice. Perhaps counter-intuitively, instead of equality, this arrangement had a tendency to produce uniformity of skill with one clear "leader" (the therapy manager) at the top. Furthermore the different values and richness brought by a multi-disciplinary team were lost.

Instead of a culture of "different but equal", a new hierarchy was created. As everybody was PCO trained, the special value and experience of the prison custody officers who were prison officers as such was lost and submerged; the people who held the power were the therapy managers and to a certain extent the counsellors. This persists to this day. In Dovegate, as in no other prison TC, a culture exists where the therapy managers are deemed to "hold the magic", and exert the power and control in a way that does not model the democratic principle however much the voting system is adhered to.

Psychodynamic Model and its Absence

The first director, Roland Woodward, had spent sufficient time in prisons (over 20 years) before undertaking the task of opening Dovegate Prison TC. He had therefore fully and ably absorbed the requirements of the operational side and in those areas where he lacked expertise he rapidly made good. It was only in the first few months that operational managers went about grumbling, "If only he'd stop meddling with things that we then have to spend extra time putting right!" Then their comments changed to, "Well this is what we could do . . . however I think we need to discuss it with the Senate".

As already noted, Roland also had tremendous and varied experience in working with difficult and dangerous prisoners specifically in the setting of a TC. His core discipline was psychology. He is a "hunter gatherer" when it comes to information and his reading and knowledge of the psychodynamic processes in a TC is very wide. It is questionable however whether he ever fully embraced the necessity for this approach to be part of the core workings of the TC. His focus, as would be expected by the customer (the Prison Service) and the general public was always towards opportunity for change and a reduction in offending behaviour. He is famously quoted as saying, "I am not in the business of producing insightful rapists".

Whilst this is an attractive comment, when repeated by a staff team it is in danger of missing the point. Aspects of pathology projected into the staff and not processed are acted out in exactly the same way as the prisoner group does this.

Whilst the senior staff team (the Senate) in Dovegate had numerous meetings within which there was the opportunity to process their own or other's material, the most important of these meetings, the Fluffy or senior staff sensitivity meeting never got beyond the basic premise of "the truth will do". There were limited attempts to acknowledge, "that's my stuff", but little or no attempt to understand process either in terms of what individuals might be carrying for their own staff teams, what they might be re-enacting or how the specific dynamics of a small group pertained to the Senate itself.

Whatever name is given to it — be it projective identification, re-enactment, or parallel process, some attempt needs to be made to understand how our clients or bits of them can get inside us and move us apparently outside our conscious control and it requires a safe environment in which to examine resonance.

The failure of this group to attain maturity led to unexamined splitting and acting-out of the senior management team, and ultimately contributed to the demise of the second director of therapy, David Lynes (see Section II).

The Numbers Game

This proved a major difficulty for the emerging TC. In *Chapter 2*, the first author, Eric Cullen, argues convincingly that the likelihood of keeping unsuitable residents in Dovegate to ensure targets were met was less than in the public sector due to contractual agreements. This was also envisioned as a safeguard by Genders in her paper.[7] Unfortunately in practice, the overwhelming necessity to keep the prison full far outweighed almost any other contractual agreement and the tyrant figure of 194[8] hung like a Sword of Damocles over the heads of the directors of therapy.

In October 2002, the riot in Lincoln Prison meant the disgorging of 200 additional prisoners into the already overstretched general prison population and a corresponding push to fill the spaces on the emerging communities.

For Dovegate TC it meant the planned admission and preparation procedure for suitable applicants had to be suspended and the places filled as quickly as possible. The lack of proper assessment meant a large number

---

7. "Legitimacy, Accountability and Private Prisons", Genders E, *Punishment and Society*, July 2002, vol. 4, No.3, 285-303.
8. The contractual need to maintain a TC population of 194 residents.

of unsuitable people were accepted on to the TCs resulting in concomitant therapy dropout as the numbers of those who had to be deselected as unsuitable or for breach of the constitution rose. As the percentage of "toxics" increased, therapy delivery became more difficult and the number of voluntary dropouts ("48 notices") also began to rise.

Due to the pressures on the prison population, the problem was further compounded by the inability to move those no longer in therapy out of the TC despite an increasingly healthy waiting list to get into it. Once begun, this process gathered momentum engendering a vicious cycle. People could not be moved out and so people could not be brought in. Even those who had completed therapy could stagnate without a progressive move for over a year.

By the time Ray Duckworth took over as the third director of therapy in June 2008, 32% were out of therapy across all the TCs and one TC had over 50% not in therapy. The therapeutic process was being smothered. Dovegate began to get a reputation for being a place you could not move out of. Furthermore those who were not in therapy had no reason other than normal prison discipline to abide by the constitution and Dovegate's reputation further began to decline and become a place where drugs were freely available.

In May 2006, Roland informed the Senate that he had decided to take up a post in private healthcare, again developing a service for personality disorder, and he left Dovegate a month later. It was perhaps at this stage that the lack of an external facilitator for the Senate made itself felt most severely.

I began this section by saying that many view that period as "the Golden Years", and I am one of those who, to a certain extent, shares this view. The gift of the first Magi was traditionally gold—a commodity valued above all others and this period is characterised as the first phase in Hobson's Therapeutic Community Disease—'the coming of the Messiah'. I quote from his paper:

> A dedicated, enthusiastic leader brings a message of brotherhood in a new society. Usually he is a sincere idealist with fascinating charisma. Bringing democratic light into the darkness of a traditional hierarchical mental hospital [or prison], he attracts a small body of followers and, at the same time, arouses fierce opposition from the establishment. When, with the help of a certain shrewd political manipulation he forms a therapeutic community, his "mana" power, his magic, increases. Although

196

he speaks of himself as "just one member of a group" he becomes for his intimates virtually an incarnation of an archetypal figure—usually a saviour hero but sometimes a great mother. To others he is a dangerous revolutionary or even the Devil. The charisma may gain admiration but it also excites envy—more overt in the enemy, more concealed in the disciple. What might have been an ideal is in danger of becoming an idealisation…an idealisation involves a splitting between "illusory good" and "illusory bad". The leader and his colleagues collude in an idealisation of the Unit which is often personified; the good Unit engaged in a battle with the powers of darkness—the badness outside which is embodied in the rest of the hospital [or prison], or the world at large. The unit is under attack.

Readers will recognise this as an accurate description of various successful new TCs and it applies to many elements of the early years of Dovegate. Thus the infant TC was ably parented by a skilled, knowledgeable and charismatic leader, who left it with the potential for growth and expansion just at the point where it was becoming adolescent and hopefully learning to stand on its own two feet.

II.   Frankincense: "The Enlightenment"

Frankincense is said to be calming, medicinal and soothing. Restorative, gently clarifying and meditative, it is said to be useful in treating depression. This aptly describes the gifts brought to Dovegate TC by the second director of therapy, David Lynes.

David is a trained psychotherapist and his immediately relevant work experience was in a TC for adolescents. He then had five years as a therapy manager on Dovegate's TCD. He therefore brought two of the three necessary requirements to the post of director of therapy.

From the start David had some difficulties in the TC due to his lack of any prison experience, which meant his community was sometimes viewed as less boundaried and less operationally sound. It is likely that some of that criticism was due to fear and envy as he was the only therapy manager who was qualified in psychotherapy (at that time all of the other therapy managers were psychologists).

The word psychotherapy means literally "healing of the soul" and this epitomised David's approach. He had long felt that some of the aspects of the TC were unnecessarily harsh and punitive and he hoped to bring in a more reflective and evaluative way of working. This was supported by the arrival as therapy manager for TCA of John Taylor, a psychiatric nurse and cognitive psychologist. For the first time words like "compassion", "tolerance" and "the unconscious" were used freely.

In addition to this there was a move to upgrade the quality and training for therapy managers.

David was determined that previously "no go areas" for discussion would now be brought out into the open, and he looked to the Senate to provide a supportive and democratic team in which solutions to difficulties could be discussed and agreed upon. In interview in October 2004, he spoke of the difficulty in walking between belief and chaos:

> It's like Theseus and his ball of string. You know if you go in and face the Minotaur you want to make sure your string doesn't break, so you can always follow and find your way back out again.

It is known that TCs are vulnerable after the departure of a charismatic leader. Unexamined transference makes this vulnerability more acute and where the previous leader has been in receipt of a powerful positive transference, his replacement receives the negative in spades.

So it was now that the unexpressed differences within the Senate came to the fore. Senate members were bruised at Roland's hurried going and their internal strife was magnified by the fact that three members had applied for the post of director of therapy, and furthermore each of them believed him or herself to be Roland's preferred candidate. They also each believed, in the company of many of the remaining Senate members that they were more able and better qualified for the post. (This author believes that it would have been preferable to search for a director who was not from within Dovegate).

In 1998 Mark Morris wrote a paper entitled "The Big Therapeutic Community Senior Staff Group".[9] In it he described how "the slings and arrows

---

9.   Mark Morris, internal paper, HM Prison Grendon.

of outrageous transferential therapy manifest themselves at a level once removed from actual client contact". He concluded that "Grendon has seen the answer several times over; the dynamics are intense and overwhelming. The senior staff team tears itself apart." He stresses the need for staff team integrity and functioning because of the constant and increased threat of anarchy. He goes on to describe the situation in Grendon as it was then:

1. The effectiveness of the senior staff group is reduced.
2. The senior staff group fragment, instead of working to contain fragmentation.
3. The senior staff group enact conflicts in the community staff groups.
4. The diagnostic function is missed.
5. The senior staff group model a chaotic style of TC leadership.

All of these symptoms were magnified in Dovegate's Senate after Roland's departure. Would an independent facilitator for the Senate have made a difference at this stage in what was to come? It is doubtful; the unexplored envy and sibling rivalry in the Senate members had by this stage become all encompassing, and the anti-psychodynamic ethos was entrenched. So it was that there ensued a series of battles which included a series of vitriolic and vicious attacks, thinly disguised as "I'm just saying what I feel". David became paralysed by the refusal of the Senate to support or ratify any decision; he constantly battled with himself as to the validity of his approach and questioned his core beliefs. In the meantime the measurable parameters in the TC were sinking.

The main prison was taking an increasing interest, sensing, with Roland's departure that the time might be right to incorporate the TC more fully into the main prison. At the same time the management of the main prison was providing, apparently, the only support available for an increasingly beleaguered director of therapy.

In October 2008, David was mending the roof at home. He put his foot on a beam that failed to support his weight and fell, sustaining a complex fracture of his arm and was fortunate not to suffer head or spinal injuries. The Senate at last decided to consider some pseudo-interpretation. However rather than consider that the director had relied upon a supporting structure which then gave way, there was much shaking of heads and comments about "rising above his station", "attempting a task beyond his ability" and "falling from a great height".

Members of the Senate, lacking the skills to process their own emotions or manage internalised projections, fell to "acting-out" in the most destructive of ways. The string of Theseus was cut and David was left to wander in the labyrinth. The result was his "managed resignation" in August 2008 and the paving of the way for things to come.

Returning to Hobson's paper, he describes this phase:

> During the 'enlightenment', the persecution occurs within the unit group where, if it is recognized with passion it can conceivably be dealt with. Rivalries and destructive alliances (for example patients versus staff, or sub-groups of each) may lead on to a state of relative disintegration from which, if the bonds of friendship are not broken, a new differentiated and yet integrated state emerges. But the disease often moves on into the third stage.

This was the case in Dovegate.

Towards the end of the David era a professor of organizational management (referred to here as Professor CB) had been commissioned to review the structures on the TC. This produced an impressive overview of the problems with some understanding of the TC perspective. He identified the need for ongoing work in the operational area; "serious disarray" amongst therapy and therapy governance, and the defective working of the Senate. He suggested a number of options some of which took the TC perilously close to a collection of Dangerous and Severe Personality Disorder (DSPD) specialist programme-orientated units.

He emphasised the importance of avoiding the build-up of out-of-therapy prisoners and professed his view (confirming the opinion of some of the auditors), that therapy as delivered at that time was dangerous to both prisoners and staff. He used as an example the fact that, sometimes, small groups ran with no member of staff present at all; all groups were run with only one member of staff; and these staff were nearly always relatively untrained. There was no opportunity for learning on the job and no safety for the small groups or the staff team with that structure. In addition:

- staff turnover was high—30% in three years;

- audited performance had dropped: in the year 2007-2008 the overall standard for compliance with the standards set by the Royal College of Psychiatrists, Community of Communities (C of C),[10] was raised to 60% plus the necessity to have obtained 50% in each section;

- the average scores for the communities ranged from 57% to 68%;

- One TC scored only 57% overall and 42% on one of the sections; and

- another TC scored 46% on one of the sections.

These results were serious indeed. Without compliance with the Community of Communities standards, Dovegate was not delivering on the contract.

Professor CB also identified the need for clear leadership and one additional suggestion he made was for "rebranding". David was caught between the powers on the main who were demanding an increased businesslike approach, a hostile and subversive "support" team (the Senate) and criticism of his main area of expertise (therapy) as being unsafe. His willingness to consider his own shortcomings led to his easy identification as scapegoat and his position became untenable. He resigned in August 2008.

III. Myrrh: "The Catastrophe"

Bob Hobson describes "The Catastrophe" as follows:

> The unit can disintegrate and collapse. Serious psychological breakdowns occur especially in prominent members of the staff. The continued persecuting situation can be damaging to patients and staff in many ways—recurrent disturbances occur within the group often with the exclusion of members, patients or staff, or by acting-out the unresolved persecution and destructiveness, in diverse ways such

---

10. The Community of Communities Quality Network of TCs described in *Chapters 2, 9* and *10*.

as violence, suicide attempts and secret sexual relationships. For it is an important fact that there can be profound effects on families who can either suffer intolerable involvement or, alternatively, envious exclusion.

When David Lynes left Dovegate, the main prison swung into action to put in place its longstanding agenda. The new director of therapy was one of the overall prison director's strongest supporters and an advocate of the authoritarian managerial way of doing things — or so it was assumed at the time.

At this stage the TC was in a parlous state. The audit results were poor and one TC had technically failed. With this came the fear of closure — if the TC was not meeting the basic standards for accreditation it could not be said to be doing the job and thereby fully fulfilling the contract. There were rumours of a hidden agenda to convert it into a Cat C prison.

In addition to that there were major anxieties on the operational side. There was a feeling that the TC was unsafe — it had perhaps not recovered from the traumatic events of a death, a suicide and a serious assault on one of the operations managers. As a result boundaries slipped and confrontation was resisted.

The numbers out of therapy continued to grow alarmingly — at one point over 50% of one community was out of therapy. The problems of moving people on persisted. It was important to keep the numbers up and this meant that those who had finished therapy could be waiting for over 12 months for a progressive move; meantime those who had opted out or been deselected remained as a toxic mix, unanswerable to community strictures so that the only means of containing them was by standard prison structures. This led to an increasing "prisonisation" of the TCs. Lastly the Senate continued to turn upon itself and refused any offers of help, denying the need. It was hard to see how a viable TC could exist under these circumstances.

It is arguable that at this stage of the process a strong leader, albeit of a totally operational perspective was exactly what was needed.

Ray Duckworth was a sound company man. A committed Christian, he came determined to make the TC a viable part of the main prison. He openly admitted he knew nothing about TCs and was on a steep learning curve. He worked endless hours and clearly spent a great deal of time reading, absorbing the theory of TCs very quickly and showing himself able to understand the requirements for audit and put them into practice.

Unfortunately, as had beset Dovegate from the beginning, he was without one of the three necessary competencies, being without the practical therapeutic experience on the TC shopfloor that would have allowed him to internalise the principles and put them into practice throughout all the layers. However, once again he acknowledged his inexperience and looked to his new senior therapist (John Taylor) for advice on therapeutic matters. Sadly John left for a new position shortly after his promotion.

One of the most important and to my mind beneficial things that Ray achieved was the acknowledgement that therapeutic skills and operational skills are different sides of the same coin and require a different background.

He grasped the nettle of moving away from the original design which, however well-intentioned an idea logically (as described earlier in this chapter), could not work in practice, particularly with the levels of staffing and the disparate experience of the therapy managers, that had been originally agreed. This instantly alleviated many of the concerns of the main prison; it also freed up the therapy managers to do what they were good at — and that was facilitating therapy.

Thus there now were community therapists and operational managers, potentially freeing up the opportunity for creative tension to re-emerge in reality as opposed to internal strife. This has not as yet been resolved. At the time of writing, it is being addressed and all the operational managers are undertaking basic training; and showing remarkable aptitude.

Unfortunately by this time the concerns of the main establishment had grown to the point where they could not be contained and the imperative was to produce a "safe" prison environment within which therapy could take place. There was not the understanding in all quarters of how the TC environment is a total environment, and more and more prison norms were running in parallel with a TC attempt at managing the process.

Ray's operational skills allowed him to capitalise on the advice given by Professor CB:

- the TCs were rebranded as therapeutic prisons;

- they were no longer TCs A, B, C and D but were to have names (chosen by themselves); and
- therapy managers were to be called "community therapists".

Whilst this seems a matter of semantics (what's in a name?), the result was a change of emphasis from therapeutic community to a prison, and many subscribed to the view that this was ultimately what would happen.

The Senate was disbanded as dysfunctional although the Fluffy (described by Roland Woodward in *Chapter 5*) continued to meet informally, and later almost secretly, albeit with reduced membership. The management structure reverted to an hierarchical shape, staff issues were dealt with using the appraisal and standard prison performance rating systems and the TC approach above the level of therapy managers was temporarily lost.

Mark Morris describes exactly this process taking place at Grendon in his paper of June 1999 as "ideological drift",[11] in which he also described its symptoms:

- lack of democratisation in managerial structures — the disregard of collective decision-making in favour of autocratic functioning;

- the marginalisation of the therapeutic brief — its dismissal as "noise" interfering with the smooth running of the prison; and

- systematisation of strategy and following current prison fashions with more enthusiasm than [therapy's] core business.

Despite its initial attempts to be different to Grendon the situation in Dovegate seemed doomed to repeat it.

Although myrrh is commonly known as a perfume or a symbol of death, (its origin in the original Arabic means "bitter") it is also dark but clear. Those days were seen by many as a time of bitterness and darkness and specialist attrition and disillusionment grew. However Myrrh was also highly valued in ancient times and was worth literally more than its weight in gold. In

---

11. Mark Morris, "Ideological Drift", internal paper HM Prison Grendon.

addition to its ancient use for embalming, it is an antiseptic and is currently being investigated for anti-microbial properties. Ayurvedic medicine uses it as a tonic and for its rejuvenative properties. The mythic origins of Myrrh lie in the legend of Myrrha, a Cypriot peasant, who, having become pregnant in an incestuous union with her father, was transformed into a tree by Aphrodite. On being pierced by the tusk of a boar she gave birth to Adonis, a deity of life-death-rebirth.

The story of the rebirth of Dovegate TC under the guidance of Ray Duckworth, including his own revolution is continued at the end of *Chapter 10*.

✫　　　✫　　　✫

Seen from the outside the development of Dovegate could be construed as chaotic with its final emergence into a healthy state as merely fortuitous. Much has been written about charismatic leadership when TCs are born, with an ultimate collapse as the charismatic leader leaves (as described at the start of this chapter by Bob Hobson).

However, another way of looking at it is to consider the growth of the community from a developmental perspective. The needs of a new baby are very different to those of a turbulent adolescent.

Dovegate is an enormous community and because of the pressures of the private sector has perforce had to develop at a remarkable rate. Due also to the public gaze (not without some *schadenfreude*), all its problems have been seen large. Continuing the analogy of the gifts of the Three Wise Men, all three were clearly deemed to be essential by the ancient sages, and this would seem to be the case with Dovegate as well.

The emergence of any TC is often heralded by a charismatic leader— "the gold" (always brighter from a distance) or "passionate mother"—and however much he would resist the description, Roland Woodward was without doubt a charismatic leader with all the gifts that that brings as well as all the pitfalls. Hence it is not surprising that when he left, the task for David Lynes was enormous. The denied dependency in the Senate resulted in extreme acting-out as described above, and it is probable that no subsequent director of therapy could have contained the process better, despite the extensive criticism of David at the time. He played the role of the teacher who loves engendering the freedom to learn.

By the time Ray Duckworth arrived, Dovegate was at the stage of being "a rebellious adolescent", needing a firm father, and the style of leadership required was very different from that needed in the early stages.

Mark Morris, taking from Manning (1989),[12] describes the central thesis that:

> Therapeutic communities require a charismatic leader to initiate them—to overcome the organizational resistance of the host service, and the cultural opposition of the new staff. Without such a figure, they are unlikely to become established. Once established, however, they require a different sort of leader: someone who is more of a bureaucrat who will protect the community via the establishment of networks and alliances. Likewise within the community, the task moves from one of the centralised manufacture of an ideology to the facilitation of pluralistic debate.[13]

If anything was fortuitous it was the arrival of exactly the right type of person at the right time to provide the right type of leadership, and their willingness to give way when the time was right.

12. Manning, N (1989), *The Therapeutic Community Movement: Charisma and Routinisation*, London: Routledge.
13. Morris, M (2004), *Dangerous and Severe: Process, Programme and Person*, Jessica Kingsley.

CHAPTER 9

EFFECTIVENESS AND QUALITY CONTROL

I.   How Do We Know It Works?

Do TCs work? What do we mean by "work"? Is it to effectively treat disorders of personality? Reduce institutional offending? Make better citizens? Reduce future offending? We would say yes to all these, but the problem is proving it and in order to determine how effective Dovegate, or indeed any TCs are, we have to know both what works in terms of the interpersonal dynamics of therapy and of the consequences in terms of the various outcome criteria cited above.

In order to ensure standards of treatment, TCs require a number of elements to be established, agreed, maintained and revised in accordance with proven criteria. Until 2000, these standards across UK democratic TCs (DTCs) did not exist. As a result it was impossible to say with any confidence what was actually happening in the name of therapy, whether one DTC was comparable to another, and how well they were actually achieving their objectives. For many years DTCs had developed within the relatively narrow professional parameters of mid-20th century psychotherapy. The media referred to the regime as psychiatric which was true insofar as the origins and traditions which informed the medical view and was the language used by the hierarchy, but could be relatively inaccurate in describing what actually occurred on the therapy units.

The core therapy activities of small groups and community meetings were staffed by non-psychiatrists, usually prison officers with little formal training, or probation officers and psychologists who also didn't have the psychiatric training or didn't subscribe to the language. The emphasis and language could change from TC to TC without check. There were no reviews, audits or inspections which addressed the core therapy. The annual HM Prison Service inspections would usually have a medical officer on the inspection team but he or she need not have psychiatric or psychological qualifications, and there were no inspectors at all with DTC experience.

The creation of Dovegate TC and the establishment of service-wide standards through national audits coincided to excellent effect. There is however some sense of concern over the extent to which these monitoring initiatives of the past decade might have a negative effect on the TCs or might impose too rigid a template, which we discuss later in this chapter.

The principal protocols for monitoring efficacy now include the Correctional Services Accreditation Panel, the Community of Communities audits, the Prison Service inspection reports, and the research into the qualitative and quantitative aspects of the DTC at Dovegate conducted by the Department of Psychology at Surrey University.

Accreditation

The Correctional Services Accreditation Panel (CSAP) was originally called the Prison Service's General and Sex Offender Treatment Programme Accreditation Panel and was created in 1996. The first appointments of experts in criminology and offender treatment were made in July 1999, when the name changed to the Joint Prison/Probation Services Accreditation Panel, changing finally to CSAP. May 2008 saw the removal of CSAP's status as an independent advisory body and the panel was brought in-house under direct accountability to the National Offenders Management Service (NOMS). Dovegate, along with the other DTCs at Grendon, Blundeston, Gartree and Send, were accredited in 2004 for use in custody and re-accredited in 2007 and 2010. CSAP consists of a panel of 15 experts in offender treatment drawn from the UK, Germany, the USA and Canada. When individuals or organizations submit proposals for accreditation, a panel of three or four CSAP members is convened to consider the application's manuals against the criteria standards agreed. An application is scored 0, 1 or 2 for each of ten criteria depending upon how well it meets detailed standards. There are four categories of accreditation ratings:

- **Accredited** The programme meets the criteria and has scored at least 18 points.

- **Recognised/Provisionally accredited** The panel has identified specific changes which could be achieved in 12 months (or a longer period where specified) and which would bring the programme up to accredited status. The programme would normally have scored 16 or 17 points.

- **Not accredited/Promising** The programme could be brought up to accredited standard, but requires a degree of development work first. The programme would normally score above ten points.

- **Not accredited/No further review warranted** A polite "there's no future" assessment, indicating that the panel "considers the programme does not merit further work being undertaken".

As can be seen above, provisional accreditation is granted for a score of 16 or 17 and full accreditation for 18 and above. Since 1999, there have been over 150 programmes submitted for accreditation, with only 70 of these given provisional or full accredited status. As accreditation is often referred to as the "Gold Standard" for prison treatment programmes and regimes, it was vital that DTCs were successful in their applications.

Effective Interventions Principles

CSAP works to the "what works" evidence-based formula, setting six principles associated with effective interventions:

- effective risk management;
- targeting offending behaviour;
- addressing the specific factors linked with offenders' offending;
- relevance to offenders' learning styles;
- promoting community reintegration; and
- maintaining quality and integrity of programme delivery.

There are ten agreed areas of scoring for DTCs, indeed for all accreditation programmes. These are the product of extensive consideration by the panel of international experts and are set on the basis of the what works models of offending programmes which in turn are based on published research proving treatment efficacy in terms of reducing re-offending rates.

These Programme Accreditation Criteria are:

1. **A Clear Model of Change** DTCs are recognised as the most effective regime-based treatment form for serious and/or multiple personality disordered offenders. To quote the Core Model for DTCs: "They give people with personality disorders the skills, strategies and understanding to manage their responses to life's stresses more competently and safely, and where possible begin a "virtuous" circle of positive experiences that reinforces the new learning". DTCs are a holistic, multi-modal treatment model. Specifically, the model of change is a combination of social learning, cognitive methods and psychodynamic approaches within a full-time living-learning setting.

2. **Selection of Offenders** To meet this criterion, programmes must include:
   - a statement of the type of offending behaviour the programme is intended to address
   - a list of inclusion criteria
   - a list of exclusion criteria
   - an account of the action taken to ensure participants are not excluded on the basis of race, ethnicity, religion, gender, disability, sexuality or age
   - a description of the selection procedure
   - a list of assessment instruments, their justification and rationale for this population; and
   - a description of any deselection criteria and procedures whereby unsuitable participants are removed from the programme.

3. **Targeting a Range of Dynamic Risk and Protective Factors** A range of dynamic risk factors known to be associated with re-offending must be addressed in an integrated manner within the programme. There are two types of risk factors predictive of future offending: static and dynamic. Static factors are historical, such as age at onset of offending or number of previous convictions, and these are of course not amenable to treatment. Dynamic risk factors are, however, and there are a number which research has established can be

modified and are therefore relevant targets for treatment. General dynamic risk factors which CSAP accept for the purposes of accreditation include:

- poor cognitive skills
- antisocial attitudes and feelings, including sexist and racist attitudes
- strong ties to and identification with antisocial/criminal models and impulsive antisocial lifestyle
- weak social ties and identification with pro-social/non-criminal models
- cognitive support for offending: distorted thinking used to justify offending
- deficits in self-management, decision-making and problem-solving skills
- difficulty in recognising personally relevant risk factors and in generating or enacting appropriate strategies to cope with them
- poor pro-social interpersonal skills
- dependency on alcohol and drugs
- contingencies favouring criminal over pro-social behaviour
- some adverse social or family circumstances; and
- weak or fragile commitment to avoiding re-offending

There are additional dynamic risk factors recognised for sex offenders. CSAP wisely identify an additional list of generic protective risk factors which frame the skill areas which treatment might most relevantly address:

- cognitive competencies (e.g. intelligence, future planning; pro-social attitudes and feelings; social models that encourage constructive coping; strong social or family bonds and support from non-deviant individuals; healthy beliefs and clear standard of behaviour; social competencies and problem-solving skills; experiences of self-efficacy and adequate self-concept; belief that change is possible; commitment to avoiding re-offending.

4. **Effective Methods** There must be evidence that the treatment methods used are likely to have an impact on the targeted dynamic risk factors. Simply put, does it work and do you have the evidence to prove it?

5. **Skill Orientated** The programme must facilitate the learning of skills that will assist participants in avoiding criminal activities and facilitate their involvement in legitimate pursuits. The skills need to be defined and demonstrably relevant.

6. **Sequencing, Intensity and Duration** Applicants for accreditation must show that the amount of treatment provided is linked to the needs of the participants and that the intensity, duration and, where necessary, sequencing of the phases of the treatment are adaptable to different participant needs.

7. **Engagement and Motivation** Successful programmes must show how motivation is assessed pre-programme, attendance and completion rates must be recorded with reasons for non-completion, and efforts made to encourage active participation.

8. **Continuity of Programmes and Services** This is essentially to encourage the overall management of the offender both during and after the treatment programme in order to ensure a smooth transition, e.g. back to another prison, and to maintain progress.

9. **Maintaining Integrity** There must be provision to monitor how well the programme functions, and a system to modify aspects of it that are not performing as expected. Three aspects of the programme need particular attention: supporting conditions, programme integrity and treatment integrity. The accreditation criteria provide detailed specifications for each of these. Treatment integrity is one of the most vital aspects and the requirements include:
   - details of the way in which treatment supervision takes place to ensure compliance with the programme manual and the competent use of specific techniques;
   - an account of methods to ensure proper use of participant inclusion and exclusion criteria;
   - a description of how the treatment style of staff is monitored, including their sensitivity to the diversity and past and current life experiences of participants; and
   - details of how circumstances or activities that might interfere with treatment are detected and managed.

The audits conducted by the Community of Communities (C of C) are intended to address these aspects of the treatment regime in the DTCs:

10. **Ongoing Evaluation** Applications are required to include an evaluation plan which should as a minimum include an assessment of:
    - the demographic, previous criminal history and clinical characteristics of participants and those not accepted onto the programme;
    - changes in the dynamic risk factors targeted by the programme; and
    - over the longer term, a reconviction study which provides any existing evaluation results in addition to a plan for future ongoing evaluation.

The process of accreditation was first instigated in 1999, when the Offending Behaviour Programmes Unit within HM Prison Service commissioned the Association of Therapeutic Communities (ATC) to develop a method of accreditation for TCs. Dovegate TC was required to provide a Submission Document summarising the entire programme proposals, as well as manuals covering theory, the programme, training, assessment and evaluation, and management and operational matters. Given accreditation in 2004, the ongoing standards of therapy in Dovegate are subject to the bi-annual audits conducted independently on behalf of the National Offender Management Service (NOMS) and the Royal College of Psychiatrists review team working jointly with the ATC.

The Community of Communities Joint-Audit Process

The Correctional Services Accreditation Panel (CSAP) does not conduct audits of DTCs directly. They are the responsibility of the Community of Communities (C of C), an "international standards-based quality improvement network for therapeutic communities". Set up in 2002, the C of C provides audits and accreditation for TCs created and agreed by network members and delivered through a system of self-review and peer-review. The DTCs in prisons are accredited offender behaviour programmes and as such must be compliant with the core model agreed by CSAP in 2007. Funding was initially with a start-up grant from the Community Fund, but is now from NOMS. The ATC had been concerned with developing some form of accreditation since the mid-1990s given the growing culture of statutory inspections and quality monitoring of treatment programmes generally.

There is a clear determination to identify and standardise essential aspects of a therapeutic regime which can then be maintained via a programme of bi-annual audits conducted by people who work within TCs both within and outside prisons.

This process is called the National Audit of DTCs. Every two years, the Royal College of Psychiatrists' Research Unit, on behalf of the C of C and the Association of Therapeutic Communities (ATC), conducts a cycle of joint reviews and audits of those DTCs which are based in prisons. After an initial improvement in standards in the first two years, performance declined in 2006-7, although all 12 DTCs were assessed as compliant with the accredited core model. An audit completed in March 2010 was accepted by CSAP in May 2010. It noted improvement in all the DTCs which had struggled, combined with the maintenance of high levels in the others to the overall credit of DTCs in prison.

Keeping Up Standards

There are a number of recognised ways in which the standards of therapy in the DTCs are checked and maintained. First among these is the bi-annual audits conducted by the C of C and Research Unit of the Royal College of Psychiatrists. At the original time of writing, the most recent audit of DTCs including Dovegate was the National Report for 2009-2010, which was approved by CSAP in May 2010. The good news was as seen in Table 8.1, where all the four TCs and the Assessment Unit had overall scores above the minimum threshold set of 60% compliance for each of the review sections of Institutional Support, Treatment and Management Integrity, Continuity and Resettlement and Quality of Delivery, and 70% overall.

Dovegate Camelot TC's overall performance had "improved enormously" since the last audit when it had fallen below the minimum standard. The report asserted that:

> Dovegate had been restructured and reclassified locally as a therapeutic prison. This development caused concern and had been raised with the prison with the result that the term therapeutic communities was reinstated for the wings.

The National Joint-Review Report of Democratic Therapeutic Communities in Prison for 2009-2010 concluded that all of the 12 DTCs (which include two assessment units) in prison were assessed as compliant with the accredited core model. The two that had failed in the 2007-2008 cycle were Dovegate TCA, which scored 42% in Continuity and Resettlement and 57% overall, and Dovegate TCC with 46% and 60%, when Dovegate TCs overall "experienced their poorest year so far".

TCs performed best in the Quality of Delivery section, with eight scoring 89% or above, a significant achievement which compares "favourably with those using the same approach outside the prison setting (the C of C audits a large number of non-prison DTCs as well). It is worth emphasising that between the earlier and later audits, there were significant improvements across the board for Dovegate and that all the DTCs are now at or above the compliance levels.

The Royal College of Psychiatrists/C of C audit team published their National Interim Report for 2010-2011 at the end of July 2011. This shows that there are 17 TCs now audited: 11 DTCs (i.e. at Grendon (four), Dovegate (four), Gartree, Blundeston and Send); two DTC Assessment Units (Grendon and Dovegate), and four Hierarchical TCs for drug offenders (first audit). See further the encouraging data reproduced in *Appendix 3*.

It is very probable that the systemic improvement at Dovegate is directly attributable to the work of the third director of Dovegate TC, Ray Duckworth and his team (see generally *Chapter 8*). Dovegate had experienced a period of disruption between 2006 and late-2008 when the founding director of therapy, Roland Woodward, had left, an event that was followed by a period of uncertainty and relative instability. It is arguable that part of the problem was a legacy of mistrust and dissent as between the main prison and the much smaller TC. Director Duckworth had the unique advantage of coming across from the main prison with an operational background but a determination to learn as much as he possibly could about TCs in as short a period as possible. A later C of C audit, the one confirmed by CSAP representatives in May 2010 (above), indicated that, despite a decrease in available time for therapy and association, budget reductions across-the-board and continuing problems with staff presence and continuity in core therapy groups, all prison TCs maintained or increased their performance. Of most relevance was the conclusion:

> *...significant improvement was shown across all HMP Dovegate TC. This impressive turnaround across HMP Dovegate is to be commended* [emphasis added].

What is clear from the latest figures for overall performance of TCs (2010-2011 interim cycle of audits: see *Appendix 3*) is that the TCs at Dovegate have significantly improved their performance overall, that Gartree continues to be one of, if not the, best DTC in the country, and that the DTCs at Grendon have declined, with three of the five now at or below the target level of 70% overall compliance with agreed standards. The concern of at least the first author of this book is that a chronic staffing problem at Grendon is having a serious effect on that prison's ability to deliver effective therapy. It has been a topic of discussion by the Grendon Steering Group during several recent sessions that significant numbers of uniformed staff on the communities there are opting-out of attending core therapy activities, creating growing pressure on the remaining staff to meet therapy commitments. This concern is confirmed by the audit's conclusion that, "Worryingly, all TCs at HMP Grendon, except the Assessment Unit, only partly met the standard requiring the TC to have enough staff members for the community to operate effectively". Again, the improvements in the Dovegate scores across-the-board be justifiably be attributed to the determination of the latest director Ray Duckworth to address the last round of audit findings and improve.

HM Inspectorate of Prisons

A full inspection of Dovegate TC took place in 2008. The summary conclusions of the inspectorate team included findings that:

* Though the therapeutic community within HMP Dovegate was generally safe and relationships were good, its therapeutic work was seriously undermined because it held too many prisoners who had dropped out of therapy, compounded by staffing and contractual issues.

- Resettlement strategy and services were underdeveloped, with a backlog in assessments, delays in parole reports and insufficient attention to the needs of lifers. Little was done to help therapy graduates sustain their learning when they moved on to other prisons.

Anne Owers, HM Chief Inspector of Prisons said:

The Inspectorate has been supportive of the small number of therapeutic communities in the prison system because they make an important contribution to managing serious and challenging prisoners. However, they are difficult to establish and sustain and require sufficient investment and senior management support.

She added, crucially:

Population pressures and a contract focused on filling beds rather than treatment integrity, compounded the problem, but with treatment standards having fallen along with staff morale, urgent action is now required by Serco and the National Offender Management Service to salvage what was previously an innovative unit [emphasis added].

The Director General of NOMS responded by referring to the improvements in reducing the numbers of prisoners out of therapy but still resident in Dovegate TCs , but there is no recorded response to the much more serious concerns expressed in the last quotation.

Internal Review of Democratic Therapeutic Communities

The part of the Ministry of Justice (MOJ) with responsibility for DTCs is called the Dangerous and Severe Personality Disorder (DSPD) Programme and DTC Unit. It is part of the Interventions and Substance Misuse Group (ISMG) of NOMS. This gives some idea of the bureaucratic nature of the organization and the target population for which HQ now consider DTCs to be most relevant. Given that DTC populations are now overwhelmingly life-sentenced prisoners with personality disorders, this is a defensible position.

The head of ISMG commissioned the DTC Unit to conduct a review of the then 12 DTCs in the prisons estate in November 2008. The terms of reference were to:

- clarify the role of TCs within the wider structure of offending behaviour programmes;

- make explicit the contribution of TCs to MOJ and ISMG objectives;

- consider the case for expansion, no change or reducing the number of TC places and their configuration; and

- identify the key areas for inclusion in the business plan and areas of work for strategic development over the next three to five years.

Before the publication of the review, Lord Bradley's independent review of people with mental health problems or learning disabilities in the CJS was published in April 2009.[1] This put back the internal review in order to consider the implications of three recommendations in Bradley:

- An evaluation of treatment options for prisoners with personality disorder, including current TCs in the prison estate.

- An evaluation of the DSPD programme to ensure it is able to address the level of need.

- In conjunction with other government departments, the Department of Health, NOMS and the National Health Service should develop an inter-departmental strategy for the management of all levels of personality disorder within both the health and criminal justice services reflecting the management of these individuals through custody and in the community.

---

1. For the report of this review, see dh.gov.uk/en/Publicationsandstatistics/Publications/PublicationsPolicyAndGuidance/DH_098694.

It is this last recommendation which may be the most significant. If it is interpreted to mean that the three departments collaborate on the management of personality disordered offenders and that responsibility for determining how treatment of such offenders is funded and managed centrally, then it is possible that the future of DTCs can be better secured against the apparently inexorable encroachment of a prison punishment and control mentality, which can then be checked.

It is worth recording that the measure by which the MOJ determines the seriousness of the offender's risk of reoffending is called the Offender Group Reconviction Scale—3rd version (OGRS3). This measure was applied to all TC prisoners on 1 January 2009. The mean score of the TC men residents was 50% compared with 48% for all cases in 2007/08. Another index used is called Criminogenic Need (CN). These measures include variables such as relationship problems, drug misuse, housing problems and attitudes to crime. The national CN score is 4.1 and the TC population mean was 5.4, with the highest being for those serving indeterminate sentence for public protection (IPPs), which was 6.2 compared with only 3.9 for non-IPP lifers.

The final version of the review of 2009 was submitted in February 2010 to the ISMG, which commissioned it. The report was conducted by the staff of the DSPD programme and the DTCs in Prisons Team, originally headed by Ed Willetts and latterly by Ian Goode, TC policy lead for NOMS. The review was only later released for public access and concluded:

> The evidence of effectiveness for DTCs has been built over 50 years. Published research indicates that they address a wide range of offender needs through reducing the risk of re-offending, and improving mental health and social functioning.

This is an extremely important conclusion and officially endorses the authors' own conviction that Dovegate and the other DTCs are the *proven* treatment programme of choice for personality disordered offenders. No other prison regime or treatment programme extant in the UK can match this record. A literature review of published research evidence for DTCs concluded:

- Meta-analyses and academic reviews have found the DTC model to be effective in reducing re-offending rates and, when compared to other treatments, to be especially effective for those with severe personality disorders.

- The longer someone stays in treatment the greater the degree of measurable improvement and the lower the likelihood that they will reoffend. The research suggests that, for many, to achieve the greatest treatment effect, a stay of at least 18 months is required.

- Psychometric test research has found positive change on a range of measures including hostility, neurotic symptoms, locus of control, impulsive feelings and mental health.

- Overall, fewer assaults, serious incidents and adjudications have been reported for those who have been through DTC treatment. Ex-residents are less likely to adhere to a negative prison culture. DTCs are thus often seen as helpful in maintaining good order and discipline in prisons and in facilitating prisoners to make constructive use of sentences.

- Research in a community setting confirms prison research elsewhere that a residential DTC experience is most profitably followed up with further treatment in the community. This is related to the known problems that patients and prisoners have with making the transition from the DTC/prison world to the outside world.

- Economic studies have found that although TC treatment can appear expensive compared to others, in the longer term it saves money year-on-year. This is because the additional costs of treatment are recovered from savings achieved once the offender has progressed from the DTC.

While many of these findings have been common knowledge in the TC fraternity for years, it is particularly important to see them summarised and agreed in an official review.

Therapeutic Integrity

Dovegate is the latest generation of DTC for serious offenders. In spite of having been created in the private sector and incorporating many innovations in offender treatment, the threats to therapeutic integrity from a variety of sources are of abiding concern. These concerns have been eloquently set out by Professor Elaine Player and Dr Elaine Genders in a paper for the *Howard Journal of Criminal Justice*.[2] In discussing the "incongruous cohabitation of a prison and a therapeutic community within a single establishment", they conclude that:

> The partnership between the two institutions is inevitably unequal and that, while the prison allows the TC a sphere of influence, penal power prevails whenever its institutional interests are threatened.

They rightly elucidate the fundamental, and possibly irreconcilable, differences between conventional prisons and TCs. Prisons are hierarchical and structured, regulated by external controls and have the primary objective of containing people who don't want to be there. TCs are collective, self-regulating and voluntary. So concerned were they about the erosion of Grendon's therapeutic primacy and the annual cycle of budget cuts, that the authors concluded:

> Our return to Grendon has left us in no doubt that the structural changes that have taken place over the last two decades have seriously challenged staff in their efforts to maintain the operation, authority and legitimacy of the therapeutic regime.

Genders and Player further argue that the therapeutic traditions of communalism and tolerance were a safeguard against the erosion stated, but concluded that:

---

2. "Therapy in Prison: Revisiting Grendon 20 Years On", *Howard Journal*, November 2010.

There comes a point where no amount of cultural commitment can compensate for the lack of staff time, the attrition of supervision, and the stagnation of post-therapeutic progression.

How then can we account for the C of C scores given Grendon and Dovegate, which seem to indicate that not only have they continued to maintain the minimum national agreed standards set for DTCs but are stronger across-the-board? The biggest question is whether audits are adequately assessing the actual strength and quality of the therapy taking place. Is it possible to get good marks on the audits and still fail to provide treatment strong enough to reduce the risk of re-offending? *Part II* of this chapter addresses many of these concerns.

Research

All of the published research on treatment efficacy concerning Dovegate TC to date has been conducted as the result of a contract agreed by Dovegate and the Department of Psychology at Surrey University under the direction of Professor Jennifer Brown. This contract was awarded as a result of an open process in which several universities submitted bids. By far the largest project was the londitudinal evaluation conducted between 2003 and 2008 to assess treatment outcome in relation to reconviction, social re-integration and psychological change. To quote the authors:

The original research specification particularly emphasised a wish to explore the nature of change in TC residents' behaviour, attitudes and psychological functioning, to find evidence of more productive and less conflictual behaviour during further imprisonment after leaving the TC and to ascertain risk reduction in re-offending after release.

The researchers devised a mixed method design of both quantitative and qualitative techniques, including repeated administration of a range of psychometric tests (many of which were already part of the core Dovegate assessment battery). These included the:

- Revised Gudjonsson Blame Attribution Inventory (GBAI-R)
- Psychological Inventory of Criminal Thinking Styles, Version 4
- Culture-free Self Esteem Inventory 2 (CFSEI-2)
- Hostility and Direction of Hostility Questionnaire (HDHQ)
- Inventory of Altered Self Capacities (IASC)
- University of Rhode Island Change Assessment Scale (URICA); and
- Cork Estrangement Scale (CES).

The results were provided in an executive summary under the heading "Key Findings" and were grouped in three aspects of "psychological and behavioural change within the TC"; psychometric change; focus groups and Card Sorts. The changes were recorded at six monthly intervals and the table is reproduced on the next page.

Reconvictions

The only published article on reconvictions for the Surrey research is Miller and Brown's "HMP Dovegate's Therapeutic Community: An Analysis of Reconviction Data"[3] The authors concluded that:

> Notwithstanding the problems with reconviction data (such as its incompleteness and the implications of types of offences implicated) we did analyse re-conviction rates.

Overall "the four year re-offending rate was 49.5% which is lower than that reported for Grendon". In fact, it isn't lower. Marshall found the four year cumulative reconviction rate for just over 700 Grendon leavers was 50%. In examining the analyses methodology, however, it would appear that the authors erroneously concluded that their sample of n=97 had been reconvicted at almost 50% in spite of the fact that they had only been released for an average of 19 months. The entire sample would have to have been at

---

3. Miller S and Brown J (2010). Article published in *Therapeutic Communities*, 31, 1, Spring.

1.4 Key findings

(I) Extent and process of psychological and behavioural change within the TC

Months	Psychometrics	Focus groups	Card sorts
Up to 6	• Little change but TC group at lower baseline starting point compared to a main prison sample	• Opening up new ways of thinking, realisation how difficult therapy is • Relationship ruptures • Sex offenders • "Phoney" residents • Staff organization • Questioning bona fide of therapy	• Avoidant/preoccupied attachment • Perception of TC as similar to other crime places • Different starting points with some able to reflect on past poor therapy relationships others more defended
6-12	• Decrease in dominance, gregariousness, and nurturance, increase in hostility, contemplation of change	• Getting answers • Importance of small groups • Relationship ruptures • Staff • Sex offenders • Power struggles	
12-18	• Increase in self-esteem • Decrease in hostility • Reversion in earlier improvements in affect regulation and inward hostility	• Increased understanding • Realisation of work to be done • Dealing with substance abuse • Relationship ruptures • Jail politics • Sex offenders • Phonies • Staff organization	• Optimism • Confusion • Engagement with TC • Struggle • Attempts to restructure key relationships
18-24	• Further increase in self-esteem. Drop in hostility, improvement in identity impairment, self-awareness and susceptibility to influence	• Insights • Maturing • Coming to terms with offending • Sense of belonging • Reciprocity • Tolerance • Relationship ruptures • Staff • Phonies • Out of therapy residents • Withdrawal from therapy	
24 plus	• Fluctuations in behaviour but more improvement in self-esteem and hostility but deceleration in rates of improvement		• Shifts in attachment styles • Seeing others' demands • Mutual/reciprocal relationships • TC shifts to non-CJS place • Crimes linked to consequences

1.4 Key Findings Table (from University of Surrey research)

risk for four years in order to be comparable. We couldn't find where in the article the entire sample had been at risk for that minimum time.

Comparing their reconviction rates favourably with those of Grendon is questionable because the original Grendon sample (see Cullen, 1993) was for a sample who had been *at risk, in other words, released,* for at least two years for all of them while it is unrecorded how many of the Dovegate sample of 94 had been released for the minimum equivalent and, in fact, most of those reconvicted (N = 44 or 48, or 91%) had been out less than one year. Equally, a sample of only 97 is too small to reach any conclusions with confidence (the Grendon research samples were Cullen N = 214; Marshall and Taylor N = 700 plus). It is reasonable to conclude therefore that not only are the conclusions open to doubt but the actual reconviction rates for the Dovegate sample, once they had been out for at least two years, might in fact be higher than for Grendon.

They also reported that three-quarters of the re-offending was for breaches of licence and "There were no reports of repeat violent offences and only one reported sex offence…" More surprising, however, is the statement that, after four years at risk of reconviction, the researchers assert that 75% of all "re-offending" (presumably they mean re-convictions; rates of re-offending are unknowable), were for breaches of licence. If this means what it seems to mean, then the types of behaviour involved in triggering the recalls *must* be listed. Being recalled on breach of licence is as much a preventative measure based on the perceived risk of re-offending as of actual crimes committed. The article continues:

> Re-offending rates are associated with length of time spent in Dovegate TC with longer periods in the TC associated with decreases in re-offending rates. Those spending less than six months in the TC were more likely and those spending over 18 months in the TC least likely to re-offend.

Again, there are no statistics to clarify this conclusion and nothing to say whether or not the differences reached statistical significance.

The first author of this work believes that the ultimate criterion against which DTCs in prisons must be judged is that of reconviction rates. It is not necessary (indeed it isn't ethically possible) to conduct a random controlled trial, where sufficiently large numbers of relevant prisoners are randomly assigned to either treatment, alternative or no-treatment groups. It is sufficient in my view to conduct carefully controlled matched samples comparing a range of relevant factors such as age, number and type of previous offences, current offence, psychiatric history, history of substance dependency/abuse etc. The research by Cullen (1994), Marshall (1997) and Taylor (2000) taken together constitute the best body of work that there is to establish a prison TC's efficacy, and these were based on Grendon samples from the 1980s.

These studies looked at reconviction rates for two, four and seven years respectively. The reason reconviction is the ultimate arbiter of treatment success is that members of the British public have a right to be protected from becoming the victims of criminals. It is insufficient to argue that the purpose of TCs is primarily to treat the individual's disorders of personality regardless of the subsequent relevance of that intervention to their risk of committing crimes in the future.

Discussion

This review of the measures in place for assessing DTCs generally and Dovegate specifically shows clearly and indisputably how thorough the process now is. As recently as 2000, none of these indices and standards existed. The only ways in which DTCs were assessed were either via HM Inspectorate of Prisons inspections or by individual efforts of internal psychologists or external academics. While this revolution in quality control and assessment is on balance a very good thing, it is not without its drawbacks. The C of C audit report of 2009-2010 confirms that Dovegate TC has achieved excellent scores across-the-board after the mixed and somewhat deteriorating marks from the previous full audit. This is a considerable achievement, especially when it is realised that it was done with fewer than two thirds of the total staff complement of Grendon and that the two TCs have roughly the same prisoner populations to deal with.

The history of Dovegate TC's first decade is a fascinating story of struggle, achievement, dissent and, more recently, revival. Seldom, if ever, in the history of the UK prison system has one establishment been so closely scrutinised.

We must however return to the original question: How do we know it actually works? What we do know is that the TC at Dovegate is accredited as effective by the C of C audits and the CSAP. We also know that, although there is some ambiguity in the research published to date, it seems there is substantive evidence that Dovegate is effective in improving interpersonal relationships for the residents and that reconviction rates are, according to the researchers, significantly lower than national rates. HM Chief Inspector of Prisons concluded in 2006 that:

> Dovegate TC remains a largely safe and well-controlled place with the impressive levels of peer support and self-management that distinguishes successful TCs. Reception and Induction were effective, bullying was under control, levels of self-harm were low, there was little evidence of drug misuse and little use of force and segregation . . . In a relatively short period of time, Dovegate TC has established itself as an important and effective contributor to the management of serious, long-term and challenging prisoners in England and Wales.

What is still unclear, however, is how Dovegate, or indeed any DTC regime, achieves these results. It is reasonable of course to conclude *à posteriori* that the consequences follow from the cumulative effects of being in a TC for a sufficient minimum period of time but it seems procedurally impossible to select out the relative contributions from any specific element or activity. What we are left with we should celebrate. What we know, we should appreciate and defend. There remain, however, vital questions concerning how best to match limited and relatively expensive resources to a particularly demanding and high-risk offender group.

II.   Effectiveness from the Clinician's Perspective.

> Guns don't kill people, it's people that kills people.
> Audits don't ensure quality; people ensure quality.
> Audits measure quantifiable targets relating to a craft.

Therapy is an art which is something else altogether.

In this time of financial stringency, the case for the complex and relatively expensive intervention of TCs has to be justified over and above offending behaviour programmes. Thus they are described as interventions that target severe offending in those with complex needs.

Whilst offending behaviour programmes address specific deficits in knowledge and behaviour, often using an educational approach, the psychodynamic and social element of the TC provides the groundwork in personality or at least relational change after which other skills can be learnt more effectively.

The analogy can be made with learning to drive a car. Offending behaviour programmes can be likened to a series of driving lessons in which an individual is taught to drive safely; however unless the individual wants to drive safely they are relatively useless. If somebody has decided that they either want to or don't care if they hurt somebody else or themselves, no number of driving lessons will make a difference.

TCs address the disturbance in an individual that makes him or her unconcerned about damage to self or others. This is not something that can be prescriptive. The first author has described the process of accreditation, the role of CSAP, audit and the C of C and looked at the hard facts of the designated outcomes. This part seeks to explore some of the difficulties with this approach and to describe how in HMP Dovegate it has worked out in practice.

Offences happen when an individual falls out of relationship — relationship with himself or herself, relationship with others or relationship with society. This may happen at an early stage in life or indeed that capacity may be absent altogether. Addressing offending behaviour therefore means addressing the absence or deficit in relationship and this is something that has to be done "in vivo" not "in vitro". TCs seek to provide a "corrective emotional experience" by which the individual learns to come into relationship with himself, his peers, authority, the community within which he lives, his family of origin and ultimately society (the community to which he or she will return).

It has been said that all of society's ills are related to the collective failure to mourn. Witness the outpouring of grief following the death of HRH

Princess Diana of Wales where it seemed the entire population of Britain mourned the passing of someone they had never known as an individual but who had come to represent something precious for them. People spoke of her in extremes, and then often found themselves led inexorably to their own experiences of loss, sometimes hidden for years; and in the re-experiencing of grief in the company of others, found a degree of companionship and healing.

Engagement with grief—for that which has been lost; for that which never was; and for that which has been destroyed—is not an event but a process, and it is individual. TCs seek to provide an environment in which this can happen. The early days of the TC movement recognised this, referring to the "Therapeutic Milieu" and "Milieu Therapy".

What *can* be measured is the quality of the environment that will allow a resident to engage with this process. The process itself *cannot* be measured or time-bounded. TCs are about relationships and it is through the medium of relationships that healing and therefore a reduction in offending behaviour can take place. It is only possible to commit an offence when the "victim" is used or seen as an object and as a means of gratifying a need or providing something for the offender. Once the offender sees the victim as a person with needs and desires similar to himself or herself it becomes impossible to offend, providing they choose to remain conscious and aware of the other.

TCs emphasise an individual and flexible approach within an overall structure. They do not seek to prescribe how long an intervention should take (how long is the grieving process?); they do not seek to prescribe the method by which somebody may change (has the most useful aspect been a relationship with a group member, a benign environment, feedback or the process of reflection?); and their holistic approach means that if during therapy an area of distress or disturbance arises it can be dealt with as part of the holistic nature of therapy within the familiar, containing and supporting community structure.

The nature of conventional programmes requires them to target one criminogenic need at a time, so that they are dealt with sequentially rather than recognising their inter-relatedness. Therapeutic learning is not linear but follows a psychological developmental model reflecting physical growth. Work is not seen as a linear process but makes use of the analogy of the spiral, coming round to the repeating patterns again and again, but from a different standpoint and view, rather than enrolment in another course, possibly in a different prison at a different time.

Again it is a process not an event. It may take as long as a year to establish a sound working therapeutic alliance. Trust is an issue, in part because of the severe trauma that has often occurred in the early years of many of the residents, but also because of learned experience in the prison environment itself.

Emphasis is placed on therapy occurring "24/7" and capitalising on the moment. Informal interaction can happen at any time, but most usually takes place in the evenings and at weekends when members, including staff, cook, eat and play together.

By the end of their time in therapy prisoners often say, "I have discovered who I truly am". This is a difficult thing to measure! Conformity of progress is equally intangible:

> The sound part of individuality, of character, is firmly rooted in the group and wholly approved by it—like a tree—the firmer it takes root the freer it can display its individual characteristic beauty above ground.[4]

How can relationship be prescribed? A recent workshop held by the Community of Communities (C of C) revisited the Core Values.[5]

1. Healthy attachment is a developmental requirement for all human beings, and should be seen as a basic human right.
2. A safe and supportive environment is required for an individual to develop, to grow, or to change.
3. People need to feel respected and valued by others to be healthy.
4. Everybody is unique and nobody should be defined or described by their problems alone.
5. All behaviour has meaning and represents communication which deserves understanding.

---

4. *Introduction to Group Analytic Therapy* (1983), Foulkes S H, Karnac Books.
5. Core Values Informing Core Standards. Working Document for Peer Review 2008. Community of Communities; Royal College of Psychiatrists.

6. Personal well-being arises from one's ability to develop relationships which recognise mutual need.

7. Understanding how you relate to others and how others relate to you leads to better intimate, family, social and working relationships.

8. Ability to influence one's environment and relationships is necessary for personal well-being. Being involved in decision-making is required for shared participation, responsibility, and ownership.

9. There is not always a right answer and it is often useful for individuals, groups and larger organizations to reflect rather than act immediately.

10. Positive and negative experiences are necessary for healthy development of individuals, groups and the community.

11. Each individual has responsibility to the group, and the group in turn has collective responsibility to all individuals in it.

It also confirmed that this is "an holistic approach, relying on the community, the existence of an inner wisdom and healer, the principle of self-actualisation and trusting the process including values such as equality, respect, creativity and play".

These are idealistic core standards which do not readily lend themselves to measurement. They can be inferred by observation however and it is this aspect that the C of C seeks to capture with its peer group visits and informal learning-centred approach of support and quality development rather than inspection.

HM Prison Service with its need for black and white thinking and measurable outcomes has devised a separate set of standards that can be audited in a more conventional sense and do have the flavour of an inspection. When a recent episode related to the realisation that hard drugs were being distributed around the TC it would have been possible to resort to cell searches, drug dogs, etc. Alternatively pressure and manipulation could have been placed on individuals to reveal their sources. Instead, trusting the process, the staff took the problem to the community and over a period of several months of discussion, involving every member on an individual and group level, new boundaries were put in place, new support mechanisms were introduced and the TC once again became (relatively) drug-free. Thus from:

- a TC perspective this was a "success". Members of the community had engaged with the problem, overcoming prison culture, taking responsibility, risking disclosure and planning and agreeing new "norms". They were required to make difficult decisions, balancing competing loyalties, expressing concern for one another, feeling guilt in many cases, recognising instances of collusion and denial. All of these were related back to [the residents'] index offences on an individual basis;

- a more conventional prison point of view it was a time of great tension. "What is this TC doing about the drug problem?", "Has security been informed?", "Who has been deselected" and "Who has been nicked?" were frequently asked questions; and

- an audit point of view how would this have been seen? It may have shown itself in the C of C standards resulting in a positive or negative comment depending on the views of the visiting community. Prison audit standards would have recorded it as a failure to maintain a safe environment.

The final "score" would have depended on the thoroughness with which it had all been documented.

One of the most important meetings on the TC is the staff team group, which meets after every group or community meeting. This is for reflection, support, clarification, recording and planning. Most importantly, it ensures the safety and integrity of the community. Dynamics in the community are mirrored in the staff team and vice versa—a phenomenon known as parallel process. Change in the dynamic of one can precipitate change in the dynamic of the other. This phenomenon is so powerful that, whenever there is disruption in the community, the staff first check their own interactions and furthermore "treatment" of the staff "condition" amounts to "treatment" of the community as a whole as well as the individuals within it.

The community was becoming increasingly impatient with *Jim*,[6] who persistently refused to join in regular activities and sat apparently impervious to all attempts at engagement. Simultaneously the staff team was attempting

---

6. Names have been changed.

to reintegrate an officer who had had a period of depression and anxiety, leaving him reluctant to undertake face-to-face duties with prisoners. A role was found for him that involved essential paperwork so that he recovered his sense of usefulness. At the same time he was encouraged to re-engage with groups but with another staff member present until he was able to take his full place in the team once more. *Jim* meantime began to undertake more taxing tasks around the community, eventually becoming "social secretary" and finally speaking in groups.

Sometimes however the process is instinctive. *Andrew*, a resident of another community for young offenders, was so alienated that he referred to himself as a visitor from another planet, and when questioned about anything would reply "life is a purple egg". The community simply "held him" for several months until a weekend treasure hunt was organized, in which each member found their own personalised treasure via a series of riddles. *Andrew* wept when he found his treasure — a purple chicken. There is not as yet a standard relating to chickens, purple or otherwise, in the audit.

With the uncovering of original trauma and core wounding, healing takes place through the group and community process. It has three aspects — the first is the recapitulation of the family group which represents the psychodynamic element of treatment; the second is resocialisation through challenge and reality-testing in the community; the third is the measurement of progress relating to risk through offence paralleling behaviour. This latter process assumes that the offence was committed because of some personality characteristic; and that this characteristic will show itself in small ways on a day-to-day basis and is therefore available for examination and change.

It is often the case that, at the start of therapy, prisoners have little sense of empathy for their primary victim even if that victim has lost his or her life. This can be very difficult for staff to understand, as it seems that if they are guilty about nothing else, they could surely be guilty about that.

However, once there is a full engagement with therapy the uncovering begins of often-severe early trauma, which has resulted in an extreme and faulty sense of responsibility. It is now commonly accepted that victims of sexual abuse, like victims of rape, can feel responsible for failing to put an end to it. Similarly, young children who have witnessed physical violence by one family member towards another weaker member, often, though not

233

exclusively, mothers, can feel responsible for failing to prevent it. Perhaps the most difficult thing is to experience repeated sexual abuse from mothers, a situation that is compounded during their son's adolescence. Abuse, sexual and physical, runs in families; many are victims of multiple abuse, have been part of paedophile rings, forced to take part in sexual acts with animals and to perpetrate them themselves.

The instinctive drive and need for love has sometimes led them to be at least in part willing participants; for this they cannot forgive themselves. Freud[7] noted that "crime is committed by individuals with tremendous unconscious guilt and overdeveloped super-egos who seek to be caught and punished".

Thus by the time they come to commit the index offence they already believe themselves to be beyond redemption, if, that is, they think about it at all. Most likely the fear, desperation and yearning has been repressed either by psychological mechanisms or with the help of drink and drugs or other acting-out. Many cope by repetitive self-harm or externalising of aggression on to others. The first task therefore is to enable the prisoner to remember, on a felt level as opposed to simple intellectual awareness, the shut off pain that was previously denied. He does this by re-experiencing it through the telling of his story to his group members, most of whom have been through something similar. In this way he is enabled to readopt, i.e. to make part of himself again the shut off experiences. At this stage there is often explosive anger or desolation.

Mike had had a succession of gruelling community meetings over the way he carried out his job on the servery. Having a mild version of Asperger's Syndrome he had laid down strict criteria about who was allowed second helpings and in what rotation. The community was demanding some flexibility on his part. The sense of hostility was growing in the room and Mike was becoming progressively more alienated. Always prone to stuttering, his desperate attempts to express himself went unheard by what had been until recently a remarkably patient and accepting community.

---

7.   Freud S (1961), *Collected Papers*, "Criminality From a Sense of Guilt", Hogarth Press. (originally published in 1916).

Two staff members spoke to him after the meeting; there was initial resistance and mild outrage followed by a sudden collapse. They were presented with a six-year-old boy in the body of a 30-year-old-man. He was sobbing with fresh feelings of abandonment at his exclusion from his family (a recovered memory), who despite all his attempts had ignored him, though not his brother, and belittled his difficulties at school, describing him as useless. His stutter now gone, he choked out his memory of his parents "forgetting" to collect him, leaving him to be beaten by bullies and find his own way home. Once there he found the house deserted and a note on the door informing him he was now to live with his aunt.

This was not the time for interpretation. He was excused work and put to bed with a cup of tea. Other prisoners visited, bringing small gifts—a piece of cake, some tobacco, an envelope with a stamp on it. He remained one of this family—a corrective emotional experience.

Before they can begin to feel remorse for their latest victims, residents need to learn to forgive themselves for these original offences, some of which have occurred in fact and some only in their minds. The disentangling of responsibility where one child has been forced to perpetrate a sexual act on another younger child is complex, and is probably impossible on a purely factual level.

The criminal feels a persecutory or oppressive guilt that is extremely harsh. Faced with such horrendous judgement or attack he can only conceive of defending himself by mounting an equally violent assault on some enemy and thus project his persecutory violence into [others].[8]

The moment he realises exactly what he has done to others and experiences true remorse, which in effect is the search for forgiveness, he opens himself to the pain and the damage that has been done to him. This in turn engenders another cycle of rage and despair.

8. "A Schema for the Transition from Cruel Object to Tender Object Relations among Drug Users in a Prison Therapeutic Community", Ronald Doctor, Consultant Psychiatrist in Psychotherapy and Clinical Director West London Mental Health NHS Trust, in *Dynamic Security: The Democratic Therapeutic Community in Prison* (2007), Parker M (ed), London and Philadelphia: Jessica Kingsley Publishers.

In moving from false victimhood as a defence, he has to reclaim the offender in himself and thereby lay himself open again to the victim within himself. The progress is not linear. He must identify first with the offender and then disidentify, then identify with his own victimhood and disidentify and so on again and again. Reclaiming themselves as offenders allows them, ironically, to identify with the experiences of their external perpetrators (generating forgiveness) and to do this by reclaiming their own victimhood as opposed to using their victim status as an excuse to offend.

Yalom describes "real" guilt as flowing from an actual transgression against another. Neurotic guilt, he says, emanates from imagined transgressions against others, ancient and modern taboos or parental or social tribunals.

He describes existential guilt as "being guilty of transgression against oneself". No longer, he says, can the individual comfortably rely on such alibis as "I didn't mean it", "It was an accident" or "I couldn't help it". He describes such guilt as being intimately related to possibility and potential, describing it as a call that brings one back to facing one's authentic mode of being. The move from neurotic to existential guilt, via the real guilt is the work of the therapeutic process.

All of the TCs in prisons have struggled with this tension between a measurable approach to delivery and standards, and a flexible interactive approach to therapy as described above. Now that there is a consensus on the basic structures and requirements for a DTC to be described as functioning as such, the time has come to consider how the process and content of the therapeutic interactions may best be ensured. In Dovegate this was first understood as a mammoth task during the "Roland era", and it was understood that the accreditation and audit standards came into being after the success of the bid. Therefore Dovegate TC was never staffed in such a way as to make the audit standards achievable within the context of a lively and active therapeutic regime. It functioned, for audit purposes, as "just good enough", and there was a belief at that time that perhaps a low or intermediate score could be used to engineer a revisiting of the original contract.

During the "David years" the collective eye was taken off the audit ball altogether, resulting in frighteningly low scores. It is questionable, however, whether or not these low scores accurately reflected communities that were failing or otherwise other than in (the equally important) institutional terms. David's thrust was to move away from the harsh offending behaviour approach and introduce more of the groundwork of relationship — "the tilling of the soil" — thus emphasis was placed on the understanding that behaviour has meaning and tolerance, and the core but harder to measure values moved more centre stage. The absence of hard results was clearly not acceptable from the point of view of the authorities or of the customer and the future of Dovegate began to be questioned.

Ray Duckworth's arrival brought with it a pragmatic approach from an operational point of view that meant that those aspects that were measurable could and should be delivered. Audit reports were examined with a fine toothcomb and protocols put into place so that in future the standards could be met. One of the first things he did was to appoint a senior administrative officer, Hannah Gordon, who had sole responsibility for the collation of statistics and the production of systems to engender them. From this it rapidly became possible to see, from an audit point of view, what was being done, what needed to be done, and what information was required to evidence it.

The collation of this evidence, from being the responsibility of the therapy managers, now fell to Hannah and her team, resulting in a quick and efficient ongoing audit of the necessary parameters — for example the production of end of therapy reports. This resulted in a dramatic increase and improvement in scores, which was met with celebration and relief all round. There is no doubt that since this approach has been adopted Dovegate TCs are far more efficient and can be seen to be so and it is evident that the required standards are being met as described in *Part I* of this chapter.

The result has been a dramatic increase in self-esteem in individuals, staff and residents and in communities as a whole. It has also increased the sense of value that residents have for their communities as being places that are worth belonging to and that can give them a sense of pride and achievement.

At the same time as the audit standards were being attended to there was a revision of the way in which risk factors were described and measured. With the penchant of HM Prison Service for the literal, rather than that evolving out of long-term observation of an individual, risk factors were now designed on the basis of examples given in the accreditation manuals and a historical and psychological/criminological basis in the Assessment Unit.

A prisoner would now emerge from the Assessment Unit with a list of perhaps as many as 20 risk factors when he arrived on the TC. Some of these were clearly unrelated to his case. Furthermore, some pertinent risk factors (because they had not been included in the examples) were left out altogether. Thus the measurement of risk became something that was part of the audit standards rather than anything that related to a particular prisoner and his crime: an example of unintended consequences! It also meant a huge increase in the required amount of recording.

All prison TCs had recognised that a major area of weakness was the lack of production of useful end of therapy reports that related to risk as well as the rather softer targets such as motivation, engagement and a sense of well-being. However, in order to tighten up the format and usefulness of these reports, more appropriate recording, particularly in relation to risk, was necessary. The emphasis on what could and could not be measured in relation to over 20 risk factors for each of 40 individuals, meant that in one community *the entire period available for post groups was devoted to recording alone*: a true example of "the letter killeth!"

In "T-Cat Training"[9] this author, in the company of others, emphasises that the most important meeting in a TC is the one that happens for the staff team after all groups and community meetings. As described above, it is here that parallel process can be examined and used to diagnose issues on the community. Detoxification of pathological projections can take place, planning of therapy and groups for the future can occur, but most of all the safety of the community and its individual members, staff and residents, is enshrined.

The abandonment of this time in favour of recording not only put the community itself at risk but obviated the whole process of the community. The fact that it could happen is a consequence of the lack of experience of the therapy managers and the climate in Dovegate at the time, which was that of "produce the goods and be seen to do so!"

Whilst Ray's arrival had rescued the TC from a watery demise within the mists of soft targets and psychodynamic theory, his lack of understanding

---

9. This refers to Therapeutic Community Accredited Training, designed for DTCs in prisons. It is accredited by the Correctional Services Accreditation Panel (CSAP) as part of the core manuals.

and experience in the TC meant that they were at risk of losing the essence of communities altogether—they went from one extreme to the other.

This lack was compounded by an absence of training for the therapy managers. The, by now, oppressive view that the TC needed to be brought under the wing of the main prison (and had to be properly operationalised), and the use of standard performance management techniques rather than DTC discussion, meant that such understanding as was available tended to go underground and there was a sense that it was dangerous to express a contrary view.

The arrival of a clinical lead, and the enthusiasm (and relief) with which Ray embraced the experiential aspect of learning about TCs suggested that this phase was to be short-lived, and already TCs in Dovegate are beginning to return to a proper balance between operational and therapeutic need.

The other aspect that can be missed in an audit/outcome-orientated approach is that therapy is about enabling the "graduate" to be able to make free and informed choices without someone always looking over his shoulder (without this in terms of risk it would be impossible for anyone ever to be released). In other words it is about giving people choice and free will. To do this, we must acknowledge that sometimes they will make choices with which we disagree and that this will be reflected badly in the statistics.

A young man spent some years in institutions during which he was exposed to therapeutic input of one kind or another. This was sufficiently powerful for him that in his mid-20s he began, during a later sentence of five years, to reflect on what he had learned. He was sufficiently moved to make changes and ultimately became a probation officer progressing to the rank of senior. Sadly, years later, he commented, "I am thinking of going back to crime" giving as his reason "you meet more authentic people there".

It has already been said that one of the things that is needed is the internalisation of authority and the development of the capacity to make free and independent choices. If this is truly the case then any community must recognise that some of the choices that will be made will not be those that the therapists would desire. This does not mean that therapy is a failure in terms of personal development although in terms of modifying offending behaviour it may be. How can this then be audited in such a way as not to punish a community because of an "aberrant success", or worse, inducing in the therapists a form of covert control? At least the overt control of the prison system can be recognised and potentially resisted. Covert control including transferential issues and powerful primitive needs is subtler but has similar potential for abuse.

If a simple alteration of behaviour is required, it may be more honest and authentic to consider the more extreme versions of behavioural modification, although it is likely that these would transgress human rights. At least however prisoners would know what they were signing up for. If they are to be "modified through manipulation" however it is a potentially dangerous path and this is where a sole emphasis on offending behaviour has its dangers.

As described in *Part 1* of this chapter, when Dovegate was set up the requirement to undertake some innovative and evaluative research was built into the bid and money was ring-fenced for this. It was clearly hoped that a sound comparative study between Dovegate and Grendon would be possible, possibly with the rather cynical subtext that if the results were "good enough", this would provide a lever to reduce staffing in the public sector to match that of the private sector.

In fact the two prisons did not have a matched population. Grendon had always taken those with a diagnosis of personality disorder, and in its early years this was a criterion for referral. A number of applicants who would today be classified as psychopathic were an accepted proportion. Dovegate, following the research available at that time, excluded those who scored highly on the psychopathy checklist revised (PCL-R).

Subsequently, due to financially straightened circumstances, Grendon actively engaged in seeking to provide a "step down" facility for the DSPD programme. Although in the event no one was accepted from a DSPD unit, Grendon became known as somewhere that would consider this difficult to place group of prisoners, and actively marketed itself as having the expertise to deal with them. It also began to speak of its *raison d'etre* as including the provision of a place of humane treatment for exceptionally difficult prisoners, without necessarily hoping to impact on offending behaviour or progression towards release.

Although the accreditation documents suggest a maximum number of high psychopathy scorers as being not more than 25% of any one community, Grendon has in fairly recent times had nearly 50% on each wing. Thus the discrepancy between the two populations increased still further.

Neither Dovegate nor Grendon have sufficient resources to allow for each individual to be tested in full; both establishments use instead the behavioural checklist which has cross validity with the PCL-R.

As described elsewhere in this book, the research project for Dovegate went out to tender and the bid was won by Surrey University, based in part on their innovative approach and the objective nature of their position being apparently uncompromised by an agenda that actively favoured TCs. This research was longitudinal and in addition to conventional parameters such as reconviction and resettlement it also looked at attachment style, and self-esteem using techniques such as drama and dance.

The earlier part of that study looked at factors related to dropout, finding a significantly higher risk of dropout or deselection from therapy in those who had a previous psychiatric history.

Professor Jennifer Brown who headed the project has summarised the results of the research as follows:

The project lasted from June 2002–July 2008 and included:

- assessment, audit outcomes and an evaluation of the treatment model; and
- a longitudinal evaluation, looking at treatment outcome in relation to:
  - reconviction
  - social reintegration
  - psychological change including: psychological/emotional functioning; anxiety; depression; self-esteem; and personal distress.

Surrey University found in follow-up interviews that self-esteem continued to increase after leaving. Alongside this, increased guilt, less hostility to others, reduced adjudications and offending were found. These results are commented upon in *Part 1* of this chapter. The researchers also looked at insecure/avoidant relating in the form of attachment styles measuring these at two different points in the resident's stay:

- dismissive
- fearful/avoidant
- preoccupied
- secure.

The measurements showed that:

- initially 13% had a dismissive attachment style, subsequently reduced to 8%;
- fearful/avoidant traits were reduced from 23% to 8%;
- preoccupied traits increased slightly from 25% to 27%; and
- secure attachment styles increased from 17% to 27%.

They commented on preoccupied attachment style:

- Can this suggest that whilst other attachment styles altered in "expected" ways, that an individual's preoccupation with regards to attachment remains a core principle of human relationships?
- More research is required to identify whether this attachment shifted from antisocial attachment (gang/subculture) to pro-social attachments (family/probation/society).

Following the theme touched upon in the section above, however, what about the view from the men? Some comments on their experiences given by residents in HMP Dovegate TC were as follows:

My experience on TP is that I can be myself and not put on a front.

I've been in out of prison since 1974 and have done over 33 years behind the door in nearly every prison and for the first time I can talk to people and staff about anything and I feel safe doing so.

I've never been on a TC before and I wish I had done so years ago, the best things are talking and listening to others and giving feedback and being myself.

I would recommend this to anyone who wants to change and live their life another way.

My sister said it has helped me by talking about things I've never spoken about in years.

It has been a massive help with personal issues.

The best thing about it for me has been working through my mental health issues and learning about these with the help of the community.

The experience is challenging but rewarding.

I have had two deaths in my family since I came here and I found the support and encouragement from staff and residents overwhelming.

In previous interventions I only looked at addiction issues—the TC looks at the bigger picture.

It is good to know that others believe we can be better people—we are so used to being told that we are worthless.

I'm glad I decided to come here it has made me look at myself and I stop justifying what I did and I'm more aware of how my behaviour affects others.

These are the softer targets and are not measurable in any quantifiable ways. Current psychotherapeutic research looks at qualitative and socio-demographic and ethnological approaches but these have yet to be embraced by HM Prison Service and in particular by those engaged in commissioning offending behaviour interventions for prisoners.

The powerful experiences related above would be unlikely to show up in any conventional research project. Nevertheless they are pertinent to risk—it is already known that good relationships have a protective effect in relation to reoffending; good relationships depend on a healthy attachment and positive self-esteem. Where they show most clearly will be in the attachment style and work on self-esteem elucidated by Surrey University.

Genders[10] suggests three types or levels of measure might be used to define successful outcome. These are similar to those decided upon by Surrey University. The first is increased self-esteem or a reduction in feelings of isolation or alienation, already parameters that have been shown to be improved by time in Dovegate TC. She makes the point however that while such changes might be beneficial to the individual involved, they have tended to be considered as precursors of behavioural change rather than as hard performance measures themselves.

The second measure, she suggests, is behavioural change in prison, and the third the direction or abatement of criminal activity after release.

There has long been debate about how to isolate the effect of therapy from other potential influences, and how to "distil" the "active ingredient" in the TC from other ancillary factors. This aim feels like searching for "Fools Gold". TCs are an holistic rather than a targeted intervention and this is part of their value. Human beings and their relationships are complex; targeting one area (for example reoffending) may result in imbalance and an increase in symptomology in another area.

The early experiments in taking young teenagers into the most frightening prisons in America did indeed result in a dramatic drop in offences committed by those involved. However a more rigorous investigation into the long-term effect showed that although these youngsters were not committing offences, the level of other disturbance such as social isolation, family abuse and mild psychiatric disorder had increased.[11] A bit like tightening only one of the four nuts on a wheel, screwing the offending behaviour nut down tight may not guarantee a more balanced or less dangerous individual.

10. "Legitimacy, Accountability and Private Prisons", Genders E, *Punishment and Society*, July 2002, vol. 4, No.3, 285-303.
11. "Scared Straight" (1978) was a documentary directed by Arnold Shapiro. Illustrations of psychological disturbance are contained in the film. In 2003, Petrosini undertook a Cochrane review, published in the annals of the American Academy of Political and Social Science (September 2003, vol. 589, No1) leading A J Schembri, secretary to the Florida Department of Juvenile Justice in his introduction to the White Paper "'Scared Straight and Other Juvenile Awareness Programmes" (August 2006) to write: "the empirical findings illustrate scared straight and deterrence orientated programmes to be not only damaging to the youth, but also detrimental to society, as they increase the victimisation rate for the general population by increasing the offence rate of participants".

Unless the "ground" of the personality has been reworked, the potential to damage others may remain and may not be recognised until it is too late, e.g. in the subtle abuse and manipulation of family members.

This is not to decry the urgent need for ongoing research into the effects as well as the effectiveness of TCs in prison and outside of it. One of the most desperate needs is for a cost-offset study.

The Central Research Group for DTCs is made up of a representative from each DTC and it coordinates and suggests direction for research. Dovegate is in the position of being able to commission its own research although financially it may have to rely on the help of student placements in the future; the opportunity for comparative studies remains a possibility. These have a natural place within the work of the C of C and their audit results.

Even without the envisioned possibilities for a comparative study between Dovegate and Grendon, the possibilities for comparison internally between the communities in Dovegate itself remains. This would require an enlightened view from the rest of the prison, involving tolerance of short term "problems" for long term gain and the possibility of comparing communities with differing degrees of specialist input or additional cognitive programmes.

A Note on Differing Perspectives

The two parts of this chapter are written from quite different perspectives, just as this book is co-authored by on the one hand a forensic psychologist (Eric Cullen) and on the other a psychodynamic psychiatrist (Judith Mackenzie), so that the contents reflect the differences and tensions that are an essential part of a healthy TC. This is eloquently described by Mark Morris, who points out that:

> The community therapist holds a particular cultural contribution which is client centred. Thus the therapist's main interest is in the well-being of his or her patients. For the therapist the process of therapy is to free the patient from some of his overbearing personality difficulties so that their lives and future are a little less wretched. The assumption is that creating victims and offending is a symptom of the wretched lives that people have led and that if they can be helped a bit, if the personality

disorder can be treated a bit, then the alleviation of the symptoms of wretchedness will mean they have to make a few other people's lives less wretched. From this perspective, reducing reoffending is not the aim, but rather is a beneficial side-effect of the aim, which is to treat people who are suffering.[12]

He makes the point that it is not possible for the community therapist to hold this role together with the role of the forensic psychologist who's focus is the task of reducing reoffending:

The difference in training and culture leads to a discipline that is much more rooted in a positivist research approach for the clinical psychologist and the effect can sometimes be that actuarial indices are overvalued. Nevertheless it is an *essential* counterpoint to the therapist's empathetic position in relation to the offender. The specific task of the forensic psychologist is to maintain the *offending behaviour focus* of the treatment.

The balance retained between these two cultural contexts (and those of the other members of the multi-disciplinary team) is maintained by debate. There are risks in concentrating in either direction and the dilemma is similar to that engendered by (in the view of the second author) a mistaken attempt to treat both perpetrator and abuser of a particular offence, or two halves of a married couple.

This creative tension is mirrored in the different perspectives of research initiatives as illustrated by the consensus of methodology for future research into therapeutic communities at the Oxford Science Meeting held in April 2008.[13] This addressed the difficult problem of randomised controlled trials and after reviewing the evidence concluded that: "There is now sufficient data in the [personality disorder (PD)] field to design a programme of Randomised Control Studies [given that] the most promising treatment interventions for PD in use or currently in development [is] the TC model".

The same meeting also looked at the three most promising areas for further research under the headings: Outcome Measures, Indicators of Behaviour

---

12. Morris, M (2004) *Dangerous and Severe: Process, Programme and Person,* Jessica Kingsley.
13. Oxford Science Meeting for Therapeutic Communities held at St Hilda's College, March 31 to April 1, 2008.

and Personality Change; and Cost-offset Studies. If one believes in coincidence, then these three areas perfectly reflect the three different stances of the three directors of therapy described in *Chapter 8*, "The Three Wise Men".

What now brings it together, and which is new in terms of a cohesive approach is the change in attachment style and capacity recorded in the Surrey University study outlined above.

CHAPTER TEN

NEW LAMPS FOR OLD: THE FUTURE TCS IN PRISON

As a helmsman for the future, the first part of this final chapter about the future of Dovegate in particular, is fittingly left for Ray Duckworth, director of HM Prison Dovegate. We follow this in Part II with comments about the way forward and, in Part III, suggest a model for the future of prison TCs.

I.   Next Steps for Dovegate

Ray Duckworth[1]

Much of the future of Dovegate as a therapeutic prison (TP) is outlined in the 25-year contract between Serco[2] and the Ministry of Justice written back in 1999. Although having a contract does have its drawbacks with continuous revision and specific contractual measures which appear stifling and restrictive at times, in truth a contract is comforting in some ways. You always have a clear reference point for clarity at times when interpretation and understanding become blurred by opinion and conjecture.

In the current political climate where value for money, key performance targets and standardisation is the emphasis in measuring operational performance, it is somewhat comforting to have a signed and sealed agreement that provides Serco and Dovegate with peace of mind for the future. Sounds

---

1. © 2011 Ray Duckworth, who since January 2011 has been Director of Dovegate Prison providing strategic leadership to almost 600 managers and staff in both the main prison and Dovegate TC. Before that he was director of the TC for three years "as a fixer" of operational and clinical performance. During that time he also renegotiated the private sector contract, realising financial efficiency for reinvestment. From 1997, he undertook a range of senior responsibilities within Group 4 and Premier Prison Services Ltd/Serco, having previously worked in HM Prison Service at HM Young Offender Institutions Lancaster Farms and Feltham (where he started as a prison officer in 1986). Educated at Sunderland University and Keele University, he is also a director of a family venture providing a network of accommodation and support to 16 to 18-year-olds leaving care—where "the rewards are priceless".
2. One of the original joint venture partners: See *Chapter 10*.

good in theory and anyone naïve enough to believe in this idea is sadly delusional. Contracts can be and are modified and tinkered with by individuals who have a limited concept of what therapy is and aims to achieve. Hours are spent weighing up the financial benefits of an offending behaviour course that on the face of it spans a colossal 18-24 months. Basically the assessment is to determine the cost-benefits of such a lengthy intervention.

Indeed, contracts are moulded and re-written to adapt and improve delivery; they can also be modified to make financial savings if necessary. The whole service is currently being measured against standardised benchmarking processes which will no doubt be used to clarify the basic minimal service delivery necessary too. Of course, standardisation is exactly that, removing innovation and difference from the service which flies in the face of individuality, difference and democratisation that underpin the fabric of TCs.

Over the last nine years Dovegate has had several "contractual custodians" responsible for managing the contract and at face value none have truly grasped the value of therapy or indeed understood the impact of the therapeutic milieu on the lives of residents in therapy.

In the summer of 2008 the contract underpinning therapy was radically changed in a bid to rescue the TC from failing miserably. The TC appeared to lose its way for a number of reasons and concerns were raised by HM Chief Inspector of Prisons and the Community of Communities (C of C) about the overall performance of the TC in its entirety.

As a direct consequence of the concerns and fears of the authorities I was introduced to therapy. My initial role was assisting the director in making the necessary changes to ensure that the TC was operationally safe, secure and in a suitable state to allow therapy to exist. Much of the contract was redrafted to reflect a massive business process re-engineering programme designed to bring therapy back to the core business. In addition the process released enough financial resources to pay for essential work that had been omitted from the original contract.

The major sticking point throughout this change process was the "194 clause" which meant that the TP as a whole had to maintain a roll of 194 to reap the financial rewards of 200. This is a good example of where "contract fit" and operational understanding were and still are miles adrift in my opinion. I use the term in the present tense because I only managed to negotiate the number down to 190 (a decrease of just four) which was better than nothing. The concept of value for money was the only focal point in this negotiation.

However, this highlights the true misunderstanding of the TP from a contractual standpoint. Focus is still placed on value for money and in filling TP beds to maintain occupancy, there is very little sympathy or concept of the therapeutic process. The logic is simple, although the need to maximise occupancy challenges the qualitative value of therapy for a quantitative rationale that places undue stress on the TP population.

So in a nutshell the contract can be changed at any point of its 25-year lifespan and such change could result in the removal of the therapeutic concept altogether. This realisation serves as a wake-up call for us all as the TP can be changed at any time.

It would be foolish just to assume that the contract is our "safe haven" and that nothing can happen to the TP whilst the contract exists. The shelving of the planned HM Prison Maghull is a sign that contracts are not as safe as was once thought.

A Way Forward

Strategically speaking, we have to look at the key drivers that influence our customer, the Ministry of Justice. They appear to be motivated by wanting to make financial savings; they naturally demand effective and efficient service that supports the reduction of reoffending. This juxtaposition resonates with Serco's core values. Our focus therefore is on providing the best service most effectively.

So confronted with this reality, the big question that the TP must ask is how can the TP maintain relevance in today's political agenda and remain true to its underpinning principles? Our recent strategic planning day highlighted a number of objectives that the Therapeutic Management Team felt would answer these questions.

Relationship with the Main Prison

Strategically our relevance to our partner Dovegate main prison is significant in the development and progress of therapy in the TP. Dovegate is indeed unique because it was purpose-built with a specifically well-designed TP. The advantages of the design have yet to be researched, but the economies of scale generated because of the shared central services afford the TP the luxury of providing credible economic advantage. However, the TP's "big brother" offers more than just economies of scale. The main prison provides a constant flow of prisoners who volunteer for therapy. The closeness of the main also provides flexibility to move prisoners from the TP to the main prison to maintain the balance of prisoners in therapy.

The TP has worked hard over the last two years to dispel some of the myths and misunderstanding about therapy that were shared by both prisoners and staff on the main prison. Relationships have been nurtured and built that have developed into a mutual understanding between both sides of the physical divide. This relationship must be developed further over the coming years to enable some of the value added benefits that residents experience in therapy to be exploited in the main prison.

The relationships that underpin the therapeutic process also serve as the key to unlocking past behaviour. Such relationships are essential in developing the culture of the main prison and through this development the main prison can reach its true potential. So a better understanding of therapy and a closer working relationship between both sides would improve the understanding of what therapy is and it would potentially increase the number of referrals to the TP as well.

Of course in the event of a resident withdrawing from therapy or being deselected, the communities need to facilitate a move out of therapy which would be simple, fast and effective. The main prison provides this alternative location with ease.

Lack of Understanding

The lack of understanding of therapy is not unusual and reflects a similar lack of knowledge across the Ministry of Justice as a whole. Offender managers have a limited understanding of therapy and therefore many prisoners who would benefit from therapy miss the opportunity because of this. Members of the Parole Board similarly lack an awareness of therapy and appear to fail to recognise the benefits of therapy when making decisions about residents who have completed such a course.

This lack of knowledge and understanding needs to be addressed on a much higher level within the Ministry of Justice, otherwise the significance of therapy will diminish or fade into a financial saving. Dovegate must continue to strategically plan regular open days for key influential stakeholders who can hear first-hand from residents the impact that therapy has had in changing behaviour.

Research

In addition, therapy needs to improve its reputation as a credible intervention. This credibility will come from research. The last promising research study from Surrey University can best be described as "encouraging". However, it failed to reach formal publication.[3] With the financial constraints that are ever prevalent in today's economic climate, we need to look at ways of partnering with local universities to tap into research possibilities.

Integration

In the spirit of true integration, I see a learning opportunity for the main prison. This opportunity will solidify the incredible work already undertaken on the main prison and support the further development of Dovegate in its

---

3. Department of Psychology, University of Surrey.

pursuit of excellence. Working in a therapeutic environment without doubt develops skill sets that are exceptional in dealing with the prisoner population.

Prison custody officers (PCOs) who work in the TP have an excellent insight into behavioural management and work in a different environment to the norm. Therapy seeks to reduce the influence of procedural and physical security in an effort to develop a true democratisation and communalism. The balance of security relies heavily on dynamic security where individuality, therapeutic activity and relationships are essential to maintain the safe and secure environment.

Therefore the skills developed by a PCO by working in a TP are markedly different to those obtained serving in the main prison. Understanding behaviour and relationship management are just some of the skills that would help to improve the personal officer scheme on the main and provide the organization with the skills to step up to the next level of organizational development described by Maslow.[4]

Multi-Agency Safety and Health Team

The greatest opportunity for achieving this synergy lies in the Multi-Agency Safety and Health Team (MASH). MASH is a prison-wide initiative involving a multi-agency team of professionals who are responsible for managing the few prisoners who end up as our most resource intensive people. The team manage prisoners who generate a disproportionate level of attention to themselves due to their unusual or challenging behaviour. Such behaviour can be manifest in the form of mental illness, poor coping or aggressive and violent behaviour.

The core team is led by a senior psychologist and other specialists from healthcare, mental health in-reach, art therapists, counsellors, Safer Custody and many other organized professionals. The team carry out assessments of an individual's challenging behaviour and establish individual care and management plans for staff to follow. Their aim is to manage the individual

---

4.   Abraham Maslow (1908-1970), the founder of humanistic psychology, is best known for developing a hierarchy of basic human needs, subsequently developed for organizations. See, e.g. Maslow, A (1954), *Motivation and Personality*, Harper and Row.

within the prison community using input from specialists and wing staff to maintain behavioural stability.

Prisoners who are unable to cope with their environment can be located in various specialist areas throughout the prison. For example, prisoners displaying acute mental health problems are located in healthcare, those who are unable to cope on normal location and are non-violent are located in the Reintegration Unit on the TP. Finally aggressive and violent prisoners are located in the Care and Separation Unit. The matter doesn't end here: prisoners' care and management plans are also developed to stabilise and eventually reintegrate them back into the community.

This development has resulted in the migration of some therapeutic PCOs into Healthcare In-patients. MASH will also introduced specialist therapeutic training into the Care and Separation Unit, equipping staff with the behavioural skills to effectively manage this difficult and challenging population. The overall result is an infiltration of therapeutic methods into working practices on the main prison. As understanding grows within the staff group, the benefits of therapeutic working will become the norm and the management of behaviour will be enhanced across all areas of Dovegate.

The new MASH Team has at its disposal other complementary therapies such as those provided by art and drama therapists who work on a one-to-one basis with the more challenging prisoners on the main prison. The impact of these therapies has significantly raised the profile of therapeutic techniques amongst staff. The value of this work serves to highlight to those sceptical of therapy the remarkable impact that it has on changing behaviour.

The April 2009 report into mental health in the Criminal Justice System[5] highlighted the need for specialised units such as Psychologically Informed Planned Environments (PIPES) that provide opportunities for prisoners to use as a stepdown from Dangerous and Severe Personality Disorder Units or TPs. There is also a desperate need for specialised units that focus on individuals with learning disabilities. A Learning Disabilities Unit would provide an environment specific to those prisoners who have low IQs or with autistic traits.

---

5. The Rt. Hon. Lord Bradley (2009), "Review of People with Mental Health Problems or Learning Disability in the Criminal Justice System". Available at dh.gov.uk/en/ Publicationsandstatistics.

The Reintegration Unit has massive potential for the development of such a unit and would provide the means to support individuals who would not be deemed suitable for the standard offending behaviour programmes. In time residents could progress to one of the four communities to undertake therapy. We have developed a partnership working arrangement with Rampton Hospital to develop the Learning Difficulties TC concept further.

Dedicated Sex Offender Community

Another area of developmental potential is the introduction of a small TC dedicated to sex offending. In truth prisoners who enter therapy with a history of sex offences find community life difficult to cope with. The tragic death of a prisoner at HMP Grendon in 2010 provides us all with a stark reminder of the dangers and vulnerability that sex offenders can face in our communities.

The Dovegate Assessment Unit has the potential to become a dedicated TC that focuses on prisoners convicted of sex offences. The relocation of the assessment function to the main prison would allow the opportunity for this to take place, although the complexities of managing such a service would need some serious thought. The advantages of a dedicated community would allow therapy to focus more on this area of offending behaviour and also provide safety and security for prisoners who traditionally have problems mixing on other communities.

Integrated Assessment and Resettlement Unit in the Main Prison

The expansion of therapy into the main prison is just the tip of the iceberg and in time I see an opportunity to develop an integrated Assessment and Resettlement Unit in the main prison. Specialised unit staff and graduate residents would assess prisoners who arrive at Dovegate for their suitability for therapy. Residents who complete therapy (elders) would graduate and leave the TP and go to the main Assessment and Resettlement Unit to help staff induct new prisoners into Dovegate as a single prison.

The assessment would focus on the four domains that therapy aims to address so that sentence planning could look at the wider issues of behaviour and not simply criminogenic factors. It would assess much more the seven key pathways of resettlement and in this way provide a much wider assessment than current tools do.

The resettlement focus would be two-fold: first to support a resident's resettlement into the normal prison culture; second preparing residents to return to their own home communities or to a supported TC outside the walls of Dovegate.

New Opportunities with a Coalition Government

The introduction of Social Enterprise initiatives by the Coalition Government present us with some exciting options which could provide the opportunity for a TC actually outside the walls linked to Dovegate TP. Such an initiative would help address some of the unanswered question posed by the Surrey University research (see particularly *Chapter 9*). The big question in my thinking would be, "What if Dovegate TCs could partner with either an existing community or could we set up a social enterprise initiative to establish a community for ex-residents who are released back into society?".

The Surrey research looked at the recidivism of prisoners who returned to society. Undoubtedly the first 12 months after discharge were the most challenging. Having a TC in the community would give the opportunity for some residents who have limited home support to use the same supportive and familiar environment that therapy has afforded them in their past. The community could also provide long arm support to other ex-residents who may need such moral and group support in the first 12 months after release.

Finally, the main strategic focus of the TP should be on the political agenda which calls for a large portion of efficiency and effectiveness together with a service that provides residents with the opportunity to change their life chances when they return to society. Much of the focus as a service is on offending behaviour, although this is only part of the conundrum faced by us all in the Ministry of Justice. Kenneth Clarke demands more from prisons by way of productive work. New initiatives such as "payment by results" are just round the corner and therefore there is a potential need to change the way we operate.

Alarmingly, future risk assessments could well decide who offending services should be provided to by simply separating those who are less likely to re-offend from those who are more likely to do so. Therapy focuses on more than just offending behaviour which is our current measure of risk. It is all-encompassing, addressing criminogenic and social behaviour. It provides a setting which fosters a living learning environment to challenge beliefs and behaviours in an effort to impart experiential learning, knowledge and understanding of the individual. This is measured pre-therapy and post-therapy so that we have a way to measure by some means how an individual changes their understanding of the environment in which they live.

Prime Minister David Cameron coined the term, "Big Society" to signify the situation in which local communities take responsibility for the running of their own communities in the still relatively new Coalition world. I would suggest the concept of the Big Society easily echoes the ethos of TCs, so I would take hope that Dovegate TP has a bright future ahead of it.

II.   Jupiter and Beyond?

Dr Judith MacKenzie

In this part of *Chapter 10* I look at the present stage of Dovegate's development in the light of the various visions of the three directors as described in *Chapter 8* together with some views of my own as second author. Despite all the trials and difficulties of the last ten years of Dovegate TCs, the results and outlook are now more than promising. How can this be sustained?

It is known that TCs in general are cyclical, having periods of growth and apparent decay. Why should a collection of TCs such as Dovegate be any different? Dovegate, however, needs to do more than simply show that it complies. To stand still when the tide is flowing against you means losing ground. Where will Dovegate find direction for the future? Robert ("Bob") Hobson suggests a way forward as follows:

> The answer can lie only in taking the risk of explorations in personal relationships, the ongoing conversations in community groups, in personal friendships, in the

dialogue of genuine science, and (as patients ourselves) in the curious friendship of psychotherapy.

In his reflections on his original TC referred to in *Chapter 8* of this work, "The Three Wise Men", Hobson was challenged to consider whether or not there may be a resurrection. His response was

Please God, not the Resurrection of the Divine Hero.

But he added that the growing sense of enthusiasm, which gradually replaced the deep fear that followed the preceding catastrophe was

A bit like rebirth, but not resurrection.

The life-death-rebirth myth is a powerful theme, which is reflected in our everyday experience, and embedded in our descriptive language. It is around us in the diurnal cycle and the changing of the seasons. It is the core of the major religions from the pagan fertility festivals through Christianity to New Age. It is part of physiological as well as psychological healing and is embedded in our relatively sterile culture of addressing offending behaviour.

Prisoners describe their experience as of rediscovering who they always were all along, and, paradoxically, as like becoming a new person. After Dovegate's initial spring of optimism, the early glory of summer, autumn gales and a bitter winter, at last there are signs of spring returning. Even the renaming of the TCs heralded spring—what could be more optimistic than Avalon, Endeavour, Camelot and Genesis?.

Nevertheless winter is known as a time of hardship. Some of the hardships for Dovegate TCs have been to bring the communities up to the required audit standards. This involves difficult, boring and often deeply resisted work on recording, observation and report writing. It depends on the collection of statistics and of the systems being in place in order to produce those statistics. Although first seen as a burden, this was eventually embraced by the therapy managers and in general the arena has been set for the freeing up of the communities to become more creative.

The chapter entitled "The Three Wise Men" (*Chapter 8*) ended with "myrrh" and the early days of Ray Duckworth as a director of therapy. It told a tale of commitment and idealism, held in faith and hope. Like all good tales it has the necessary ingredients of Heroes and Demons, Challenges, Battles and Impossible Odds. The all too human qualities of fear and anger lie cheek by jowl with those of sacrifice and courage.

Like my predeccessor, Hobson, of a quarter a century ago, I am beginning to move from a sense of catastrophe towards a growing sense of hope. No longer do I believe that the current "sanitised" version of TCs in prison has had its day and that they will have to be reinvented in a new and different form with a different name in the future to maintain their diversity and creativity, but I am beginning to believe that they can renew themselves in a meaningful way in the present. Myrrh, perhaps has given birth to Adonis!

It has already been stated that much depends on the vision of the director of therapy. Roland Woodward's vision was for a kind of "University of Anti-Crime". He had in mind a campus model where individuals could gain qualifications and an understanding of the business model. Residents could expand their creative abilities and learn more about the external world as well as their own internal and inter-relational worlds. He wanted to take the emphasis away from the pure model of therapy as the key deliverer for change. This is in keeping with his worldview as a psychologist, existentialist and businessman.

David Lynes, as a psychotherapist, had different goals. In interview in October 2004 he said,

> My goal is, you know, to reintegrate people's personalities if you like. I mean I know that sounds a bit over egotistical but people need to take the damage and make the damage into advantage. I mean, I think that's probably my kind of cornerstone for myself as a psychotherapist.

For the institution he said, "My moral pressure is to make sure that the treatment — I don't like the word treatment — the place that I'm head of is — is humane and positive and real". He was always interested in how staff were affected by and how they could get alongside their charges:

I feel that it's necessary if I'm to work as a therapist for me to have some under-standing of what mental and emotional shapes a person happens to be in, in order to allow them to do what they've done. And in order to understand that, I have to be able to put myself into that shape so that I can understand why a person, how a person might have done something or just to understand how un-understandable it is.

Ray's background is of coming "through the ranks" from a basic grade officer in the days of Feltham Borstal. He had experience of working with Mary Ellis who had long espoused TC principles in working with this diffi-cult and disturbed population. Mary had always understood that the basics of a TC came from the humanitarian principles which were espoused in the training of good borstal officers. She knew too that TCs had emerged from a culture of "anti-specialist", and that they are traditionally counter-culture. She embodied the capacity to put this into practice in an environment that was rigidly pro-specialist and deeply ingrained in prison custodial culture She recognised that many officers come to work in prisons out of a wish to "make a difference", but that the environment can corrupt them in the same way as prisoners have been corrupted themselves by their own background. She had a significant faith in the capacity of human nature for regeneration and that given the right environment this would come to the fore.

I was asked years ago in Grendon to justify the existence of TCs in prisons. After prevaricating around the areas of safer prisons, offending behaviour and personality change, I eventually responded testily, "*Because it's Right!*"

Ray has embraced the TC culture with a vengeance, seeming able to recognise that the therapeutic jargon often seeks only to express in an accept-able manner what has been inwardly known all along. Once understanding that he could facilitate the emergence of basic personal officer skills and the deconstruction of the specialist role to embrace the common values, as enshrined in the TC core values, the way was clear for the TC to continue its original developmental path.

He has always freely acknowledged his lack of experience in TC practice and clinical expertise and he therefore actively sought a new senior therapist He found this in Maggie Evans, a senior forensic psychologist with exten-sive prison experience in risk-assessment as well as being counsellor trained and crucially having undertaken her own therapy. Between them they have produced the perfect marriage of operational and therapeutic abilities and furthermore respect and listen to one another. With the help of Maggie, Ray quickly understood the need for all members of the TC to undergo basic training, and again, despite resistance, he insisted that his new (soundly operationally-minded) unit managers undertook the same TC training that is mandatory for all other TC staff. He modelled this by undertaking it himself. The result has been the return of open debate and the recognition of the necessity for clearer communication and a place to process difficulties between staff as well as their own internal processes.

The Fluffy was reborn as the senior management sensitivity meeting. Further innovations have begun to emerge such as the resettlement scheme from Camelot and the assessment procedures on Endeavour. Horizons have broadened with further appointments for art and drama and Rezart is in the process of being revisited.

What is likely is that if everyone associated with Dovegate were to be polled for their ideas for the future there would be a rich and diverse list to choose from. That the establishment is not unwilling to consider alterative futures is evidenced by their use of Professor CB (the organizational consultant referred to in *Chapter 8*) for a way forward. He came up with five options for the future all of which were dramatically different but all of which remained close to the TC principles on which Dovegate was founded. One of these was the possibility of specialisation. Dovegate is fortunate in possessing two small units (assessment and resettlement), both of which lend themselves to small, more highly specialised, prototypical units.

The Correctional Services Accreditation Panel (CSAP) has given provisional accreditation to the submission for the modification of the mainstream manuals, contextualised for learning disabilities. Not only is this group relatively neglected in terms of intervention, the need for provision is given increased potency with the result of the judicial review relating to Dennis Gill in 2010 which concluded in the words of Mr Justice Cranston

Thus the claimant is entitled to a declaration that the Secretary of State has breached his duties towards him by failing to take steps to enable him to undertake some type of offending behaviour work.[6]

The intervention described as a learning difficulty TC has as yet not been trialled. Dovegate TC provides a perfect environment for this to take place.

Small specialist units have other possibilities as well. It is known that schizophrenic patients also do well in TCs provided these have been appropriately modified or contextualised. Most prisoners diagnosed with a psychotic state are excluded from conventional programmes as well as TCs. Secure NHS provision however will not admit them until discharge is imminent unless their condition is intractable and unresponsive to prison prescribed medication. For a partially symptom-controlled schizophrenic life-sentenced prisoner this can delay admission and thereby release almost indefinitely. The same applies to other less noticed groups of people: "deniers", the elderly and the very young, to cite three such.

Sex offenders against children do less well than other kinds of offender, and Grendon's experience suggests that they may be more successful within a designated unit where the Sex Offender Treatment Programme (SOTP)[7] can be incorporated. The way is open for a specially designed TC for such prisoner groups, and particularly within this climate, for an organization such as Dovegate as a private prison to take the lead.

A TP senior management Strategic Away Day illustrated the new openness and collective sharing of experience and expertise. It was a day of hope, energy, creativity and inclusion, in which differing areas of expertise could be seen to have equal and essential value.

Lastly, despite its difficulties, this author agrees with the third director, Ray, that the advantages of conjunction with the main prison outweigh the disadvantages. The problems of a "stand alone" TC such as Grendon remain those of a perception of "difference" and "specialness" and all too often an apparent belief that "prison" is not for the likes of them. Hence

6. *R (Dennis Gill) v Secretary of State for Justice*, 26 February 2010, [2010] EWHC 364 (Admin).
7. This is the standard accredited programme for sex offenders (at progressive levels).

there are often many difficulties when those emerging from therapy return to a normal location.

Should there be a third "Big TC"? This debate will no doubt continue!

III. A Model for Prison TCs

Eric Cullen

The Story So Far

The story of Dovegate TC has, to date, been replete with lessons concerning the challenges and opportunities of opening, developing and successfully defending a liberal and innovative therapeutic regime within both the financial imperatives and corporate restrictions of private sector enterprise, and the security/operational imperatives of the much larger, dominant category B prison just the other side of the fence. There are a number of obvious problems, limitations and tensions with this scenario, some of which were raised at both the bidding stage (see *Chapter 1*) and at subsequent early phases of opening the TC (see especially *Chapters 2* and *5*). These were always trumped by the economic advantages/security implications of either having a physically separate establishment or a completely independent staff profile. They also made the achievements of the management, staff and residents of Dovegate TC all the greater.

Sustaining Dovegate TC has demanded so much of the staff and residents through their first decade. Therapeutic integrity flows from, and is sustained by, maintaining a number of linked factors, including:

- organization, physical and dynamic;

- setting and maintaining the necessary professional experience and expertise to guide and defend the community;

- keeping the boundaries between the TC and the main prison while remaining part of the whole;

- supporting staff in both their therapeutic endeavours and personal well-being;

- targeting optimal rather than minimum viable funding for the treatment programme and staffing strength within it. This funding should be informed by the "what works" literature and the findings of *Breaking the Cycle: Effective Punishment, Rehabilitation and Sentencing of Offenders*[8] Department of Health/Ministry of Justice initiative; exploring the advisability of applying for Dovegate TC to be a "payment by results" leader as promulgated in that Green Paper.[9]

There are certain themes, small in number, which also fall within the ambit of this final section's overall theme and these are dealt with in the remainder of the chapter.

Dovegate and Grendon Co-operation

Before Dovegate opened, there was a spirit of great optimism towards the opportunities for the two large TC s of Grendon and Dovegate to establish a collaborative approach in taking forward best practice and sharing ideas. Sadly, this has not happened. In fact, relationships between the two establishments could at best be described as fragmentary. Much of this failure is ascribed to the fact that one is a public sector undertaking, the other part of the private sector, with their conflicting managerial imperatives and Dovegate's commercial sensitivities about sharing practice, procedure and information concerning costs. There is such great potential if these two DTCs could find a way to meet and share ideas on a regular basis.

---

8. (2010), Cmnd. 7972.
9. See *Chapter 2*, Footnore 15 for comments on the Government's response to the Green Paper.

Offender Personality Disorder Strategy 2011

In September 2010, the responsible office within the National Offender Management service (NOMS) submitted a formal strategy to the Health and Criminal Justice Board, which was approved for onward submission to ministers, Paul Burstow (Department of Health) and Crispin Blunt (Ministry of Justice) proposals for public consultation as announced in the Green Paper, *Breaking the Cycle: Effective Punishment, Rehabilitation and Sentencing of Offenders* mentioned above. The relevant extracts are:

> There are a group of high-risk, sexual or violent offenders whose offending is linked to severe forms of personality disorder. These offenders pose challenging behavioural or control problems in prison, and a high risk of reoffending if in the community. There are currently a number of pilot treatment and case management Projects underway as part of the Dangerous and Severe Personality Disorder Programme.[10] The projects provide services within prisons, secure hospital services and the community, aimed at reducing the problems and risk that this difficult group presents and protecting the public. We think this approach needs to continue to build on the experience of the earlier programme.

> However, it is important to ensure that these services are as effective as possible and we have agreed with the Department of Health that we should *reshape the use of these point resources.* It is proposed that the National Health Service and National Offender Management Service *reconfigure existing services in secure and community settings to manage and reduce the risk of reoffending.* This will acknowledge that there is a *joint responsibility* for this population across the two organizations and that services will be delivered through coordinated and, at some stages, joint operations. This approach will improve the management of this population, including: *earlier identification and assessment, evidence based psychologically informed interventions, and progression units* where offenders can be monitored in secure settings to support their rehabilitation and eventual return to the community. We estimate that by organizing these services differently we would be able to *increase treatment capacity by 2014 from 300 places up to 570, mostly in prisons.* In addition, we will aim to

---

10. Which is also responsible for DTCs.

provide *additional psychological support for up to a further 800 places* (in prisons and the community) for those making progress, and strengthening oversight for those released from custody. *The implementation plan for these changes will be subject to a separate consultation by the Department of Health and the Ministry of Justice.*

The potential to improve services for personality disordered offenders is considerable but there are equally a number of significant logistical and managerial issues raised by the creation of a joint initiative with the Department of Health.

There are to be a series of public consultation events early in 2011, transition plans for existing patients and prisoners; a scoping exercise for research put out to tender, and community and Psychologically Informed Planned Environments (PIPES) specifications drafted. These are clearly momentous developments in the provision of treatment facilities for mentally-disordered offenders, the population for which Dovegate and all the DTCs cater.

A Model for the Future

A task force was convened in 1993 to "determine the need for further 'Grendon-style' therapeutic regimes". It estimated that by 2001 there would be at least 2,400 prisoners in the system not falling within the scope of the mental health legislation who would benefit from therapeutic regimes. The main recommendations of the Task Force were:

- a second therapeutic establishment with category B security should be established in the north of England;

- there should be a further six therapeutic units in the existing establishment;

- one of these should be for women and should specialise in treating drug dependency; and

- full implementation of the recommendations of the 1989 Working Group on the Allocation of Disturbed Young Offenders.

267

The authors of the task force report described this as a "mixed economy" of therapeutic prisons and smaller units, combining the advantages of each. An internal "state of progress" document from January 1995 stated:

> The Directorate of Health Care are responsible for advancing the decision of the Prison Board. At their August 1994 meeting, the decision "appeared to have been taken" to go for 2 x 250 bed prisons AND some smaller units (units for Women and Cat As were mentioned specifically).

The official advice to bidders for the second TC in November 1997 was:

> The second therapeutic community prison should be situated in the North of England. (As envisaged by the Executive Committee, a third therapeutic prison should also be established to these general specifications. It is recommended that it be situated in London or South East England).

These references clearly indicate the intention to build not just a second DTC (which became Dovegate), but a third as well and, a minimum of six smaller TCs in larger establishments. In spite of these exhortations, only Dovegate was funded.

In 2010, NOMS completed a review of Democratic TCs, having consulted widely throughout penal TCs. Their recommendations include:

- DTCs may benefit from being located in each region with 40-place units with a smaller one, about 20 places, for prisoners with learning disability;

- young offenders and learning disability—both of these populations may benefit from DTC provision [there is none at present, but the CSAP approved a pilot DTC for adult males with learning disabilities]; and

- the community for women at HMP Send should be expanded to 40 places.

Some Facts and Assertions about DTCs

Fact DTCs are the only regime-based treatment in UK Prison Services with published research which proves a significant correlation between completing treatment in a DTC and fewer reconvictions on release after two years.

Fact There are significantly more prisoners who could benefit from DTCs than there are places. Every review to date has indicated even the most modest figure of several thousand relevant prisoners for this treatment modality.

Fact DTCs are not significantly more expensive. The appropriate cost per prisoner place comparison must be with where these prisoners would be if there were no DTCs, not the average for adult prisoners. The overwhelming majority of DTC prisoners are serving very long sentences (over 80% in Grendon, Gartree and Dovegate are lifers) with serious, frequently multiple, personality disorders and the gravest of crimes. If there were no DTCs, they would be in higher security prisons, which are more expensive.

Assertion There is an even larger number of prisoners, not necessarily described as "personality disordered", who would benefit significantly from attending a DTC, due to the benefits in more stable conditions, and of less disruptive prison behaviour, quite apart from post-release comparisons.

Assertion There is a strong and proven case for expanding the number of DTC places to provide for the unmet need.

Assertion The funding for DTCs should not be devolved from the centre because: (a) they are a national resource and; (b) devolved budgets make small regimes more vulnerable to "cost-saving" measures or other local, transient imperatives or opinions.

The existing division within the National Offender Management Service responsible for TCs (and for dangerous and severe personality disordered (DSPD) offenders) should be expanded to assume the administrative (but not managerial) responsibility for all TCs, whether democratic, hierarchical or hybrid.

The authors also propose a more ambitious schedule of DTC expansion to best meet the large and growing unmet need in the prison population, (which has several thousand prisoners with personality disorders), sentences of sufficient length, and we believe, the motivation to change. We therefore recommend a new configuration for TCs in prisons.

Recommendations

1. Prison-based TCs should all be part of a national, integrated network with central funding and co-ordination, but with local clinical and operational management. This cluster of establishments/units should fall within the Department of Health/Ministry of Justice cooperative and consideration should be given to giving primacy to the former.

2. Structure and capacity:

   • Three large and independent (with their own discreet staff complement) DTCs of between 200 and 230 beds. These to include Grendon in the south, Dovegate in the Midlands and a third new DTC to be built in the north. These three TC Centres should have specialist DTC units for specific groups including, e.g. young offenders (3), a learning disabled TC for adult offenders (1) and a shorter-term substance dependent/personality disordered TC (1).

   • Ten DTCs of approximately 30-40 beds, one each in the DOM catchment areas, or now they are to be replaced, appropriate geographic areas.

   • Four hierarchical TCs for drug offenders; and

   • A range of hybrid TCs for convicted offenders with or without personality disorders. There should be more prison regimes based on the TC principles of collective responsibility, group and community meetings and direct, supportive staff involvement within the traditional criteria. These regimes should be available for those of varying sentence lengths between six months and indeterminacy. The initiative entitled Psychological Informed Planned Environments (PIPES) is of this type. The Kainos[11] regimes are also in this category.

These proposals would realise minima of 630-beds for the large independent DTCs, 300-400 for the ten small regional units, at least 220 for the HTCs and an additional potential to generalise DTC principles and procedures across a range of non-TC prisons. The total TC places would thus exceed 1,200, a significant improvement on current capacity.

A Few Loose Ends

TCs are now thoroughly audited and inspected, but there is very little to determine the quality of clinical supervision and progress. It would, we suggest, be a welcome addition to the existing audit process to have a *clinical* section which addresses the more qualitative aspects of therapy such as the therapy managers judgement of progress in therapy and the state of health of the communities. Improvements for DTCs are also apparent in other areas including:

Referrals
Over the past decades, the population of the TCs at Grendon and Dovegate have changed significantly. The current Grendon population, and most of Dovegate, are serving life sentences or indeterminate sentences for public protection (IPPs) and are therefore imprisoned mainly for very violent and/ or sexual crimes. It is uncertain whether this is the group best suited for TC therapy or whether it is simply an effect of other forces, e.g. acquiring a reputation as the best type of imprisonment in which to serve large sections of their sentences.

---

11. Kainos Community is a charity dedicated to reducing reoffending "by lives being changed". See wix.com/kainoscommunity.

Progress in Therapy

Therapy managers in the main DTCs are reluctant to make their clinical judgements as to how successful or not the residents have been in therapy, a matter of record. As a consequence, there is no way of determining either qualitatively or otherwise how well men are judged to have progressed at their time of leaving.

Research into Re-offending

The emphasis within DTCs has shifted subtly but significantly away from rates of reconvictions towards post-treatment indices more relevant to post-transfer prison behaviours such as rates of institutional offending. This is a seriously retrograde shift. The first concern should always be the safety of the public, not the stability of the prison.

Summary

This is about trying to change lives in order to save lives. We have a chance to increase the opportunities for those men and women who, having committed terrible crimes, have determined to try to look honestly at the damage they've done and stop. I was reminded by a good friend, Pam Turney, of something Tim Newell the former Governing Governor of Grendon Prison used to say to the residents there:

TAKE RESPONSIBILITY.

Anyone who knows TCs will recognise much of their nature in this book, full as it is of a range of sometimes conflicting but hopefully stimulating and challenging views, assertions and experiences. It may well be possible to create and run offender treatment programmes which are more operationally precise, more programmed and clear-cut in their procedures and outcome measures. What, we would assert, however, is unique to DTCs in prison is that they alone give dangerous offenders, many with serious disorders of personality and histories of alcohol and drug abuse, the best chance they will ever have of changing their lives in order that they will have no more victims. Dovegate TC does that.

APPENDIX 1

The Development of Core Standards and Core Values for Therapeutic Communities

Briefing Paper: Royal College of Psychiatrists' Centre for Quality Improvement, August 2008[1]

This paper describes the development of a set of Core Values and Core Standards for therapeutic communities (TCs) and their application in therapeutic communities and the Community of Communities (C of C) Quality Network[2]

Background

Evidence-based mental health care is generally accepted as necessary, but it has been strongly argued that it is not sufficient without reference to underlying values (Fulford, 2004; Cloninger, 2006). Attempts to develop a values-based framework have therefore been developed to complement it (Woodbridge and Fulford, 2005). Therapeutic communities have their origin in 'moral treatment' (Bloor, 1988, Kennard 1998) which were only value-based. This, together with other critiques of modernity in psychiatry (Bracken and Thomas, 2005) and the successful development and growth of the Community of Communities Quality Network (Haigh and Tucker, 2004), has given the impetus and opportunity to develop an explicit value base for standards in therapeutic community practice.

Development of Core Standards and Core Values

Provisional 'Core Standards' were first published as an appendix in the C of C Service Standards for Therapeutic Communities 4th Edition (Hirst and

---

1. © 2008 The Royal College of Psychiatrists: enquiries@cru.rcpsych.ac.uk
2. See www.communityofcommunities.org.uk

Paget, 2005). The 16 standards were developed through a series of workshops and consultation and refined by the project team following a literature review. The standards were further refined and agreed by an advisory group of experts before full publication in the Service Standards for Therapeutic Communities 5th Edition (Keenan and Paget, 2005) as standards critical to TC practice.

The Core Standards were included in the C of C annual cycle of self- and peer-reviews and are regarded as the minimum standards for member TCs. The Core Standards have become integral to the C of C accreditation processes for TCs within the NHS and the prison sector.

In 2007, C of C developed three new sets of service standards for communities working with people with addictions, children and young people and people with learning disabilities. The first editions of the Service Standards for Addiction Therapeutic Communities (Shah and Paget, 2007) and Therapeutic Communities for Children and Young People (O'Sullivan, Shah and Paget, 2007), adopted the existing Core Standards after consideration from their respective advisory groups incorporating them into their review processes. The Service Standards for Communities for People with Learning Disabilities (Wood and Paget, 2007) did not adopt the Core Standards, their advisory group deciding that they were not wholly applicable to all their communities. A set of 'Core Values' was first developed by the advisory group for communities for people with learning disabilities and was published in the first edition of their service standards in an attempt to ground the standards in a philosophical base that reflected the model of work. Similarly, the advisory group for children and young people TCs devised their own set of Core Values to describe the philosophy within their own approach.

Towards the end of 2007, C of C held a series of workshops to revise the Core Standards and develop a common set of Core Values in an attempt to identify key elements of the TC approach and philosophy irrespective of client group or sector. The resulting draft was sent to all TCs in the UK for comment. Responses were considered by the C of C project team and the advisory groups and a new set of 10 Core Values and 15 Core Standards was agreed.

The Core Values describe the journey of processes an individual experiences in order to develop good mental health by explaining the journey undertaken by a member of a therapeutic community, beginning with attachment and progressing to responsibility. The Core Standards detail the necessary structures and commitments required for these values to be operationalised and will be used as an integral tool in C of C's quality assurance and accreditation cycles.

Using the Core Values and Core Standards

The Core Values can help therapeutic communities articulate their mission statements and basic beliefs to themselves and others describing their service as one grounded in a sound theoretical and philosophical base. Therapeutic communities may also use the values for training, using them to reflect on aspects of the TC approach.

Therapeutic communities will want to use the Core Standards to quality assure their service using the Community of Communities annual cycle of self- and peer-review.

Regulators may wish to use the values and standards to better understand the relationship between existing regulatory frameworks and the therapeutic application in services. Commissioners may also wish to use the Core Standards to assist them in matching needs to placements, and identifying appropriate therapeutic placements for individuals. They will be of use to commissioners when establishing if a setting is, and continues to be, therapeutic in its principles and practice.

Most importantly, the Core Values and Core Standards can be used by non-TC services to develop a TC-centred approach, helping them to foster a culture and attitude to implement the structures necessary for TC practice. This process of development will be complimented by participation in the C of C Quality Network.

Conclusion

This set of Core Values and Core Standards is the first joined up attempt by therapeutic communities to identify their common core beliefs and the basic structures required for these beliefs to be realised. The extensive development and consultation process means that these values and standards represent broad consensus and reflect current TC philosophy and practice. The desire to regularly review this work ensures their organic and dynamic nature will remain relevant. This work leads the way for a common ground on which all therapeutic communities can stand and identify themselves as a value-based service.

At the outset of this work, some TC practitioners expressed the view that the need for common Core Values and Core Standards was preaching to the converted and not in keeping with a modern mental health service however the vast majority contend that this is not true. The challenge for all services identifying with these values and standards is to convey their message to those who need to hear it.

Core Values	
CV 1	Healthy attachment is a developmental requirement for all human beings, and should be seen as a basic human right
CV 2	A safe and supportive environment is required for an individual to develop, to grow, or to change
CV 3	People need to feel respected and valued by others to be healthy. Everybody is unique and nobody should be defined or described by their problems alone
CV 4	All behaviour has meaning and represents communication which deserves understanding
CV 5	Personal well-being arises from one's ability to develop relationships which recognise mutual need
CV 6	Understanding how you relate to others and how others relate to you leads to better intimate, family, social and working relationships
CV 7	Ability to influence one's environment and relationships is necessary for personal well-being. Being involved in decision-making is required for shared participation, responsibility, and ownership
CV 8	There is not always a right answer and it is often useful for individuals, groups and larger organisations to reflect rather than act immediately
CV 9	Positive and negative experiences are necessary for healthy development of individuals, groups and the community
CV 10	Each individual has responsibility to the group, and the group in turn has collective responsibility to all individuals in it

Core Standards	
CS 1	The community meets regularly
CS 2	The community acknowledges a connection between emotional health and the quality of relationships
CS 3	The community has clear boundaries, limits or rules and mechanisms to hold them in place which are open to review
CS 4	The community enables risks to be taken to encourage positive change
CS 5	Community members create an emotionally safe environment for the work of the community
CS 6	Community members consider and discuss their attitudes and feelings towards each other
CS 7	Power and authority in relationships is used responsibly and is open to question
CS 8	Community members take a variety of roles and levels of responsibility
CS 9	Community members spend formal and informal time together
CS 10	Relationships between staff members and client members are characterised by informality and mutual respect
CS 11	Community members make collective decisions that affect the functioning of the community
CS 12	The community has effective leadership which supports its democratic processes

CS 13	All aspects of life are open to discussion within the community
CS 14	All behaviour and emotional expression is open to discussion within the community
CS 15	Community members share responsibility for one another

© The Royal College of Psychiatrists: enquiries@cru.rcpsych.ac.uk

Dovegate

APPENDIX 2

Aspects of Psychodynamic Theory Pertinent to *Chapter 7*

(Written with a view to assisting those who have little or no understanding of psychodynamic theory; with apologies to those who have studied it in depth for whom these brief descriptions may seem simple, not to say simplistic).

Psychodynamic therapy focuses on the psychological roots of emotional suffering. It requires the capacity for self-reflection and self-examination, and makes use of the relationship between therapist and patient. This is seen as a reflection or mirror of the relationship patterns in the client's life. It includes concepts such as the unconscious, defence mechanisms, transference and counter-transference.

Psychodynamic psychotherapy, supported by current neuroscience, understands that the way that we relate to others and the world around us is laid down in infancy and early childhood (the Early "Maternal" Care System).

Patterns are established that become more entrenched with repeated use and form the basis of how we are across the different domains of our lives. They are reinforced by experience and circumstance, most particularly by those close to us, our caregivers, but also by influences from others such as school and peer groups. There is also a genetic element.

Learning in this way is not a cognitive function although behaviour control can be. However, true change is engendered by revisiting past experience, releasing trapped emotion and experimenting with new ways of being. It requires the safety of a trusted relationship that includes boundaries as well as care. Brain plasticity suggests that these changes can become physiologically entrenched.

In therapy, healing takes place within a relationship between the client (or resident) and the therapist, in this case the community. The therapist acts as a mirror to the client, reflecting back both what the therapist sees and what the client expects to see. This expectation may be rooted in transference. Transference involves experiencing the other as if they were a key person from the past. It is not conscious (i.e. it is not the same as being reminded of somebody), and usually involves powerful emotions and impulses.

In counter-transference the therapist finds himself or herself responding as if they themselves were that original key person. Although their own genuine feelings may be elicited, and their own material activated, sometimes feelings are evoked which are echoes of the client's experience. This can be seen as simple patterning—for example, a client who has habitually found himself rejected may behave in a manner that is either ingratiating or hostile thereby engendering a rejecting impulse in the therapist. The therapist's feelings may also be a reflection of the client's own denied feelings.

This is why the enhancement of the staff member's personal awareness, and particularly the therapy manager's awareness is so important.

Because many memories are painful, and are often "buried deeply", defence mechanisms prevent them coming into awareness. Thus the processes described are not conscious to the client though should be to the therapist. Clarifying these processes is the work of supervision and the post-therapy group, so that damaging patterns are not repeated unconsciously by the therapist.

In supervision the same process as has happened between the therapist and residents may occur between the therapist and the supervisor. This is called "parallel process". The scenario given at the start of *Chapter 7* is an example of this.

The most important arena for the examination of parallel process is the staff team which will often mirror what is happening in the resident group. The bringing into awareness of these processes and their alterations in the staff team will have a similar effect on the resident group. This is why so much attention is paid to staff team dynamics.

Further parallels occur in the way the senior management group relates to the staff group, and in particular how the views of the director of therapy "trickle-down" through the senior management team to the staff team and thereby inform and colour the work with the residents. Hence the extensive description of the various directors of therapy in *Chapter 8*.

In group therapy, a number of "curative factors" have been defined. One of these is the "Recapitulation of the Family Group" which is a manifestation of transference within a group setting.

The "Early Maternal Care System" is understood on the TC as the recapitulation of the family group within the group setting.

The capacity to develop identity is dependent upon relationship with another. Part of the tension between separateness and belonging is the need to be included by a particular group and not excluded by it.

Early or "primal" wounding is the result of an assault to our sense of self caused by failures of nurturing environment. Whilst it can produce feelings such as shame, abandonment or anxiety, it can also produce empathic failure which is a key element in the maintenance of offending behaviour.

Dovegate

APPENDIX 3

Service Standards for Therapeutic Communities

The following bar chart and accompanying table of percentages illustrate the overall percentage of standards met for all the TCs following peer-reviews of the Service Standards for Therapeutic Communities 5th Edition (for DTCs) and the 1st Edition of the Service Standards for Addiction TCs in the interim years 2008/09 and 2010/11.

There is no 2008/2009 data for six communities, HMP Dovegate Avalon and the HTCs participated for the first time and HMP Dovegate Camelot underwent a repeat audit. The Assessment Units (AUs) are compared against their performance in the last cycle (2009/2010). In addition, it is important to note that the data reflects the change of names at Grendon A (formerly G) and Grendon D (formerly A).

The Community of Communities memberships' overall average percentage of standards met is indicated by the black line on the bar chart on the next page at 77%. Whilst it is not possible or useful to directly compare performance of DTCs and HTCs, the data does identify a number of useful similarities and joint difficulties which are reflected in the text.

Source: Choudhury, A and Paget, S (eds.) (2011), Royal College of Psychiatrists College Centre for Quality Improvement (CCQI) National Interim Report 2010-2011, Integrated Audit of Therapeutic Communities in Prisons. Reproduced by kind permission of the College Centre.

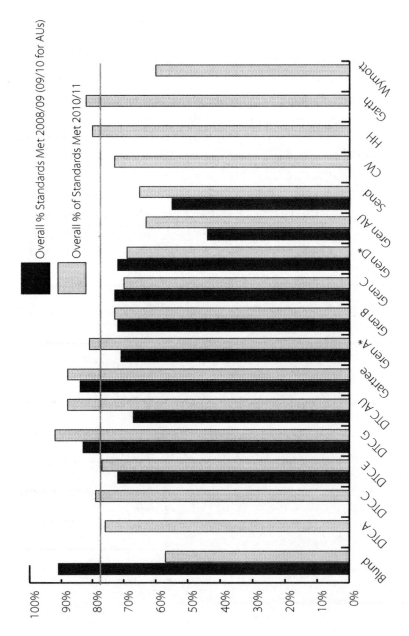

*These scores represent quality improvement activity which whilst part of the TC audit cycle does not contribute to compliance scores.

	Overall % Standards Met	Overall % of Standards Met
	2008/09 (09/10 for AUs)	2010/11
Blund	91%	57%
DTC A	TC in development	76%
DTC C	TC underwent full audit	79%
DTC E	72%	77%
DTC G	83%	92%
DTC AU	67%	88%
Gartree	84%	88%
Gren A*	71%	81%
Gren B	72%	73%
Gren C	73%	70%
Gren D*	72%	69%
Gren AU	44%	63%
Send	55%	65%
CW	N/A	73%
HH	N/A	80%
Garth	N/A	82%
Wymott	N/A	60%

*These scores represent quality improvement activity which whilst part of the TC audit cycle does not contribute to compliance scores.

Argyle, M (1972), *The Psychology of Interpersonal Behaviour*, Harmondsworth, Middlesex: Penguin.

Bion, W (1961), *Experiences in Groups*, London: Tavistock

Brown, J, Huston, S, Lewis, L and Speller, G (2004), "An Evaluation of Dancing Inside: A Creative Workship Project led by Motionhouse Dance Theatre in HMP Dovegate Therapeutic Community". Two-year programme. Forensic Psychology Research Unit, Surrey University.

Chazan, R (2001), *The Group as Therapist*, London, Jessica Kingsley.

Correctional Services Accreditation Panel (2009), Programme Accreditation Criteria.

Cullen, E (1993), "The Grendon Re-Conviction Study, Part I", *Prison Service Journal*, 90, 35-37.

(1994), "Grendon: The Therapeutic Prison That Works", *Therapeutic Communities*, 15, 4, 307-311.

(1998), "Grendon and Future Therapeutic Communities in Prisons", London: Prison Reform Trust Achieving Prisons Reports.

Cullen, E, Jones, L and Woodward, R (eds) (1997), *Therapeutic Communities for Offenders,* Chichester: John Wiley & Sons.

Cullen, E and Newell, T (1999), *Murderers and Life Imprisonment,* Winchester: Waterside Press.

Cullen, E and Miller, A (2010), "Dovegate: Birth, Bid, Growing pains and Survival", in Shuker, R and Sullivan, E (eds.), *Grendon and the Emergence of Forensic Therapeutic Communities* (25-44), Chichester: Wiley-Blackwell.

Doctor, R, (2007), "A Schema for the Transition from Cruel Object to Tender Object Relations among Drug Users in a Prison Therapeutic Community", in *Dynamic Security: The Democratic Therapeutic Community in Prison* , Parker M. (ed), London and Philadelphia: Jessica Kingsley.

Dolan, B and Coid, J (1994), *Psychopathic and Antisocial Personality Disorders, Treatment and Research Issues*, Gaskell, Royal College of Psychiatrists.

Dolan, B (1996) , "Therapeutic Communities for Offenders", *Therapeutic Communities*, vol. 15, No. 4.

East, W N and Hubert, W H de B (1939), *The Psychological Treatment of Crime*, London: HMSO.

Edgar, K and Newell T (2006), *Restorative Justice in Prisons: Making It Happen*, Hook: Waterside Press.

Firman, J and Gila, A (1997), *The Primal Wound, A Transpersonal View of Trauma, Addiction, and Growth,* New York: State University of New York (SUNY Series in the Philosophy of Psychology).

Foulkes, S H (1964), *Therapeutic Group Analysis*, London: George Allen & Unwin.

Genders, E and Player, E (1995), *Grendon: A Study of a Therapeutic Prison*, Oxford: Clarendon Press.

Genders, E (2002), "Legitimacy, Accountability and Private Prisons", *Punishment and Society*, vol. 4(3), 285-303.

Gildard, H (2010), "Dovegate Therapeutic Prison Annual Report", April 2009-April 2010, Serco.

Guardian (2001), "Softly Does It", February 2.

Gunn, J, Robertson, G, Dell, S and Way, C (1978), *Psychiatric Aspects of Imprisonment*, London: Academic Press.

Haggerty, J (2006), "Psychodynamic Theory", psychcentral.com/lib/2006/psychodynamic-therapy

Harding, R (2001), *Private Prisons and Public Accountability*, Milton Keynes: Open University Press.

Hemmings, M and Rawlinson, J (1995), "Ladies and Lady Killers", *Prison Service Journal*, 111, pp 24-25.

HM Chief Inspector of Prisons, Reports.

Hinshelwood, R D (2001), *Thinking About Institutions,* Jessica Kingsley.

Hodkin, G and Woodward, R (1996), "Another British First: Gartree's Therapeutic Community for Lifers", *Prison Service Journal*, 103, 47-50.

Hobson, R F, "The Therapeutic Community Disease", Lecture given to the Royal College of Psychiatrists.

Kennard, D (1998), *An Introduction to Therapeutic Communities*, London: Jessica Kingsley.

Kennard, D (1998), "Therapeutic Communities are Back: And There's Something a Little Different About Them", *Therapeutic Communities*, 19, 4.

Kennard, D and Lees J (2001), "What is a Therapeutic Community: The Kennard and Lees Audit Checklist (KLAC)", Association of Therapeutic Communities, therapeuticcommunities.org.

Klauber, J (1982), *The Elements of the Psychoanalytical Relationship and Their Therapeutic Implications,* New York: Aronson.

Lacan, J (2001), *Ecrits* (Translation: Alan Sheridan), London: Routledge.

Main, T (1946), "The Hospital as a Therapeutic Institution', *Bulletin of the Mennings Clinic,* 10, pp 66-70.

Manning, N (1989), *The Therapeutic Community Movement: Charisma and Routinisation,* London: Routledge.

Marshall, P (1997) "A Re-conviction Study of HMP Grendon Therapeutic Community", Research Findings 53, London: Home Office Research and Statistics Directorate.

Miller, A (1964), "After The Fall", (4th edn. 1967), Viking Press.

Miller, S, Sees, C and Brown, J (2006), "Key Aspects of Psychological Change in Residents of a Prison Therapeutic Community: A Focus Group Approach", *Howard Journal of Criminal Justice,* vol. 45, pp 116-128.

Miller, S and Brown, J (2010), "Dovegate's Therapeutic Community: An Analysis of Reconviction Data", *Therapeutic Communities,* 31(1), Spring, pp 62-75.

Morris, M (1999), "The Big Therapeutic Community Senior Staff Group", Internal Publication, HMP Grendon.

(2000) "Ideological Drift", Internal publication, HMP Grendon.

(2004), *Dangerous and Severe: Process, Programme and Person,* Jessica Kingsley.

Neville, L, Miller, S and Fritzon, K (2007), "Understanding Change in a Therapeutic Community: An Action Systems Approach", *Journal of Forensic Psychiatry & Psychology,* June, 18(2): 181-203.

Newell, T (ed) (1997), "Therapeutic Communities in Prisons", *Prison Service Journal,* No. 111.

Newton, M (1973), "Progress of Follow-up Studies and Comparison with Non-patients carried out at HMP Oxford", Grendon Psychology Unit Report, Series A, 15.

(1998), 'Changes in Measures of Personality, Hostility and Locus of Control During Residence in a Prison Therapeutic Community", *Legal and Criminological Psychology,* 3, 209-223.

(2000), "Psychological Variables as Dynamic Risk Factors for Reconviction Among Residents in a Prison Therapeutic Community", unpublished research study.

Norton, K (1992), A Culture of Enquiry: Its Preservation or Loss, *Journal of Therapeutic Communities*, 13(1), 3-25.

Pines, M (1999), 'Forgotten Pioneers: The Unwritten History of the Therapeutic Community Movement", *Therapeutic Communities*, 20, 1, 23-42.

Rapaport, R (1960), *Community as Doctor,* London: Tavistock.

Rawlings, B (1999), "Therapeutic Communities in Prisons: Research Review", *Therapeutic Communities*, vol. 20, 3, pp 177-193.

Restorative Justice Consortium (2000), "Restorative Justice from Margins to Mainstream".

Rose, M (1997), *Transforming Hate into Love*, London: Routledge.

Segal, H (1964) "Introduction to Melanie Klein".

Shine, J and Morris, M (1999), *Regulating Anarchy*, Spring Hill Press.

Shine, J (ed.) (2000), "A Compilation of Grendon Research", Leyhill: PES.

Slevin, P (2001), "Promise of Private Prisons Still Unfulfilled", *Wilmington Morning Star,* 4 February 2001.

Smartt, U (2001), *Grendon Tales: Stories from a Therapeutic Community*, Winchester: Waterside Press.

Symington, N (1986), *The Analytic Experience, Lectures From the Tavistock*, Free Association Books.

Taylor, R (2000), 'A Seven Year Reconviction Study of Grendon Therapeutic Community", Research Findings 115, Home Office Research and Statistics Directorate, London: Home Office.

Travis, A (2001), "Jail Terms: Privatisation of the penal system may not be the answer after all; in some cases the public sector's bids have been cheaper and better", *Guardian*, July 12.

Wexler, H K (1995), "The Success of Therapeutic Communities for Substance Abusers in American Prisons", *Journal of Psychotropic Drugs*, 27(1): 57-66.

Whitely, J S (1977), "Dilemmas of Leadership in the Therapeutic Community and the Large Group", Paper given to the Scientific Meeting of the Group Analytic Society, London.

Woodward, R (1991), "Banging Your Head on a Sponge" (Unpublished Grendon article).

Woodward, R and Hodkin, G (1997), "Surviving Violent Death", *Prison Service Journal*, May 1997, No. 111.

Woodward, R (1997), "The Selection and Training of Staff for the Therapeutic Role in the Prison Setting", in Cullen, E, Jones, L, Woodward, R (eds.), *Therapeutic Communities for Offenders*, Chichester: John Wiley & Sons.

(2006), "Symbiosis: Therapeutic Communities within Non-Therapeutic Community Organisations", in *Dynamic Security*, Parker, M (ed), John Wiley & Sons.

Woodward, R, Cullen, E, Hemmings, M, Moore, C., Checkwas, E, Angeli, G and Jameson, A (2000), "Dovegate Therapeutic Community: Staff Training Manual", London: Home Office.

Yalom, I D (1995), *The Theory and Practice of Group Psychotherapy*, 4th Ed., New York: Basic Books.

INDEX

Symbols

48 hour rule *74*
194 requirement *73, 134, 195, 250*

A

abandonment *182, 283*
abnormal and unusual types of criminal *89*
abuse *117, 165, 244, 245*
  abusive parental/care-giver relationships *182*
accessibility *101, 146*
accountability *31, 46, 50, 52, 53, 54, 56, 70, 158*
  'creative accountability' *53*
accreditation *xix, 64, 67, 82, 92, 127, 151, 180, 191, 202, 208, 212, 213, 236, 240, 262*
  Accredited Treatment Programme Suite *64*
  Correctional Services Accreditation Panel (CSAP) *127, 208*
acting-out *174, 176, 180, 182, 195, 200, 201, 205, 234*
Adam Smith Institute *48*
addiction *37, 243, 285*
addressing offending *209*
adjudications *111, 158, 241*

advances *xix*
Advisory and Steering Group *50*
age *210*
aggression *156, 176, 180, 234, 254*
aims *129, 145, 150*
Albatross Unit *94*
alcohol *38, 160, 211, 272*
alienation *121, 179*
  feelings of alienation *244*
allocation
  TCs to *150*
amends *60*
American Civil Liberties Union *44*
anachronism *84*
analytics *82*
  democratic-analytic TCs *87*
anarchy *199*
Angeli, Gustavo *147*
anger *114, 120, 142, 161, 234*
  anger control *37*
antisocial
  antisocial attitudes, etc. *38, 211*
  antisocial behaviour *60*
  antisocial people *96*
anxiety *37, 70, 108, 123, 142, 150, 152, 177, 183, 191, 283*
apology
  letter of apology *61*
application *40*
armed robbery *129, 183*
art *152, 153, 255, 262*
  arts festival
    Rezart *130*
  art therapy *79, 254*
Asperger's Syndrome *234*

Education Department *103*
education manager *137*
education phobia *144*
EduCom *110, 114, 115, 117, 144, 150*
  peer tutor model *144*
effectiveness *62, 209, 257*
efficacy *57, 226*
  protocols for monitoring efficacy *208*
efficiency *50, 58, 63, 257*
"effort syndrome" *87*
ego *162*
  ego strength *179, 183*
  overdeveloped super-ego *234*
elders *256*
electronic gaming *153*
Ellis, Mary *261*
emotion *121, 160, 168, 281*
  corrective emotional experience *174, 182, 228*
  emotional management *40*
  emotional relationships *185*
  emotional suffering *281*
empathy *84, 181, 233*
  empathic failure *283*
  victim empathy *164*
empire building *122*
employment
  meaningful work *143*
energy *263*
enfranchising *102*
engagement *143, 212, 232*
enlightened approach *59, 83*
enterprise
  sense of enterprise *54*
enthusiasm *115*

entry criteria *39*
environment *81, 127, 130, 159, 171, 203, 229, 230*
  corruption by *261*
  interpersonal environment *130*
  physical environment *130*
  safe and supportive environment *187, 195, 232*
envy *179, 186, 187, 197, 199*
equality *193, 231*
  different but equal *194*
escalation
  collusive escalation *182*
escape *70, 100*
ethics *xix, 43, 46, 51, 56, 69, 113*
ethnicity *210*
ethos *69, 169*
European Convention on Human Rights *62*
evaluation *64, 213, 218*
Evans, Maggie *74, 261*
Evans, Val *102, 150*
evidence
  evidenced-based design *131*
excellence *127, 154, 254*
exclusion *132, 210*
expansion *64, 218*
expectations *35, 144, 151*
experience *79, 193, 281*
  echoes of *282*
  experiential groups *146*
experimentation *281*
experts *58, 76*
  experts in criminology, etc. *208*
  organizational experts *178*

Putting justice into words

Restorative Justice in Prisons
A Guide to Making It Happen
by Tim Newell and Kimmett Edgar

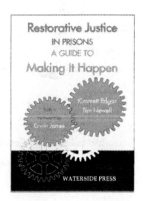

Leading edge information and ideas from two of the UK's
most respected practitioners and authorities. A handbook
for people who want to make a difference when working with prisoners. It suggests the tools for this and offers
guidance — and is wholly up to speed with what is happening in UK prisons.

- One of the most important penal reform
  books for years — part of a major initiative across UK prisons
- Essential reading for every RJ practitioner and student
- Designed to be used in conjunction with the free toolkits available for download from WatersidePress.co.uk

**'Successfully translates theory into practice and provides a model for organisa-
tional and cultural change in prisons'**: International Review of Victimology

Paperback ISBN 978-1-872870-25-2 | Ebook ISBN 978-1-906534-61-5 | 134 pp | 2006

visit **WatersidePress.co.uk**

Grendon Tales
Stories from a Therapeutic Community
by Ursula Smartt
Foreword Lord Avebury

Ursula Smartt's ground-breaking Grendon Tales lifts the lid on a highly acclaimed regime that was developed at Grendon Underwood in Buckinghamshire from the 1960s onwards. Grendon Tales is essential reading for anyone wishing to understand:

- What therapy with offenders consists of
- What it can achieve
- How Grendon Prison with its therapeutic communities became a world leader
- What drives some people to commit heinous and unspeakable crimes
- How 'prison democracy' works
- Why Grendon is 'the last chance saloon'
- Why some prisoners struggle to 'get into' Grendon whilst others avoid the place
- The impact on prisoners when they first arrive at Grendon
- What happens during their time there
- The pressures they face on their return to the mainstream prison system
- The approach in relation to different types of offenders (including sex offenders)
- The effect on prisoners' lives and relationships
- The aims and mission of the those who work at Grendon; and
- Moves to replicate its success

'**As readable as a novel ... I could not put it down until finished**': The Magistrate

'**A breathless personal slide through her year talking to some of the country's most difficult prisoners**': Community Care.

Paperback ISBN 978-1-872870-96-0 | Ebook ISBN 978-1-906534-51-6 | 232 pp | 2001

visit **WatersidePress.co.uk**

The Curious Mr Howard
Legendary Prison Reformer
by Tessa West
Foreword by Clive Stafford-Smith

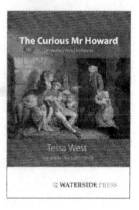

- Looks at Howard's immense achievements and his fascinating life
- Sheds new light on what drove the UK's most famous prison reformer
- A key work in social and penal history

In modern times John Howard (1726-1790) is perhaps best known as the man after whom the UK's oldest penal reform charity, the Howard League, is named.

Tessa West's book breaks fresh ground by looking at both Howard's legacy in terms of reform as well as his fascinating character. Based on extensive research in the UK and abroad, it provides a vivid picture of his life's work which will be invaluable in understanding why prisons and imprisonment demand constant scrutiny.

'**A much better picture of penal reformer John Howard than I had believed possible**': Dick Whitfield, trustee and former chair of the Howard League

'**A remarkable book about a remarkable man**': Sir Louis Blom-Cooper QC

'**This book is a timely reminder of the dreams that inspired one man many years ago, and a reminder that we need John Howard as much or more today**': Clive Stafford-Smith (from the Foreword)

Hardback ISBN 978-1-904380-73-3 | Ebook ISBN 978-1-908162-05-2 | 384 pp | June 2011

visit **WatersidePress.co.uk**